Mab Segrest, the Fuller-Maathai Professor Emeritus of Gender and Women's Studies at Connecticut College, is the author of *Administrations of Lunacy: Racism and the Haunting of American Psychiatry at the Milledgeville Asylum* (forthcoming from The New Press). She was a fellow at the National Humanities Center and lives in Durham, North Carolina.

ALSO BY MAB SEGREST

*Administrations of Lunacy: Racism and the Haunting of
American Psychiatry at the Milledgeville Asylum*

Born to Belonging: Writings on Spirit and Justice

My Mama's Dead Squirrel: Lesbian Essays on Southern Culture

Quarantines & Death: The Far Right's Homophobic Agenda
(with Leonard Zeskind)

Sing, Whisper, Shout, Pray: Feminist Visions for a Just World
(with M. Jacqui Alexander, Lisa Albrecht, and Sharon Day)

MEMOIR OF A RACE TRAITOR

Fighting Racism in the American South

Mab Segrest

THE
NEW
PRESS

NEW YORK
LONDON

Requests for permission to reproduce selections from this book should
be made through our website: https://thenewpress.com/contact.

Originally published in the United States by South End Press, Boston, 1994
This revised edition published in the United States by
The New Press, New York, 2019
Distributed by Two Rivers Distribution

ISBN 978-1-62097-300-4 (ebook)

LIBRARY OF CONGRESS CATALOGING-IN-PUBLICATION DATA

Names: Segrest, Mab, 1949– author.
Title: Memoir of a race traitor : fighting racism in the American south / Mab Segrest.
Description: Revised edition. | New York : New Press, [2019] |
Revised edition of the author's Memoir of a race traitor, c1994.
| Includes bibliographical references and index.
Identifiers: LCCN 2018049332 | ISBN 9781620972991 (pbk)
Subjects: LCSH: Civil rights movements—Southern States. | Southern States—
Race relations. | Segrest, Mab, 1949– | Civil rights workers—North Carolina—
Biography. | Lesbians—North Carolina—Biography. | Feminism—Southern States.
Classification: LCC F220.A1 S38 2019 | DDC 305.800975—dc23
LC record available at https://lccn.loc.gov/2018049332

The New Press publishes books that promote and enrich public discussion and
understanding of the issues vital to our democracy and to a more equitable world.
These books are made possible by the enthusiasm of our readers; the support
of a committed group of donors, large and small; the collaboration of our many
partners in the independent media and the not-for-profit sector; booksellers, who
often hand-sell New Press books; librarians; and above all by our authors.

www.thenewpress.com

Composition by dix!
This book was set in Fairfield LH

Printed in the United States of America

2   4   6   8   10   9   7   5   3   1

For Wilson W. Lee
and
John Fletcher Segrest Jr.

Racism is so different from prejudice; it would be helpful if people could begin to use words precisely, giving them their actual meaning. . . . We have scarcely begun to probe this illness. Let's call it what it is: evil. I'm not sure it is an illness, it may simply be evil.

—Lillian Smith, *How Am I to Be Heard?*

Contents

Introduction to the New Edition

This year I turned seventy years old. A quarter of a century ago, this book was an alarm bell in the night; now it is clanging louder yet. This is still a story about the ravages of racism, the meanings of race in the United States, and what we must do about them. *Race Traitor* is also one glimpse into a trajectory of the great battle that still rages in the United States about who controls resources and who is human. It touches us all in intimate ways that white people often have not realized. The memoir part of this book is a story about how that impact of white supremacy happened across generations in my white, conservative southern family. Also, as a treatise on "the souls of white people" (to borrow W.E.B. Du Bois's phrase), the book was one of the first attempts by a white person to mark the encompassing whiteness that is everywhere on our radar screens, an always present reality that finally comes into sight for us white people as we take it on.

Memoir of a Race Traitor was also written by a lesbian who could not look at race in an uncomplicated way. Rather, it is part of a much larger story about my generation as we variously came out and grappled with what in 1978 the Boston-based Black feminist Combahee River Collective formulated as "the particular [generational] task of integrated analysis and practice based upon the fact that the major systems of oppression are interlocking." The Black feminism that Combahee articulated was, its proponents argued, "the logical political movement to combat the manifold and simultaneous oppressions that all women of color face."[1]

In 1989, this concept of interlocking and simultaneous oppressions became a basis of what Black feminist critical legal scholar Kimberlé Crenshaw termed "intersectional feminism." As Crenshaw recently explained, intersectionality is "a lens through which you can see where power comes and collides, where it interlocks and intersects," with its primary standpoint the Black and Brown women who are subjected to the multiple effects of systemic power. The intersectional aspect presented the standpoint from which to see; the interlocking part provided the action then required to push through the gates and doors. Locks can be opened, if all the tumblers fall right. The goal was to forge more vital integrities of self, more vibrant communities, and more powerful movements for justice, driven from the margins that become the centers (in bell hooks's terms).

But Black feminism also called white women to account for white supremacy, as did the "women of color" feminism that burst forward in *This Bridge Called My Back: Radical Writings by Women of Color*, edited by Cherríe Moraga and Gloria Anzaldúa and published by Kitchen Table Women of Color Press.[2] I was one of those white lesbian women who received this charge from my friend Barbara Smith, who was on the Combahee Collective and was an editor at Kitchen Table Women of Color Press. Most notably, Barbara would say, "I don't live in the women's movement, I live on the streets of North America." *Memoir of a Race Traitor* was my attempt as a white person to stand at the intersections of power in order to articulate them in a way that could help figure out how to unlock their tumblers.

The variously gendered queers who are my people brought our struggles into the open during a rising right-wing insurgency that put its scapegoating targets on our backs and tried to make us their political pawns. We did not let them do so: we cared for each other during the AIDS epidemic and, when necessary and now still, walk or carry our loved ones to their graves or cremations.

So from this new edition, hello to old friends. Some of you were there before this book's beginning or at its origins. I met many more of you through this book. And welcome, new readers. Many of you will have come of age in the quarter century since *Race Traitor*'s first publication, with the years since then bringing their own distinctive set of tumults, from Katrina to 9/11 to the yet unending War on Terror, from the 2008 economic crash to uprising against police shootings to Donald Trump's election. This narrative reads as a precursor to the subsequent dizzying years in which all the plots thickened.

Now white supremacy tweets from the White House in a presidency as surreal as it is just one more f*ing thing. The president is a bag of gale-force winds that blow into the sails of white nationalist movements across the globe. On March 15, 2019, in New Zealand, one of white supremacy's foot soldiers brutally attacked two mosques in Christchurch, killing at least fifty Muslim worshippers at prayer while he live-streamed the slaughter on social media to 1.5 million people. In a manifesto posted online before his rampage, he cited the inspiration of recent mass murders by white supremacist terrorists across the globe, including Dylann Roof, who shot to death nine worshippers at Emanuel AME Church in Charleston, South Carolina. He festooned his clothes and weapons with the symbols of neo-Nazi movements and the names of their leaders. Those organizations also maraud through this book.

The killer hailed President Trump as "a symbol of renewed white identity and common purpose."[3] Like the current U.S. president, the New Zealand mass murderer spouted fears of hordes of immigrant invaders threatening the white homeland as harbingers of "white genocide."[4] White Patriot Party leader Glenn Miller, one of the antagonists of this story, also declared race war in his intersectional diatribe against "Niggers, Jews, Queers, assorted Mongrels, white Race traitors, and despicable informants," declaring in 1987: "And so, fellow Aryan Warriors, strike now." Keep reading to see his results. Glenn Miller now sits on death row in Kansas after a 2014 attack outside a Kansas City Jewish community center in which he murdered three people.

Of course, in the New Zealand attacks against Muslims praying in their mosques, the antecedent is much older than the U.S. Civil War. It's the Crusades.

A quarter of a century after the initial publication of *Memoir of a*

Race Traitor, the stakes are higher, the waters are rising, and so are our resources, our solidarities, and our insistence.

As one marker of time, I spent the greater part of March 11, 2019, in Raleigh, North Carolina. I was there at the Wake County courthouse to support people who were arrested on November 23, 2018, after Immigration and Customs Enforcement (ICE) seized Samuel Oliver-Bruno from his family—his wife and his nineteen-year-old son. On November 23, 2018, Samuel left eleven months' sanctuary in CityWell Methodist Church to go to the U.S. Citizenship and Immigration Services (USCIS) office in Morrisville, outside of Raleigh, as part of a scheduled appointment to move forward his application for reprieve of deportation. Knowing the dangers of this journey, CityWell congregants caravanned with Samuel to the USCIS office, where dozens of other supporters waited. So did undercover ICE officers, who had collaborated with USCIS prior to the appointment. Once Samuel was inside the office, undercover ICE agents tackled him, and other ICE agents appeared from behind closed doors to haul Samuel to a waiting ICE van. His son, Daniel, was charged with assault on a government official for refusing to let go of his father in the tumble, holding on as all children do when faced with separation from a loved parent. After ICE moved Samuel to its van, protesters surrounded the vehicle, arms locked and singing, extending the sanctuary of the church building to the streets for as long as they could. Three hours later, the twenty-seven people surrounding the van were arrested and Samuel was taken into detention.[5]

Family separations are a cruelty familiar to many whose people have suffered them, from slave auction blocks to the Trail of Tears, from the forced attendance of native children at racist boarding schools to the dispersal of residents of New Orleans's Ninth Ward after Hurricane Katrina to queer parents losing children to the state. It is a system that is expert in roiling white fears to break Brown people's hearts, or any heart open to such human suffering and courage. Soon after his arrest, Samuel was sent to an ICE deportation center in Georgia, where his petition to defer deportation was denied. After being moved around to a disorienting number of locations, Samuel was flown to the Brownsville, Texas, Port Isabel Detention Center, then dropped off at the international bridge to walk into Mexico. On the other side of the bridge/border, he was met by Casa del Migrante members, who helped him call his wife. They drove him back to the international bridge, where he and Daniel, who had been brought to Brownsville, reunited.[6]

At the March rally outside the Wake County courthouse, I was happy that Pastor Cleve May from CityWell was at the mic to explain the real gospel: *Seek and ye shall find. Knock and it shall be opened. Love thy neighbor as thyself.* I learned those basic principles from the stained-glass windows in my segregated Methodist church back in Tuskegee, Alabama, many years ago, even as my father and other church leaders locked its doors to keep out the Black people praying on the church steps.

Recently, I have grieved the decision of the United Methodist Church to strengthen its ban on same-sex marriage and LGBT clergy. In my childhood, the United Methodist Church aligned with a social gospel, although many white southern congregations did not. Today, institutional Methodism has put itself inside a locked church without realizing that whatever locks other people out locks them in. As someone who has lived and organized in small southern towns, I know that acceptance and blessings from the church can make a life-and-death difference for queer and trans young people.

Also in the crowd among the arrestees that November day was my daughter, Annie Elizabeth Culbertson-Jolly Segrest, now thirty-two, and her nineteen-year-old friend Jemma Barton-Lippin. Annie was one of the very first children of an openly queer family in the Triangle, and she has many stories to tell. Nineteen years ago, Jemma's moms, Betsy and Tobi, brought her to meet me soon after they arrived with her from Guatemala. When Annie was in the eighth grade, she became Jemma's babysitter, and she held that position off and on for years. In November, Jemma and Annie stood shoulder to shoulder in the face of ICE agents in the group defending Samuel before Tobi, Jemma, and Annie were placed in different transports after their arrests. I was in New York for Thanksgiving when Samuel was arrested, and Annie called me with a report.

At the mic at the Wake County courthouse at the March rally, Annie's Peace Camp counselor from twenty-five years ago spoke. Manju Rajendran now trains marshals for demonstrations and strategizes with people across the United States on combating racism and compounding oppressions. Manju's mother, Vimala, was also there in the crowd but was not arrested. The deportation threat that Vimala faced because she but not her children was undocumented mirrors Samuel and Daniel's situation. Now Vimala owns and operates Vimala's Curryblossom Café in Chapel Hill and was voted top chef in the Triangle recently; she cooks delicious meals and advocates for food as a human right.

In the crowd that March day were also queer gender-nonconforming or non-binary younger folk from Workers World, the group that allegedly toppled Durham's Confederate monument on August 12, 2017. The twelve people identified as instigators in this toppling were hunted down and arrested in their homes by the Durham County Sheriff's Department (the sheriff was recently defeated for reelection), and they received multiple death threats in the days and weeks after the incident. The day they were arraigned, two hundred people from the Durham community dressed in black and lined up to confess to the same crime. Eventually, in spite of multiple videos of the event, none were convicted, testimony to the continuing pressure of #DefendDurham.[7] The Confederate monument at the University of North Carolina at Chapel Hill came down a year later, after decades of protests led by African American students, faculty, and staff. In both cases, those tried got leniency in part because local judges and prosecutors took into account the North Carolina legislature's gerrymandered Republican supermajority that made it illegal to move any "historical" monument without its permission.

To understand why such monumental Confederate soldiers might be a bit exhausted on their pedestals, see Constance McCurry, *Confederate Reckoning: Power and Politics in the Civil War South* (Cambridge, MA: Harvard University Press, 2010). In that war, Confederate soldiers died at three times the rate of their Union counterparts. Because the North had so many more people than the South, the Confederacy drafted 75 to 80 percent of its white men into the army, leaving families at home to starve and very upset wives, many of whom conducted food riots across North Carolina and the South in 1863. As its white soldiers deserted, the Confederacy tortured their wives to reveal their places of hiding, levied a 10 percent tax on anything they produced and sent revenue collectors to their door to get the Confederate tithe, and even punished them with execution. If many of these statues of regular foot soldiers across the South had their way, I think they would have climbed down a while back, happy to be finally done with a war and a history that has been so distorted in their names.

Durham's statue of a Confederate soldier fell the week after the torch-bearing "Unite the Right" rally marched through Charlottesville, Virginia, drawing groups of the most blatantly fascist stripe for "blood and soil" and in defense of the city's Confederate monument of Robert E. Lee. Saturday afternoon, as police watched, they clashed with protesters, and white supremacist James Fields drove his car into a crowd, killing Heather Heyer and injuring nineteen others. In response to this outbreak of fascist violence, President Trump not only refused to condemn white supremacy, given how much of his base was represented in Charlottesville, but embraced them by saying there were "good people on both sides."

The week after Charlottesville, with feelings running high, the Durham County sheriff circulated word that the Loyal White Knights intended to demonstrate at the statue site. In response, two thousand people gathered at the former monument base for a spontaneous party with West African and Afro-Brazilian drumming. It was emceed by Manju and by Serena Sebring from Southerners on New Ground (SONG). SONG is a vibrant queer liberation organization (and, like this book, twenty-five years old). Its current campaign is to end money bail, the reason that so many poor people spend time in jail waiting for their trials, often on negligible charges, incurring numerous fees that run them into debt. The overall goal is to end a system of mass incarceration that swelled from 300,000 prisoners in the 1980s to 2.3 million today, and actively to reimagine our communities in the process. In 1993, Pat Hussain, Joan Garner, Mandy Carter, Pam McMichael, Suzanne Pharr, and I founded SONG at the National Gay and Lesbian Task Force conference in Durham, the first location for this conference in the South.[8] (The text of a keynote speech that I gave at that founding SONG weekend, on creating change, ends *Race Traitor*.)

On that August day in 2017, the handful of white nationalists who showed up quickly fled, and the partiers continued to dance and kept their joyful cool on a sweltering August afternoon. Together they refused the Charlottesville terror.

In cities across the United States, the quarter century's time is measured in such days and generations of work for justice and peace.

One week after the August 2017 party downtown, I returned to Durham for a gig at the National Humanities Center in Research Triangle Park to work on a book on southern insanity (that redundancy) that The New Press will soon publish: *Administrations of Lunacy: Racism and the Haunting of American Psychiatry*. The next summer I moved back to Durham for good, hauling what's left of my worldly possessions in a fifteen-foot U-Haul down I-95. I have loved many people in New London, Connecticut, where I taught for twelve years, and then in Brooklyn, New York, two places where I spent most of the twenty-first century to date. Back when Annie was still in high school, I returned to Durham from New London as often as three times a month and for holidays and summer vacation. Relocating myself fully back to Durham was a wrenching departure from people I love in Brooklyn. But I was obeying some powerful homing signal. It is Durham and North Carolina where my life comes clearest. This book explains why. There are joys and fights behind us, and joys and fights coming. I see them best from home.

Now that I am seventy, the work documented here is a quarter of a century behind me. I look back on the much younger dyke who wrote it with gratitude for how she charted my adult life. Her picture graces its new cover. The New Press wanted to replace the image that was on the original cover: my great-grandfather's family, which stood in for my family's history and its complexities that I explored. For a while I resisted replacing it with an image of myself, which seemed narcissistic. But I came around after editors explained that readers needed an image with which to identify the author in what is, among other things, a very personal story. And, honestly, I really love the cover shot. It was taken of me in 1979 at the beach with my *Feminary* buddies just after I finished my dissertation. On the back of the new edition will be a Klan sign condemning, among other "mud people," all "Queer Scum." And there I am, hairy armpits, no bra, straw hat, jauntily leaning against the door frame, looking at a group of women I adore, free and happy—as we queer scum will continue to be, whatever must come.

Rereading, I am struck by how *Race Traitor* bleeds across my family's history in Alabama, which reaches back into the nineteenth century, and into my coming of age in North Carolina. In Durham in my twenties and thirties I jumped the tracks to the right side of history. I carried in my baggage, out of the apartheid of my Alabama childhood, the genealogies of family members whose legacies included the destruction of Reconstruction, the Ku Klux Klan, the White Citizens' Council, segregated private schools, and the murder of civil rights worker Sammy Younge in my hometown of Tuskegee, Alabama, in 1966. It left me lots to unpack and sort through, to discard or mend, or to wrap around me. The last major portion of the book, "On Being White and Other Lies," is my attempt to provide a concise history of the evolution of racism and white supremacy in the United States over a period of five hundred years.

In my unpacking of both white and queer identities, I also discovered at deeper levels my parents' love for me and their respect, even during the years in which I increasingly disagreed in very personal terms with their worldview. If you read to the end, that dialectic unfolds in surprising ways. Anyone who has struggled with a mama, a daddy, a sister, or a brother might recognize themselves here. My parents each in their own way granted me the freedom not only to disagree but to work to displace them and the segregated world they raised me in. Perhaps they knew I would do it anyway, and perhaps they knew their love could strengthen me in that process.

Once out of Alabama, I came out into a vibrant, multiracial, lesbian feminist movement of people across a range of genders. Combahee, anti-racist feminism, and the friendships it engendered opened my door into a more vital life than I ever would have had if I had stayed on the segregated side of the tracks. *Race Traitor* is one piece of evidence of those earlier struggles, their dangers, and their great rewards. In the twenty-first century, Black Lives Matter again embraces the vision and politics of Combahee as the movement for Black lives brings to the forefront of anti-racist social justice struggles the vision and determination of queer feminists of color.

Circles turning amid circles—live long enough and it all comes around. The work recorded in this book and its reissue a quarter of a century later is (still) my effort to live up to, and live into, this vision of the future.

So go again, little book.

Mab Segrest
Durham, North Carolina, 2019

Preface to the Original Edition

This book is the work of one white woman, who is also a lesbian, thinking race, feeling race, acting against racism in a sustained way over one bleak decade in her country's history. I write it from the vantage point of Alabama and North Carolina, the American South whose history presented me in my adolescence with a continuing preoccupation about my country and my people. I have written this treatise on the souls of white folks with an urgency that it be exemplary, a template into which white readers can read themselves. Then I have worried that its very particularities will create ruptures in the identification I seek: "No one in my family ever killed a Black person or joined the Ku Klux Klan." So let me phrase the broader question clearly: "What does it mean to be a post-colonial European—anywhere in the United States, anywhere on the planet?" The problem of the twenty-first century—to extend W.E.B. Du Bois's insight—will also be the color line, and it is time we figure this out.

This book is by a lesbian, who cannot look at race in an uncomplicated way, who has worked to articulate the many interfaces among misogyny, racism, and homophobia in a culture ravaged by all three.

This book is by a woman who has never yet gone to bed hungry for lack of food, who has never yet slept outdoors for lack of shelter, who has never yet not worked for lack of a job, who is trying to understand a capitalism that denies many of her fellow humans all three.

I could never have written this book alone. Fortunately, there were many people who helped me bear its burdens and share its satisfactions. Thanks, then—to my editor, Loie Hayes, at South End Press, who believed in the book at all the right moments, prodding, cajoling, and encouraging me over its many rough spots; to my father and sister, who generously gave me the freedom of my own memories, even when they conflicted with their own and did not always put family members in the best light; to Theresa Foley and Marc Miller, who gave me careful editing that helped to untangle the skein of stories— my narrative mess of worms; to friends who kept me accountable to high standards, whose advice (though hard at times to hear) kept me going eight months after the book was due: Dorothy Allison, Leah Wise, Minnie Bruce Pratt, Jacqui Alexander, Lynora Williams, Steve Schewel, Adrienne Rich, and Tobi Lippin; to the other editors of *The Third Wave: Feminist Essays on Racism,* who provided the context in which I could write "On Being White and Other Lies": Jacqui Alexander, Lisa Albrecht, Sharon Day, and (for a while) Norma Alarcón; to Lenny Zeskind, Lynora Williams, and the Board of the Center for Democratic Renewal for their continuing friendship and courage; to Christina Davis-McCoy and Linda Shealey-Williams, staff of North Carolinians Against Racist and Religious Violence, to the NCARRV Board for their support and encouragement and for access to the NCARRV files; to Cynthia Brown, who called me from the airport in Vermont to tell me how exciting she found the manuscript; and to my other co-workers Joanna Miller, Coleen Lanigan, Barbara Taylor, Karen Hayes, and Gina Chamberlain, who gave encouragement and advice as I worked and reworked the memoir in the final eighteen months while working full-time; to the Steering Committee of the U.S. Urban-Rural Mission—Leah Wise, Mac Charles Jones, Young Shin, and John Boonstra—for allowing me the flexibility to write and work full-time for them; to the people who gave financial support and/or physical space in which to work: "Country Dyke" at the Funding Exchange; Albie and Susan Wells and their Windcall program; Greg and Debbie Warren, who generously lent me their trailer at the beach for a week; for legal advice to Catherine White, Lucy Lovrien, Ruth Walden, and Cathy Packer; to the people whose lives I also recounted, who helped me shape and remember: Leah Wise, Lauren and Paul Martin, Betty and John McKellar, Junior Cummings, Mac Legerton, Christina Davis-McCoy, Faye Melton, Lewis Pitts, Rosetta Jones, Flora, Betty Jo, Pat, Lenny Zeskind, Barbara, Elizabeth Freeman, Allan Troxler, and Alice Lee; to others who read all or parts of the manuscript and gave valuable feedback: Ronnie Kolotkin, Chrystos, Nancy Bereano, Len Stanley, David Jolly, Lisa Albrecht, Barbara Smith, Loretta Ross, and Jan Montgomery; to Annie and Barbara, for their patience when I worked through family vacations and holidays, and for their impatience when they refused to allow me to, who continue to anchor me with their love.

MEMOIR OF A
RACE TRAITOR

Part One

MEMOIR OF A RACE TRAITOR

For Christina Davis-McCoy

The oratorical traditions in the South are a real way of molding perceptions.

—Joe Freeman Britt, *Southern Magazine*

Things that are cheap and tawdry in fiction work beautifully in non-fiction because they are true. That's why you should be careful not to abridge it, because it's the fundamental power you're dealing with. You arrange it and present it. . . . But you don't make it up.

—John McPhee, *The Literary Journalists*

The southern [white] woman played it ear by ear, day by day—and never, afterward, turned back to see what significance, what meaning, lay in what she had actually done and said and thought and recorded. She could not form a gestalt and say: This has been my life and my people's life.

—Lillian Smith, *The Winner Names The Age*

1

Osceola's Head

I had become a woman haunted by the dead. The time was the mid-
to late 1980s. Organizing against a rampaging far right movement in
North Carolina, I traveled back roads that roiled beneath me like a
riverflow on a journey into the ravages of racism and the meanings
of "race" as those forces framed southern and national culture—the
people and ideas that had shaped me from birth.

My immediate adversaries were Ku Klux Klansmen seeking to restore the apartheid world of my Alabama childhood and neo-Nazis
looking toward a cataclysmic future, a globe in which only Aryans
would survive their wars to purify the white race. These extremists
could operate because they served the purposes of numb and greedy
men and their systems built on dark-skinned people's bones and blood.
I had come to see, time and again, that when any of these foot soldiers
outlived their usefulness to their more powerful white cousins, they
were eminently expendable. I have even helped to bring a couple of
them down.

I have struggled to find a voice to bring you back these stories.
Almost a decade ago, when my part of this story begins, I started
to chronicle the seemingly isolated events—the cross burnings, the
threats, the gunfire or the knife thrust, the violence of annihilating
ideas. I did so out of the certainty that, in the face of evil, good people do not respond because they can pretend they do not know. This
denial is the metaphysic of genocide. Thus, in the face of enforced

ignorance, I struggled to shape an "objective" language, the procession of crisp black letters across the empty page, like the ones you read in your morning paper that say this happened, at this place, at this time, in this way. Could I turn bits and pieces of a large, bloody, violent puzzle into a coherent story that would move both ordinary and powerful people? I became a pack rat, a collector of verified details, my files stuffed with authenticated facts, like what the district attorney said, how many men we counted at what march, the lynch message on the Klan phone line in May, the number of pounds of C-4 explosive pilfered from Fort Bragg. I put numbers to the violence and charted it each year in jagged upward lines. And it worked, up to a point. But behind and around the marching letters, I felt a growing horror. The winter came when my throat began to close. The doctor said it was some virus or infection, but I was choking on the stories. I had to quit the work to find again "subjective" language, what poet Muriel Rukeyser called "unverifiable fact." But I insist also on the documentary, accountable to the laws that govern how the public perceives what is real.[1] You'll know when the tone shifts. I cannot write a "whole" book about a broken world.

In the white household where I was raised, themes of race permeated our family interactions. After my parents bought our first television in the mid-1950s, civil rights battles on the noon and evening news became a fare as regular as tomatoes or iced tea at family meals. I often replicated these battles with my siblings as white reactions increasingly repulsed me. Then in 1966 Marvin Segrest, one of scores of Segrests in Macon County, shot and killed Sammy Younge, a Black student activist. The murder came at a moment of rising white violence across the Deep South that was wearing out the patience and faith of Younge's Black comrades. "The murder of Sammy Younge marked the end of tactical nonviolence," James Forman later reflected, "the long marches where Blacks were expected to undergo harsh treatment by white Southern crackers, not protecting themselves, not fighting back."[2] A decade after Marvin shot Sammy at the Tuskegee Greyhound station, I recognized I was lesbian, a self that I first fled and only later came to celebrate. Two decades after Younge's murder, I heard a call, clear as a bell, to oppose the white supremacist forces that kill both "niggers" and "queers." As I did that work, I reread the biography of Sammy Younge's life in my hometown, finding in his angers, fears, and resolves a deeper understanding of my own outcast self. As I traveled the courtrooms of North Carolina, I also recognized in myself my now-dead kinsman Marvin Segrest, white and poor, also angry and afraid. My terror and my fury—from whom do they come?

Three breaches in identity underlie the preoccupations of my life: race (my own and others), my gayness, and my mother's sickness. I search each one for clues to meanings of the others. They constantly bleed into one another, like watercolors on wet paper.

My mother would break out all over her body from a skin disease everybody could diagnose but nobody could cure. We could tell when she began to get bad, tearing at her arms and face with a constant, nervous, and sometimes savage movement that left her bleeding and raw. Then she started taking cures, every two or three years. There was a metaphor in the itching and inflamed skin that I learned too well, this sensitivity to environment that left our mother tearing at her own flesh, like she was allergic to life itself. When racist violence in Alabama erupted like the lesions on my mother's arms, I was not surprised when it all came down to skin. Then there is my father, who organized a network of segregated private schools all over Alabama. I have made a profession of being better than him.

Searching for an antidote to family pain, I have become an aficionada of cures. I have dragged myself to therapists and peer counselors and pored over books on "dysfunctional families." With difficulty and with help, I have gained some understanding of my subjective life. But something was missing, some more transparent view of the interweave of race and family that white folks usually miss. Race does not happen to us genetic humans.

Or perhaps it does. Consider the story of Osceola's head. I first heard of Osceola from my father, who has an intense interest in Macon County and Alabama history. When I was a child, he took me to find Osceola's birthplace near Tallassee, in the northern part of the county. I remember standing in an open field with grass the color of straw up to my shoulders. My father pointed to a tree: "That's where he was born." We turned and trudged back to the car. Much later, Charleston novelist Josephine Humphries told me the story of Osceola's decapitation, having found it in a guidebook to her city.

Born Billy Powell in 1804 to an Indian mother and white father, Osceola was a Muskogee, a group of tribes called "Creek" by white settlers. His uncle, Peter McQueen, was one of the Muskogee warrior-prophets who fought the growing white encroachment, an Indian uprising defeated by Andrew Jackson at the Battle of Horseshoe Bend. McQueen took the Muskogees who still resisted the settlers' presence down to Florida. In the 1830s, Osceola (Anglicized from the Muskogee Asi:yaloli) became a leader in a guerrilla insurgency of Seminoles and escaped slaves. Andrew Jackson's troops finally captured him and sent him to Charleston. During his brief captivity there, Osceola was tended by Dr. Frederick Weedon, who visited frequently and claimed to be his friend. At Osceola's death, however, Dr. Weedon wanted a souvenir, an artifact, so he took his surgeon's saw and cut off Osceola's head. According to Weedon family stories, the doctor took the head to St. Augustine, where he displayed it in his drugstore window among the pharmaceuticals. When one of the doctor's adolescent sons did not sufficiently obey, Weedon would take out Osceola's head and tie it to the child's bedpost.[3] What fear, what furious dreams must his young white sons have dreamed, the apparition of their father's clinical brutality rising in the savaged Osceola's head?

What therapist would tell us to read history, would help us see how this fetishized racism circulates within white families? We wash it down with gin and violence. It surfaces as anger or depression, passed down and down and down, refracted for generations to children who inherit sometimes houses and land but always jumbles of terror and anger. And how could we divine their source, the headless Osceola, dodging outside in the trees?

My friend Leah looks over my shoulder: "The book's title is wrong. That's not what you were doing." I flush. I do struggle with betrayal. My Klan folk had me spotted: a race traitor. Even in this beginning, the "I" of memoir betrays, when this story belongs to many people, many of whom in large ways or small do not agree about the facts I assemble, much less their interpretation. To reflect what some of us know as collective struggle, the hard disagreements and fallings-out among people who work toward a transformed world, is difficult enough, as is writing about violent white kin I still live among. I also need to find a way to write about my white family that explores the primal hurts that both drove me forward and held me back. Race and family, the intimate and the historic, action and reflection, Marvin Segrest and Sammy Younge: I straddle chasms that make the Grand Canyon seem like some little creek.

It's not my people, it's the *idea* of race I am betraying. It's taken me a while to get the distinction.

2

The Typical American Democracy

I had a phobia about Nazis. Storm troopers at the door, the kind of midnight visit after which friends wonder where I disappeared, or I knock to find their apartments empty, their cats unfed.

I was not totally in the grips of paranoia. Events going into the 1980s were not reassuring. Black schoolchildren had begun to turn up murdered in Atlanta. A Black cab driver in Syracuse, New York, had his heart cut out. In the Midwest, a white racist shot civil rights activist Vernon Jordan while Jordan was jogging.

Violence in these places echoed in gunfire in Greensboro, North Carolina, an hour's drive west of my Durham home. The people at the intersection of Carver Drive and Everitt Street in Greensboro had also felt the country's ugly mood. They were at an anti-Klan rally in Morningside Homes, a public housing project of mostly African Americans. It was a rainy Saturday morning, about 11:00 a.m. on November 3, 1979, one year and three days before Ronald Reagan would be elected president. The Ku Klux Klan, the 112-year-old terror organization indigenous to the American South, was on the march again after a decade or so of relative quiet. The spring before in Decatur, Alabama, Klansmen had attacked civil rights demonstrators. Various Klan factions, with names like Invisible Empire and Carolina Knights and arcane titles like Imperial Wizard, Exalted Cyclops, and Grand Dragon, were also on the march in the Piedmont, the hilly central

part of the state, as were neo-Nazi factions such as the National Socialist Party of America.

Two centuries before, this part of North Carolina had echoed the
gunfire from Revolutionary War battles like the one at King's Mountain, where Carolina boys "made their country a hornet's nest for Lord
Cornwallis in the darkest days of the cause of liberty," as native son
and racist novelist Thomas Dixon Jr. wrote. For Dixon, North Carolina was "the typical American Democracy," sending "more boys to the
front than any other state of the Confederacy—and [leaving] more
dead on the field."[1] Carolina had fired the last volley at Appomattox,
although for many Carolina Klansmen the Civil War was not over, nor
the question of slavery finally settled.

In the 1890s all across the New South, northern capitalists and
a new southern owning class built a network of cotton mills on the
rivers and streams of land only thirty-five years removed from chattel slavery. Into those mills flocked poor whites out of the hills and
off depressed farms. They entered into a pact to provide non-union,
low-wage labor in exchange for the exalted privilege of being white.
Another native son, North Carolina journalist W.J. Cash, explained
the deal they cut:

> Not only was [the poor white person] not exploited directly,
> he was himself made by extension a member of the dominant
> class. . . . Come what might, he would always be a white man.
> And before that vast and capacious distinction, all others were
> foreshortened, dwarfed, and all but obliterated.[2]

In the 1970s, a declining national economy was squeezing these
blue-collar workers once again. An Arab oil embargo sent gas prices
through the ceiling, initiating a spiral of double-digit inflation and
unemployment. Third World men and women, working for subsistence wages, undercut North Carolina labor in the same way Carolinians had undercut unionized Yankee workers for generations. And
when white workers got squeezed, true to their old bargain with the
devil of white supremacy, they looked for revenge—not to seemingly

faceless corporate boardrooms but to the nearest person with darker skin.

These whites had plenty of help in making this illogical leap. Republican Party strategists began telling them in 1972 that the problem was affirmative action programs, niggers getting their jobs. Forget the fact that Black folks were still far worse off than whites. And the Klan was around again to focus white discontent. The leaders at the Morningside Homes rally in Greensboro realized what was happening. "We invite you and your two-bit punks to come out and face the wrath of the people," the rally's organizers had intemperately proclaimed. "Death to the Klan."[3]

Some of the people who organized the rally at the intersection of Carver and Everitt Streets on November 3 had worked in textile mills themselves: factories like White Oak, Haw River, and Revolution. Many of them did not grow up in the mill towns across the Carolinas but were drawn there in the belief that the country was in a countdown to a second American Revolution that would confer not only life and liberty but a fairer share in the country's material wealth. Only a month before, some of these people had decided to call themselves the Communist Workers Party (CWP), a dramatic (most said crazy) move in an era when communists were considered devils. Communism was anathema in North Carolina, where government officials advertised a docile labor force to entice even more cheap jobs.

Someone at the intersection looked up the street to see a line of cars approaching. "It's the Klan," the alarm went out. The cars were filled with white men from almost all of the state's Klan and neo-Nazi organizations.

Less than five minutes after the Klan caravan had arrived, four of the CWP's leadership—Jim Waller, Bill Sampson, Sandi Smith, and Cesar Cauce—were dead, their blood pooling on the pavement beneath them or soaking into the earth. CWP supporter Mike Nathan lay sprawled in the street fatally wounded by a shotgun blast to his head. He died two days later. Television cameras captured the eighty-eight seconds of gunfire on videotape that would be played and replayed hundreds of times on state and national television and in courtrooms for the next five years.[4]

No one who has seen the footage can forget the images of Klansmen coolly removing weapons from the trunk of a blue Ford Fairlane, a cigarette dangling casually from one man's lips. Or of white supremacist Jerry Paul Smith running down the sidewalk with a pistol in his hand, firing a .357 Magnum bullet into the neck, heart, and lungs of an already wounded Cesar Cauce.

Greensboro police arrived only as the Klan vehicles were pulling out. The Greensboro Police Department later explained that its officers had misunderstood the starting time and place of the rally, although an officer had followed the Klan caravan all the way to the rally site. In the weeks and months after the bloodbath, the public learned that two government informants had been inside the coalition of Klan and neo-Nazi organizations that went to Morningside Homes—Ed Dawson, who informed to the Greensboro Police Department, and Bernard Butkovich, an agent of the federal Bureau of Alcohol, Tobacco, and Firearms (BATF).[5] Police on the scene stopped one van and arrested the men inside for four counts of murder and one count of conspiracy to commit murder.[6] They also arrested several of the demonstrators.[7] One survivor, her face wild with shock and grief, turned to the cameras to charge a government conspiracy in the killings. Signe Waller knelt over the body of her husband, Jim, her black hair framing her anguished face, her fist clenched. "Long live the Communist Workers Party!" she cried. "Long live the working class."[8]

Four of the "CWP Five," as their friends and comrades called the dead, had lived in nearby Durham, where I had settled eight years earlier to attend graduate school at Duke University. I heard about the attack that evening. I was shaken. I had seen the rally signs on telephone posts and had considered going. The next morning in a picture on the front page of the Sunday *Durham Herald* a white woman cradled the head of a wounded white man. I recognized Jim Wrenn and Kate White. I had met Kate in the mid-1970s. We kept up with each other, periodically meeting to compare notes and debate my emerging lesbian-feminist and her communist politics. There they were on the front page, Kate looking urgently over her shoulder toward the sound of gunfire, Jim's eyes glazed, his face webbed with blood. Jim had been wounded, I later learned, as he crawled to help the fatally wounded Mike Nathan, who had been shot as he attempted to help the dying Jim Waller.

For days I wanted to call Kate to offer comfort. But I was living in the country by myself, and I dreamed the old farmhouse was surrounded by crosses, dry grass ablaze and me inside the burning circle. Kate's phone was probably tapped. I had been an openly lesbian activist for several years. Out of fear that I might attract similar violence, I didn't call.

Ideological certainty generated self-righteousness and closed the CWP members off from the genuine dangers of calling out the Klan, many people felt. They had put other lives at risk as well, especially those of the Black residents of Morningside Homes, who had had little say in bringing carnage to their neighborhood. On the other hand, the Communist Workers Party members argued that the assault proved their analysis about the state's violence in repressing workers. "Under the direction and aid of the FBI, the KKK and Nazis with military precision assassinated five members of the Communist Workers Party," they declared in a press statement. "The murders of the CWP5 is a clarion call to U.S. workers and oppressed people to rally around the banner of the Communist Workers Party to turn this country upside down."[9]

Regardless of their political differences, civil rights organizations recognized the Greensboro massacre as part of a rising tide of racist violence and far right activity sweeping the United States. Lucius Walker, C.T. Vivian, Anne Braden, and Leah Wise were among the organizers who convened the National Anti-Klan Network with strong support from churches and civil rights organizations. The network hired Lyn Wells, a working-class white woman who had been active in the anti-war movement, as its executive director. The emerging coalition called for a national march in Greensboro on February 2, 1980, the twentieth anniversary of the day Black students launched a series of sit-ins at segregated lunch counters in the city. Only days before the event, the march's organizing committee expelled Communist Workers Party representatives when Nelson Johnson, pressed repeatedly by reporters, refused to advise people to come to the march unarmed.

These factional struggles were remote to me as I marched with lesbian friends and ten thousand other people through Greensboro on February 2, down streets lined with police in riot gear, helicopters circling overhead.

In June 1980, six Klansmen and Nazis went on trial for the Greensboro murders in an atmosphere of anti-communist fervor. The white supremacists in court claimed self-defense. Their arguments hinged on the Communist Workers Party's inflated rhetoric, how the people at the rally had closed in on the Klan vehicles, and on the weapons some anti-Klan demonstrators had brought to the march. Key also was a highly technical debate on whether any of the first eleven gunshots had come from anti-Klan demonstrators (later trials showed they probably did not).[10] In November 1980, an all-white jury acquitted the defendants of all charges. To the average Carolinian long antipathetic to the communist menace, the incident was over—like the papers said, it was a battle between extremes, with the neutral middle unaffected.

Boosted by their victories, Klan and neo-Nazi factions began organizing all over North Carolina, running men for various state and local offices, marching through towns, and bragging publicly of paramilitary organizing. In Iredell and Alexander counties, residents reported a rash of cross burnings and attacks on interracial couples. Across the state, four different Klan groups emerged: the White Knights of Liberty, suspected in the Iredell activity; Virgil Griffin's Invisible Empire; the old and secretive United Klans of America; and, most worrisome, a neo-Nazi formation, the Carolina Knights of the Ku Klux Klan. In early 1983, National Anti-Klan Network director Lyn Wells drove up I-85 from Atlanta to Statesville to investigate an attack on the home of a Black minister, Reverend Wilson Lee. Together, Lee and Wells documented twenty-five cases of Klan violence between 1979 and 1983 in western North Carolina. That summer, she took Reverend Lee to Washington, DC, to meet with Justice Department officials, and a federal grand jury in Asheville, North Carolina, began an investigation. After the investigation went nowhere quickly, the network's lawyers helped Reverend Lee and eight other victims of racist violence sue the Justice Department for inaction.[11]

A second front in the emerging anti-Klan efforts opened in January

1983 after someone burned a cross on the lawn of the Martins, who had moved into the little community of Bahama, just north of Durham.[12] Lauren is white, and Paul is racially mixed, a tall man often mistaken as white; he is an officer in the Durham Police Department. After the attack, Lauren spent weeks of sleepless nights, taking her pistol to the mailbox in the mornings. The Martins, like Wilson Lee, went looking for help and got in touch with the National Anti-Klan Network in Atlanta. Lyn Wells contacted Leah Wise, a network board member from Durham, urging her to organize a response to what was a growing crisis.

Leah Wise is an African American woman whose southern activism goes back to the Student Nonviolent Coordinating Committee (SNCC), the 1960s organization of young Black radicals that was the cutting edge of the civil rights movement in the South. She later moved to Durham to attend graduate school at Duke, and then worked as a steel fitter before injuring her foot. Leah had helped to organize the February 2 march in response to the Greensboro murders. In 1982 she became director of Southerners for Economic Justice, an advocacy group based in Durham. Leah is a striking woman, six feet tall and highly analytical. She can intimidate the bejesus out of just about anybody when she tries, and sometimes when she does not. Over the years, Leah would become my most trusted mentor.

A core group of ten people formed to respond to mounting Klan violence.[13] Mardie McCreary, who began working for Southerners for Economic Justice part-time with the emerging anti-Klan effort, recalls: "I remember the severity of the events with no media attention to them, and the isolation of the victims. There were cross burnings, shootings, the racially motivated murder of a Black man near Gastonia. How could we pull everything together to get public attention?"

By midsummer, the ad hoc anti-Klan group had assembled a chronology of extensive white supremacist activity and racist attacks, drawing heavily on the research of Lyn Wells and Reverend Lee in the western part of the state. They got an appointment with Governor Jim Hunt's lawyer, but he met them at the door with a remarkable statement: "Ms. Wise, before I let you go further, I must remind you that it is not the role of the state to enforce the law." Lauren recalls the moment: "Here I was suffering from sleep deprivation and fear and this guy says this. We were outraged." They began to modify their original expectation that when they sounded the alarm, the appropriate organizations and government agencies would act. Instead, they found profound fear and denial.

I joined the group that summer of 1983. I had just left a closeted college teaching job with six months of unemployment benefits. I intended to spend much of my free time writing, but the anti-Klan organizing drew me. North Carolina had the fastest-growing white supremacist movement in the country, Lyn Wells said. I had left Alabama to get away from violent repression. It had followed me. But I was an adult, not an adolescent. I had unfinished business.

Our ad hoc anti-Klan group organized a local petition drive when Klan posters showed up in downtown Durham, a press conference to release our report chronicling the upsurge in racist activity, and a conference on the Klan's threats to put armed guards in public schools to protect white children. Jimmy Pratt and Bobby Person joined our efforts. They were Black prison guards from Moore County, a couple of hours south of Durham. On May 29, 1983, Person had requested a copy of the employment manual for the Moore County Correctional Unit. He wanted information on how to apply for the rank of sergeant. The next day, a cross was burned in front of his home. The following October, armed Carolina Knights Special Forces showed up on his doorstep to threaten his family. They vandalized his and his father's property, ran his wife off the road, and threw hate literature onto his lawn.[14] The Klan had targeted both Person and Pratt because they had raised issues of institutional racism on their jobs. They complained of racist treatment of prisoners and tried to take the sergeant's test in a prison with no Black officers. Bobby and Jimmy got little satisfaction from the sheriff or the governor, and they came to us in fall 1984. Leah tried to publicize their case and put them in touch with Morris Dees, director of the Alabama-based Southern Poverty Law Center and its Klanwatch program. Dees filed suit against the Klan in Person's behalf.

The resistance to our message continued when a local television station postponed for two months a Black public affairs program that featured Reverend Lee, Jimmy Pratt, and Bobby Person.[15] It took another petition drive and letters to the Federal Communications Commission to have them air the program. In early January 1984, nine of the white supremacists involved in the Greensboro assault went on trial again, as a result of a vigorous campaign by the survivors—this time in federal court for civil rights violations.[16] On Palm Sunday (April 15), Mike Nathan's widow, Marty, called me from the courthouse, a deadness in her voice, to let me know the jury's decision: all defendants innocent again of all charges. We called a vigil at the Durham post office to protest the verdicts.

By fall 1984, we decided that we needed to formalize our efforts into a watchdog organization. We named the new group North Carolinians Against Racist and Religious Violence (its acronym, NCARRV, pronounced "en-carve"). We assembled a board, and Leah asked me if I would be coordinator. I was ready, but I knew I needed the freedom to link homophobia and racism. I also knew I could no longer hide my sexual orientation to any employer. I made sure that all the board members knew that I was gay and that under the state's "crime against nature" statute some people might consider me criminal. One Black minister clarified, "You mean we are hiring an acknowledged homosexual with a profile as an activist?" I nodded. They voted unanimously to give me the job.

3

Statesville

Reverend Wilson Lee was maybe the bravest man I ever knew, and the most soft-spoken. On an early February morning in 1983, he and his wife, Alice, woke to gunfire outside their parsonage in Statesville. A young neighbor was beating on the door.

"Reverend Lee, Reverend Lee, the Klan burned a cross!"

Wilson walked through his home in his pajamas to answer the door, the light from the burning cross casting strange shadows on Alice Lee's carefully kept living room. The glass blown out of their front windows crunched beneath his slippers.

"Oh, the Klan?" he said, calming the young man. He called the police, dealt with them when they came, cleaned up, and went back to sleep. The next morning, he began systematically calling friends across the state.

In choosing Wilson Lee as a target, the Iredell County White Knights had made a mistake. For months, the klavern had been terrorizing interracial couples, people whose relationships tended to separate them from both white and Black communities. But until he died of a stroke in 1988, Reverend Lee lived at the heart of the African American community, and he had friends all over the country. He had come to the Klan's attention when he wrote a letter of protest to the *Statesville Record and Landmark* after sheriff's deputies had allowed fifteen Klan members to visit the jail. The Klan had offered to "bond out" a Black man accused of raping a white woman. The prisoner refused the offer, which amounted to a threat of lynching.[1] The sheriff's department had made no move to identify any of the Klansmen, in spite of the county's rash of unsolved Klan-like attacks.

After Reverend Lee's letter, the threatening calls began. "Have you ever seen a Klansman? Well, you're going to see one." Two nights later came the cross burning.

It was almost strange that the Klan had waited so long to visit the Lees. Reverend Lee had come to Statesville in 1957. Born in 1917, he grew up near the Carolina coast in the Perquimans County town of Woodville. His parents died when he was seven, their deaths two months apart. His grandmother had raised him, sitting him in her lap and telling him of her experiences during slavery. "I began to have strong feelings against slavery and the quasi-slavery I was brought up under," he later explained.[2] He left his family's tenant farm to work in the Norfolk Naval Shipyard until 1941, when he joined the army and fought in North Africa and Italy. After the war, he served two stints in the merchant marine and graduated from Raleigh's Shaw University and Crozer Theological Seminary in Chester, Pennsylvania. Then he was called to St. John, the lovely small Baptist church on the west side of Statesville that he would pastor for three decades. When the civil rights movement heated up in the central part of North Carolina in the early 1960s, he was on the front lines.

Reverend Lee's first arrest came in the late 1950s when he attempted to use a "whites only" restroom. (The indignity of the segregated bathroom would ignite Sammy Younge's final explosive confrontation with racism.) In 1962, Alice Lee spent her very first night in Statesville alone because her husband had left her and her furniture in the middle of the parsonage floor to "go down town for a little while"—where he and a friend sat in at the Woolworth's lunch counter. He called Alice that evening: "Sugar, I'm in jail."

Demonstrations at Woolworth's and Howard Johnson's continued in coordination with the Congress of Racial Equality's "Freedom Roads" campaign to desegregate public facilities along interstate highways. At the jail, demonstrators sang, played cards, fixed each other's hair, and ate the good food their supporters sent in. Reverend Lee slept on several inmates' mattresses pushed together, while the others watched over him, forbidding cursing in his presence. One evening, Statesville's Black citizens marched five hundred strong from a church meeting to the jail, where the crowd was twice sprayed with insecticide by a city vehicle. Reverend Lee on several occasions pointed out to me the corner where it happened, shaking his graying head in disgust. Attorney General Robert Kennedy called the local judge and urged that demonstrators charged with trespassing be released.

Eventually, in 1963 (that intense year of school desegregation in Alabama), all of this pressure led to the desegregation of all public eating places in Statesville, although whites continued to resist the court orders. A new, more conciliatory city council agreed to integrate a city park and swimming pool. Outraged white citizens voted the entire council out in a special recall election. The years between 1965 and 1972 brought court-ordered desegregation of schools, hospitals, and housing, with Reverend Lee (whom his people considered, by then, "the Martin Luther King of Iredell County") in the lead.[3]

A meticulous man, he always wore a coat and tie in public. At least, I never remember him in more casual dress. Other ministers might have larger churches and bigger salaries, but no one else in Statesville's African American community had the kind of love and admiration that his people gave to Wilson Lee. Whenever police beat up a young Black man, whenever there was a shooting, people called Reverend Lee. Even when he was clearly old and tired, with high blood pressure and his doctor warning him to slow down, he would always rise from his bed in the middle of the night to help. He reminded me of the Good Shepherd in Jesus's parable, who left ninety-nine of his flock safe to go after the one that was lost. The family whose house was shot up might live on the wrong side of the tracks or run a liquor house, but Reverend Lee answered their calls. Each life was precious, and the wolves who fed on five hundred years of African flesh could easily enough pick off his flock one by one.

In 1985, Wilson Lee became president of the board of the newly incorporated North Carolinians Against Racist and Religious Violence. Overt racist activity in Iredell County had quieted in 1984 after Reverend Lee and Lyn Wells had brought the upsurge in the western part of the state to the attention of the U.S. Justice Department. But violence flared again in 1985, and I soon began to work in Iredell County with Reverend Lee and Christina Davis, an African American whom NCARRV hired to lead our community organizing. I had first met Reverend Lee when he, Leah, and Lyn had led an educational forum in Durham in the summer of 1983. It was also my first contact with the emerging anti-Klan coalition. Reverend Lee had been skeptical of me at first. I think he doubted my staying power, but at some point his attitude shifted. He began to trust my commitment. As local representative of NCARRV, he served as mediator between us and the people in Statesville and as adviser to our work. Like Leah, he became a mentor to me, one of my first and most important guides on the journey I had begun, my descent into the racism of my culture. A couple of times he called me his "little sister." It was perhaps more as a father than as a brother that I needed Wilson Lee.

In fact, Wilson Lee and my own daddy were the opposite sides of a coin. My father spent much of my adolescence organizing white private schools all over Alabama to avoid integration. Like Wilson, he spent many of his evenings out of the house at meetings. When I went to Black community meetings in Statesville with Reverend Lee, I had an eerie feeling that my father was out there somewhere organizing the other side.

I listen with fascination to friends who grew up as "red diaper babies" during the McCarthy era, brought up by leftist parents. I was a "white diaper baby." My father was a Republican in Alabama before the "southern strategy"; in fact, he turned Republican in 1932 in response to FDR. In 1964, my family supported Goldwater for president, the Republican debacle from which the New Right would emerge triumphant via the populist presidential campaigns of George Wallace, which we also cheered on. We enthusiastically followed Ronald Reagan in his passage from *General Electric Theater* to the California governor's mansion. Stacks of conservative publications like *Human Events, None Dare Call It Treason*, missives from the Heritage Foundation, and William Buckley's *National Review* spilled from bookshelves in my father's room. If a person sneezed, she could be buried under an avalanche of right-wing ideology.

Daddy grew up on a small farm ten miles out of town on land

Segrests had owned since the U.S. government moved the "Creeks" west in the 1830s. In his youth, he had risen early in the morning to help with the farm chores. Then he would walk with his younger sister May down the clay road that wound like an orange ribbon through the pines, to where the bus would pick them up for school. My mother's people lived in town, part of the ruling class that had regained control of the county after Reconstruction, her grandfathers a judge and a college president. Little capital remained after my widowed grandmother raised three young children, sending the two sons to medical school. My inheritance was more a dose of snobbishness. I cared little about my father's family beyond my aunt and cousins. Sundays, Daddy would take us out to the country to visit Grandma, to the clapboard house where he grew up, shotgun hall down the middle and two rooms on each side heated by fireplaces. Playing barefoot outside, I would dodge chicken droppings and acorns, waiting to go back to town.

My father was appointed postmaster by Eisenhower Republicans. He began organizing private schools during the Kennedy administration. After attending a meeting in Selma, he received harassing letters from the assistant postmaster general in Washington. The possibility that he could lose his job was palpable, if not stated. He warned us repeatedly that the phones were probably tapped. He was probably the first organizer I knew, and one of the best.

But into my work I carried an anger at my father that I did not totally understand and a determination, also hardly articulated, to out-organize him. It was complicated: all the energy he put into establishing segregated private schools was for my brother and sister and me. Why did it feel like betrayal?

With Reverend Lee and Christina in my first months in Statesville, I crossed and recrossed more racial boundaries than I had ever managed in the eighteen years I had lived in my similar Alabama hometown. With them, I had access to the Black community, and I saw white people through their eyes.

At Mitchell Community College, near the center of town, one of four Black instructors told me he was carrying a gun because of anonymous threats to kill him and his family.[4] One of these letters read:

"Once and for all drop your grievance and keep your mouths shut. . . . Children are quite often involved in unexplained accidents or . . . just disappear."[5] The school's four Black employees had received ten such letters over the previous two years. Then we visited Reverend Robert Young, a United Methodist minister in the uptown church of many white town fathers. He explained their concern that bad publicity would keep businesses away from Iredell County, and he puzzled over how to encourage his parishioners to act. Christina and I suggested they generate positive publicity by opposing the Klan. Then Reverend Lee took us across the railroad tracks into the factory section of town and poorer neighborhoods. On Meeting Street we talked with a Black family that four white men with semiautomatic rifles had attacked in the course of what police called a "neighborhood quarrel." Two of the family members and a friend had been wounded in the attack, which left nineteen bullet holes in the walls of their small house.[6] Then we went to talk with a state legislator, a crusty old white man from whom I heard a refrain that was to become familiar: news about the county's epidemic of racist violence was giving the place a bad name, as if the victims of numerous cross bumings had planned it all just to undermine the Chamber of Commerce.

"This is just a normal Scotch-Irish community," he explained of a town that is one-third African American.

"Yes, and I'm very proud of my Scotch-Irish ancestry," Christina answered without missing a beat, her brown face gathering up the light. We both rolled our eyes toward the ceiling as we exited the office.

What *was* "normal" in North Carolina and the United States in 1983? This particularly normal county was founded in 1788 by Scottish, Irish, and German settlers. It had three separate integrated school systems, its two cities with systems 50 percent Black, its county system 85 percent white. The per capita income of residents of Iredell County in 1982 was $7,232, with workers concentrated in textiles, furniture, and apparel.[7] Although 17 percent of the county's population and almost one-third of Statesville's population were Black, there had never been a Black elected official.[8] After the integration battles of the 1960s came a decade-long struggle against brutality by the city's all-white police and fire departments. The result was a federal order, which came down shortly before the Klan entered the county, mandating that the departments start hiring Blacks. The NAACP next targeted the electoral system, getting a federal order that required the city to reshape municipal and school board seats to include seats for predominantly Black wards.[9] "The power of this city is in the hands of the White population," one of the anonymous Mitchell College letters had read, reacting no doubt to these events. "All Whites are born leaders." The letter writer concluded, almost plaintively, "We don't mind you being here, just please let things get back to normal."

Christina and I were both in our thirties and had known each other from past projects. But NCARRV work required an intimacy that built quickly. We developed a style that would see us through six years together, lending an easy rhythm to the kind of interviews we began in Statesville. In the process, Christina became my first really close Black friend. I had other Black folks I cared about and with whom I worked. But Chris and I spent days together, on the road sometimes a week at a time, similarly feeling urgent and amused, building a bond between us. Her mama and brothers and sisters, with their squabbles and support, their family reunions in Raeford with acres of food, became familiar through Chris's stories, and I matched them constantly with my own cast of characters on our rides together or nights unwinding. Evenings in Statesville, we stayed at Jubilee House, a white Christian community whose members had opened their doors and hearts to us.[10] We laughed and cooked and recounted the day's events with the Jubilee adults—Kathleen, Sarah, Mike, and Margaret— while their kids did homework or played. Chris herself had a huge heart and a hard head—a stubborn streak as wide as mine, or so she said. She had an easy way with people, for which I was grateful, since it balanced my shyness, and a range of skills that sometimes surprised me, probably because I figured I was supposed to know everything, as a white person.

What we were doing required teamwork. I learned how to repeat the message heard from Reverend Lee or Chris to white audiences, sensing that my words would be heard differently, as if my vocal chords were tuned more to the frequency of white ears. At first, I was

surprised when Black folks let me in the doors of their homes and
meetings, given the disaster racism was inflicting on their lives. But
the Black people I encountered seemed to know as many versions of
white people as words Inuits in Alaska had developed for snow, and
my place on the white spectrum seemed recognizable immediately in
my inflection, body language, and, especially, deeds. I read in these
responses that I was hardly the first white person to venture into this
territory. I could feel Black strangers opening toward me or closing
down, a constant calculus of distances. I learned also to cipher the
distances in Black friends, when in the middle of a conversation I
would feel the attention drift or shift, a sudden space between us.
Sometimes their challenge would be direct and swift, though seldom
sharp; other times I would look back and recognize a subtle contradiction or rerouted conversation that left me searching through my
words to find the point where I had thrown the switch. There was a
constant possibility of small betrayals that could invoke the specter of
much larger crimes.

There are always at least two versions of any story, and sooner or
later a person has to choose, I thought as Christina and Reverend
Lee drove me back and forth between white and Black citizens. I had
begun to question the law of physics that no two objects could occupy
the same space at the same time. Like residents of Mars and Venus,
the Black and white people of Statesville might as well live on different planets. To many white Statesville residents, Reverend Lee often
sounded strident, but I saw how he had to hike up the volume many
decibels before it even registered to them as sound.

Christina and I began to fill in the blank spaces on the Carolina
map, highways that ran like rivers, like streams inside the body, major
arteries that split to smaller vessels then to capillaries, State Road
1099. Then the road back, like veins, like a different journey, un-
wound a different way: the angle on a field, a ramshackle wall on a
tobacco barn, or the endlessly gaudy series of billboards for South
of the Border, a kitschy truck stop on I-95. Very soon, I could no
longer drive with innocence down any of these highways. Every exit
announced a town or city written in bigotry or blood: China Grove,
where the Communist Workers Party had stood down the Klan a few

weeks before their Greensboro encounter ended in a blaze of gunfire; Cliffside, Sanford, Grover, Rocky Mount, all sites of Klan rallies; Garner, Clayton, Lexington, where white and Black students clashed over racism in the schools; Henderson and Fayetteville, where white supremacists were arrested with illegal explosives and armaments; Otto, home of the neo-Nazi Church of the Creator. And on and on and on.

I soon began to talk to reporters about Klan violence and racism, and often the question would come: "Why do you do this work?" Probing for a human angle, no doubt, the interviewer was also casting me as an anomaly. As the years progressed, it was all I could do not to grab the mike and shoot back into the camera's eye, "Why doesn't everybody?"

The insanity of racism affects children deeply, and, born in Alabama in 1949, I soaked in the anxiety, fear, and resistance that had been building in Macon County since the end of World War II. Macon County, home of Tuskegee University and a predominantly African American Veterans Administration hospital, had one of the largest Black populations of any county in the country—close to 90 percent through much of my childhood. My mother recognized that "nigras" would raise significant and far-reaching challenges to segregation in the South, and, to the southern whites of my parents' generation, *Brown v. Board* came as no surprise. It was a question of how to respond, and within a year the forces of fear and reaction won out. I honestly cannot remember now how much I knew about the riots at Little Rock in 1957, when I was eight, or the outbreak of violence when Autherine Lucy attempted to integrate the University of Alabama. But I am sure I knew in 1957 about attempts in my town to redraw a four-sided municipality into an "uncouth twenty-eight sided figure"—as *Gomillion v. Lightfoot*, the landmark Supreme Court decision that struck it down, observed—to eliminate 395 of its 400 potential Black voters.[11] *Gomillion* opened the door to voter registration and the eventual demise of white rule in Macon.

In 1963, history came to dinner. We watched ourselves and other Alabamians on state and national news every evening over supper. The year began with George Wallace's inaugural address, in which he promised "segregation forever." The spring brought demonstrations in Birmingham at which police turned fire hoses and dogs on children. Over the summer, Wallace was grandstanding again, this time at the University of Alabama, where he "stood in the school house door" to deny entrance to two Black students, then rapidly backed down under federal pressure. On August 13, federal judge Frank Johnson ordered the desegregation of Tuskegee High School on September 2, when doors would open for the fall, an unexpected move that shocked local residents. Birmingham, Mobile, and Huntsville also had desegregation suits pending.

I was preparing to enter the ninth grade at Tuskegee High. I was on the Student Council, which met through August to discuss how to respond to integration. The most popular suggestion was just to freeze the Black kids out by starting all-white sororities and clubs. I was not sure I could go along.

The Sunday before school was to open, I went outside to think. It was the weekend of the March on Washington, in which King dreamed his dream of little Black boys and Black girls in Alabama joining hands with little white boys and white girls as sisters and brothers. That event seemed far from me that afternoon as I dragged my foot in the gravel of the front driveway, tracing a figure eight as I tried to imagine the next day's school. How would it be to walk into homeroom after the first bell and see the Negro kids there? How would everybody act? I could see the rows of desks in my mind, scribbled and carved on by years of bored students, with the teacher up at the front of the room, impatient. Where would they sit? Would they be scared? Weren't they asking for trouble? Would I be friendly? How would the white kids treat me if I was? I pondered these questions a very long time, my foot and leg up to my calf covered with dust from dragging it through gravel.

I finally resolved, out loud: "If I like them, I will be their friend. If I don't, I won't." I was ready for school.

The next morning, Governor Wallace sent two hundred state troopers to surround the building, closing the school for a week in hopes that white resistance to integration would build. That day, the town was chaotic, filled with reporters, troopers, and angry and confused townspeople milling about. On Wednesday, Birmingham's schools integrated, but when some whites responded with bombings and riots, they were closed again. Wallace closed the Huntsville schools, as he had Tuskegee High, and Mobile delayed opening day. The second week the troopers were there again to deny the thirteen Black children entrance, although four Black children made it to Huntsville's schools. Then the Justice Department got a restraining order against Wallace, who called out the National Guard. President Kennedy promptly nationalized the Guard and ordered them back home. On September 10, Tuskegee, Mobile, and Birmingham desegregated.

I was lying in the bushes in Mrs. Fort's yard looking through onlookers' legs that September morning when the thirteen Black students in a lone school bus rode through the crowds of white folks and armed men. People in front of me shifted to let the bus through, some muttering about "niggers." A few minutes later, three of the Negro kids were coming down the steps to walk across the breezeway. I could see them walking across the breezeway just as I had done for nine years with Sandra and Hilma and Lana, going from grammar school to high school. Then it was as if I were outside myself, looking down on Mab-under-the-bushes, and the Negro children, and the ring of policemen with their guns, and many of the white people with their hate. I knew how the Negro children felt then. They looked lonesome. They could be me. It was as if my heart went out of my body, out through the feet in front of me toward those small human figures crossing the school breezeway. Then they were up the stairs and in the door, and it was over.[12]

The week that Tuskegee High integrated, my father was elected president of the Macon Academy Private School Foundation, which immediately began plans for a private school that would eventually draw off most of the county's whites. Three days later, the rising racial tension crescendoed in Birmingham when Klansmen planted a bomb under the steps of the Sixteenth Street Baptist Church, and the explosion left four girls my age dead in the rubble.

I heard about the Birmingham bombing in my own church that morning when Reverend Sellers (one in a long line of liberal preachers the Methodist Conference sent to try to persuade our church to integrate) announced that four girls had died. Weeping, he asked us to pray for their souls and ours. I was immediately saddened. They had been in the women's bathroom between Sunday school and church when the explosion occurred, the same place I had been with my girl-friends only an hour or so before. After church, I heard adults talking among themselves, saying that the explosion was probably the work of Black Panthers looking for publicity, or of the FBI.

"The preacher's tears were inappropriate," my father said.[13]

Inappropriate? I was shocked. Those girls were my age. Why did this man say such awful things? When he did notice me at the table, it was often to criticize: "Don't eat so fast" or "Don't put so much salt on the food, it will dry up your blood." He seemed to work all the time, then go out to meetings at night, and when he was home he just watched TV and went to bed earlier than anybody else. He was wrong, and it made me angry. Like him, I withdrew into silence.

I was confused and felt increasingly isolated. I still believed in states' rights and was sure most white Yankees were hypocrites, but I also believed segregation was wrong. I would get into bitter arguments with my older brother, my younger sister chiming in on his side, as we watched the evening news.

"You believe these Yankee newsmen," he would taunt me. "You are Walter Cronkite's dupe."

"Them being hypocrites don't make us right," I would counter.

This separation from my brother was painful. He was three years older than I and a boy, so as a child I had been allowed to go wherever he could go, and that was everywhere: to East End and back, to the turnpike and back on the longest July day. By April we would be beg-ging to go barefoot, though Mother never allowed it until the first day of May, when early in the morning we would run out the front door, hop across the gravel on tender winter feet, brush through new grass wet with dew, and race to the giant magnolias. We would shinny to the lowest limb, then mount, branch by branch, until the trunk swayed against the sky. From there, flushed with summer, we could see the whole town. Holding tight to the trunk amid masses of leaves slick like green patent leather, it seemed that summer would last forever. But in adolescence, we looked at each other across a great divide.

The next Alabama flash point came in Selma in 1965, when police went on well-publicized rampages against demonstrators, and Jimmy Lee Jackson, a young Black man, and James Reeb, a white minister, died at the hands of racist whites. People from all across the country flocked to Selma to join the march to Montgomery. Then Klansmen shot to death Viola Luizo, a white volunteer who was driving participants back to Selma.

My brother said Luizo was a whore and deserved to die. "Nobody deserves to die," I yelled, picking up whatever was nearest my hand (keys? a fork?) and throwing it at his head. Sometimes my mother would follow me to the kitchen and tell me she agreed with me, but at the dinner table I was on my own. After a while, I just stopped talking and plotted to get out of Alabama. Years later, my younger sister reduced me to tears in the middle of the kind of white southern family argument where politics mixes with inchoate currents of emotion: "You always were crazy."

"Race was always somewhere inside southern whites' family arguments," a white woman observed to me years later in a comment I recognized immediately as true. A Black lesbian at an anti-racist workshop provided elaboration. White people use Black people to draw boundaries in homes where family members' identities are enmeshed, she explained, in response to a white woman's pleased story of how upset she had made her parents in her adolescence by dating Black men.[14]

I was not the only Tuskegee youth moved by these events. Sammy Younge was among Black students at Tuskegee Institute who participated in the Montgomery rally and came back home determined to press the pace of change in Tuskegee. They picked the town's churches.[15] On June 27, 1965, they began attempts to integrate my church. Sunday after Sunday I would see a flurry of activity by the ushers at the back of the sanctuary. The church board had appointed a new officer, the "welcomer," to let white people in and lock the door when any of the Black demonstrators approached. The irony was not lost on me as I looked out from the choir loft at the stained glass windows, the one nearest the back, portraying a fair-haired Jesus knocking at the door. "Knock, and it shall be opened"—I knew the verses

by heart—"Seek, and you shall find." I had been raised in the Tuskegee Methodist Church by people who loved and nurtured me. Along
with my parents, they had taught me all the values I knew. "Love thy
neighbor as thyself," as we had studied in Sunday school; "Let justice
roll down." Like most adolescents, I was an idealist, and this rupture
between my teachers' lessons and their behavior shook me profoundly.
If we could decide who could not come into our church, then it was
just a building that belonged to us, not God. It took me years to articulate my disquiet. Didn't the same act of locking other people out
also lock us in?

On the third and fourth Sundays when the demonstrators returned,
white men from town attacked them, beating Sammy Younge and two
other student leaders.[16] I was away at the time, and after I heard about
that incident I never quite came back to church. I was not particularly
pleased with God, either. I decided to develop a sin to register my
protest. After considering drinking, smoking, and screwing, I settled
on cussing as the safest bet.

During the campaign for church desegregation, I met my friend
Ann on an errand near the town square. We sat down on the bank
stoop and started to compare notes on how totally fucked up (she was
cussing now, too) the whole town was. Nor did theology make much
sense to us. How could all those Africans be condemned to hell when
white missionaries had not had a chance to get to them? How could
God exist in the midst of this confusion? Then my friend Sandra got
a new boyfriend from Union Spring who was a poet and an agnostic. I
asked him what "agnostic" meant, and he said it was someone who did
not know if God existed. *Hot damn*, I thought. *That's me.*

The confrontation between my sixty-seven-year-old kinsman Marvin Segrest and Sammy Younge at the Standard Oil station next to
the bus depot came on January 3, 1966. After the demonstrations at
the church, Sammy and the other young Black radicals had lost the
support (and the protection such support brings) of established Black
leadership. Anonymous whites had threatened to bomb Sammy's parents' home, and he himself had received death threats directly from
white men in the town. His friends later commented on his "constant
compulsion to fight racism," which often took the dangerous form of

slipping off to Montgomery or Auburn with a friend to test restaurants.[17] "I'm going to die from a bullet," he said.[18] Under increasing
pressure, he dropped out of the movement that fall, then he returned
shortly before his death. On the Monday he died, he helped bring
Black rural voters into town to register. That night, he left a party at
the Freedom House to buy mayonnaise and cigarettes. At the gas station a block off the city square, he asked to use the bathroom. Marvin
Segrest, working that night, tried to send him around to the Jim Crow
bathroom. Sammy refused.

I remember Daddy reporting Marvin's version of the event: "Marvin
said Sammy wanted to use the white bathroom and he wouldn't let
him. Said Sammy left and came back with what looked like a rifle. It
turned out to be a golf club. Marvin got his rifle from the gas station
and shot a warning shot at the pavement. It ricocheted up and killed
Younge. They're saying it's murder."

Well, I tried to reason it through, the autopsy will show that the
trajectory of the bullet proves Marvin was right.

Years later I found James Forman's oral history of Sammy Younge.[19]
The book shook me profoundly. It gave the other side of my adolescence in Alabama in the 1960s, and I read that the young SNCC
worker whom my cousin had killed had been a moving force in shaping
my teenage years. According to Forman's account, Younge was killed
by "a single bullet in the back of the head."[20] An eyewitness testified
that Younge was moving away from Marvin when Segrest fired, and
the location of the young Black man's body on the far side of the bus
terminal supported that version of events.[21] When an all-white jury in
Opelika found Marvin Segrest not guilty of second-degree murder,
Tuskegee Institute students rioted. The views on Sammy Younge's
death were as different as the views of white and Black inhabitants of
Statesville would later be.

In Statesville these old voices and stories swam in the air around
me. I was driving back into familiar terrain. I'm not acting out of guilt,
I would tell myself, just working on the Segrest family karma. And
there was Reverend Lee, impeccable and enraged, ushering me in and
telling me his stories.

"When I was a teenager," he said, "I was playing in the woods with some friends. We came across a creek where a couple of white girls were swimming naked. My friends and I took off, and we ran and ran and ran back home. We knew what could happen to Black boys who saw a white girl like that!" I knew as well: lynching, mutilation, being burned alive. My friendship with Reverend Lee was built, among other things, on our knowledge of the violated taboo.

Wilson Lee loved to "walk with the people." "There was always a burning love in my heart for my people," he explained. "I was determined through the help of God that racism would not persist." He read widely, from Marcus Aurelius to Sandinista philosopher Ernesto Cardinal. He always made it clear to me how thoroughly institutional racism allowed Klan terrorism to happen, a point he also made repeatedly in letters to local papers. In a typical message, he wrote:

> The Ku Klux Klan indeed is dangerous and mean. . . . But this is really not the greatest danger to us, their victims. Our greatest danger is sympathy and cooperation by millions of American people with the Klan. And at best it is apathy on the part of people who do not have sympathy for the Klan, nor do they cooperate with the hooded men and women. [They just] don't do anything to require the law to take actions against this mob.[22]

Alice Lee was as brave as her husband. She told me once about a series of threatening calls to their home. She would answer the phone, only to hear a white male's voice. The first time he called with a string of obscene insults, she said, "That's your mama." The second time he called to harass her, she said, "That's your grandmama." The third time, she said, "That's your great-grandmama." The fourth time, she said, "I can't go back any farther than that, or we will be related." He hung up and did not call again.

In 1986, Reverend Lee had his first stroke. Alice let us know he was in the hospital in Salisbury. Chris called and found that only family were permitted in.

"We'll tell them we're family," Chris said, and I agreed until I looked down at my skin.

"Chris, I'm white, they'll never let me in!"

"We'll tell them you are family, too," she repeated. She did, and we both got in to visit.

I reported to Reverend Lee on recent events in town, but in a voice he obviously thought was too loud, given that we did not know who was in the next bed.

I told him what Chris had said, and he repeated it: "You are family."

So now, like Alice said, I was related. I had a white family and a Black family. Maybe we even shared a great-grandmother or great-grandfather, a white slave master and rapist.

Chris and I traveled back and forth to Statesville through the spring and into the summer, responding to growing Klan presence in the area. Joe Grady, the White Knights' Grand Dragon, showed up at a Board of Education meeting to protest the "obscene" presence in the local library of *In the Night Kitchen*, a well-known children's book, because one illustration showed a naked boy tumbling into dough.[23] In June, the White Southern Rebels, a splinter Klan faction, staged a "cross lighting" in a predominantly Black neighborhood in nearby Mooresville, to angry reaction. (Ingeniously, they used lightbulbs, since the fire codes prohibited real flames.) "In this day and age, Blacks will not sit back and be silent, we will fight back," one resident warned at a town meeting.[24] The Rebels began to hold armed rallies in other parts of the county, as well as paramilitary training. All the activity attracted Invisible Empire leader Virgil Griffin, whose group marched into the county in August, then rallied on private property with a show of arms.[25]

Chris and I were following through the courts the trial of the white men who had attacked the Black family on Meeting Street. We worked closely with the staff of the *Iredell Neighbors* (a weekly magazine of the *Charlotte Observer*) and the Black-owned *Iredell County News*. Keith Williams, the only Black reporter at the *Iredell Neighbors*, had begun covering the county's Klan activity and got the attention of white readers. We organized a meeting of white liberals to solicit their help and began responding to a request from Black activists for community trainings in leadership skills. It was often slow going. People were skittish of outsiders. Many people assumed that Christina and I were members of the Communist Workers Party, in town to instigate a riot, or some other radical group with a hidden agenda. Chris and I brought Leah Wise over for a couple of meetings, but middle-class Black leadership blanched at her talk of better wages and working conditions as a long-term answer to the Klan.

In spite of the difficulties, the work began to pay off by midsummer. One turning point came when two young white men monitored a White Knights meeting. Michael Woodard was one of the residents of Jubilee House. Jeff Byrd was the editor of the *Iredell Neighbors*. It wasn't hard for Mike and Jeff to locate the rally. The *Record and Landmark*, Statesville's daily, had been printing advertisements for and directions to these rallies for several years. One of our organizers, following the directions, located the spot, then took me there one day. I had expected to ride down some winding dirt road into a corn field, but I was surprised. There, in a suburban neighborhood, in a grassy empty lot with houses all around, lay a big cross made of two pine trees lashed together. Every couple of weeks, the White Knights would wrap it, soak the cloth in gas, and light up. The material burned, leaving the charred pines for later use. Recycling, Klan style.

At the rally, Klan "nighthawks" or security guards recognized Michael and Jeff and forced them to leave. But the men had seen enough. Jeff went home and wrote an editorial: "Almost all of the men had guns—pistols strapped to their legs, rifles over their shoulders. . . . These gun-toting, self-proclaimed 'followers of Christ' probably could have fired 475 rounds without reloading." Jeff and Mike brought back samples of Klan literature, including an "Official Running Nigger Target." The stereotyped silhouette of a Black man indicated ten points for a hit from his head down to his trunk, with crosshatches over his skull and genitals. "Are we subtly supporting this maniacal fringe by our racial attitudes?" Jeff asked, and called on people to speak out.[26]

Like I say, white folks have a habit of listening to other white folks with different ears. Jeff's editorial brought an outpouring of letters and inspired Bob Young, the white Methodist minister, to call together other Black and white clergy. Their "Resolution of Conscience and Concern" stated the facts of Klan presence in the county, requested that law enforcement do its job against illegal Klan activity, and asked civic bodies in the county to join them in passing the resolution. They also asked that each of the state's Christian denominations pass the resolution at the highest administrative level. "The concern surfaced from within the community," Young explained to the press. "People are resistant when outsiders try to tell them what they ought to be doing."[27] I remembered the conversation with Young in which Chris and I had suggested that town leaders concerned about the negative Klan publicity could generate some positive publicity of their own. We had spent several months shaking the trees. Something finally was beginning to fall out.

A second major breakthrough came in late July. Keith Williams, the Black reporter at the *Iredell Neighbors*, told us that the Justice Department was about to enter indictments for the string of cross burnings. As Keith's stories made their way into the *Charlotte Observer*, the parent paper of the *Neighbors* and the state's largest daily, events became real in the public mind.

The White Knights of Liberty rapidly unraveled under FBI scrutiny. First came plea bargains of Grady Herman Rector Jr., twenty-six, the driver in many of the night rides, who turned state's evidence in July in exchange for a sentence of thirty months. Then Alvin Wayne Childress, the nineteen-year-old son of the Iredell klavern's leaders, Mary and Jerry Suits, was charged with a federal civil rights violation. The week before he came to trial, Mary Suits's niece, Kathy Eidson, also copped a plea in return for her testimony against Childress.[28]

Childress, who had been sixteen at the time of the 1983 night rides, came to trial in late August. Rector testified about one of the cross burnings. He explained that the Black family had heard them outside and turned on their light, scaring the attackers away before they lit the cross. But Childress had stopped at a phone booth and called back to the young Black man in the house he had just left, who had once been his friend and in whose house he had sometimes slept: "Ten minutes later," Childress told him, "and you'd a been one dead nigger." The judge found Childress guilty. He was ordered to pay a $300 fine and placed on probation until his twenty-first birthday.[29]

It was at this first trial that I met other people who would join the core of the Statesville anti-Klan efforts. Flora, a white woman in her fifties, had been attacked because of her relationship with Joe, who was Black. I got to be good friends with Flora, who shared the story of her life with me. When she was a child, her father beat her often. One day in her teen years, he came at her and she stopped him cold. "Don't you ever do that to me again," she told him, and left the house. She spent the day by a stream in the woods, imagining how to live a different life. When she returned to the house, her father had her brother beat her severely. She married to get away from home, then her husband beat her, too. After her husband died, she met Joe, and he was treating her more decently than any white man ever had. Then the Klan started in on them.

Flora found a blackened cross when she was backing out of the drive-way in November 1982, during the first wave of attacks in the county. Her body shook like she was having chills. The next spring, Joe's car was spray-painted and she found "KKK" on her mailbox.

"My nerves just sort of went," she told me. "We kept wondering what was going to happen next. Sometimes, during a Klan rally, we'd sit up all night watching, one in the front room, one in the kitchen, with a gun on the table."

Their next-door neighbor began harassing them, yelling slurs over the fence into the garden where they worked together, the only place they had felt safe. After that, they just stayed inside.

By now, Joe, Flora, and other families who'd been attacked were meeting regularly. Romley, an organizer connected with the National Anti-Klan Network, had pulled them together. Romley was a short, intense white man in his late forties with years of organizing experi-ence. He had grown up in a mill village near Greensboro. The group soon expanded. Flora and Joe had a police radio, and on August 1 they picked up word of a cross burning in the northern part of Iredell County.[30] The next day, Flora called up Betty Jo, the white woman in front of whose trailer the cross had burned. She talked fast enough to get Betty Jo the message she was a friend. Soon Betty Jo and Rick, her Black lover, joined the group. It was the second cross burning for the two.

Betty Jo and Rick lived in a trailer on her daddy's land, and her daddy was not pleased. He had stopped talking to her and turned off the trailer's electricity. The first time I met Betty Jo, she was heating water on a camp stove in the trailer. Mattresses blocked the windows, and rifles stood in the corners of the room.

She told me about the first cross burning, which had happened two years earlier.

"Rick came to bed about three o'clock and looked out the window and saw a light. 'Oh, my God, it's a cross!' It was setting up close to the road right in front of our bedroom. We just stared at it, waiting for the Klan to march by. I really expected to see white hoods. Rick jumped up and got the gun. I was really just frozen. I kept hearing little plops against the bedroom wall. I thought it was bugs or something. You know how loud bugs can be against a trailer. Then I heard a crack and I knew that was a gun, they shot straight up in the air. We sat on the floor until daylight."

Betty Jo and Rick told her children but not anybody else. Then two years later, August 19, 1985, came the second visit on a foggy, rainy day. Her son saw someone suspicious and alerted her and Rick. They got their guns and stood in the doorway, where they saw a light flicker as a man in fatigues trotted back up the road. Then the cross burst into flames. The man in fatigues broke out running.

Betty Jo commented:

First cross, I thought it was somebody local, even family, to get a message to us. This last cross—I figured after two years, people would have accepted it—it must be more to this thing, somebody out there that really is set on getting rid of us or something, right? It was like being in the dark, you're scared and just flailing out. I knew there was something I needed to fight, but I didn't have anything to fight with, right? I got more and more paralyzed. As a matter of fact, by the day Flora called, I was totally depressed. You feel so powerless. You feel like there's nobody. All my life, I felt like there were other people like me. Here I was in a community where I had grown up with Christian people, supposedly, the church I went to all my life is half a mile down the road, and after the cross burning, not one person came here and said anything. In fact, that Sunday morning after church, everybody left

church and drove by to see the cross. The road was lined with
cars. Not one person stopped to see how we were.

That summer also brought changes in Christina's life. Something
in her was settling down. She met and married Rody McCoy in a
whirlwind courtship. She also cut off her dreadlocks. She was shifting
from an activist-based community to a community of family and nation, as she described it, relocating to Greensboro, where Rody lived
and where she had grown up. Rody is a Muslim, and Christina is a
strong-minded woman.

In September, nine more people were indicted on civil rights violations, including both Jerry and Mary Suits.[31] White folks then had a
hard time saying Reverend Lee had burned a cross on his own lawn
to give them a bad name. That fall, the "Resolution of Conscience and
Concern" moved from the county to various state and regional church
bodies, and in October the sheriff's department made three arrests in
two cases of racially motivated intimidation. In October elections, the
first Black won a seat on the Statesville City Council.

On a more difficult note, the district attorney allowed the white
men indicted in the Meeting Street shooting to take a plea bargain for
six months in prison, with work release, out of a possible sentence of
fifty years.[32] It was a hard verdict to take. The next morning, Reverend Lee and I had breakfast together at Hardee's—ham biscuits and
coffee that were not recommended for the health of either one of us.
I was very pissed off. "Pace yourself," he told me, probably hinting at
the arrogance in my white expectations about what I could achieve in
a year against centuries of racism. "Don't try to do it all at once. We
need you."

In December 1985, we were all in federal court again. A flock of
White Knights violated their Klan secrecy oaths, plea-bargaining and
turning state's evidence, to bring a "sudden and unexpected flood of
guilty pleas," as one news account explained. Jerry Suits bargained for
a maximum sentence of ten years and agreed to testify if his wife got
no active prison time.[33]

In April 1986, eight Klan members went to trial in federal court in

Statesville, with Jerry Suits as the star government witness. In court testimony, he recalled how he had joined the Klan in the summer of 1982 and quickly became the Iredell leader. He said that Joe Grady had asked him to start a unit in Alexander County, and Suits was soon sworn into the "security forces," the duties of which were night riding. Their first activities were lessons in how to construct a cross to Klan specifications. Then they began looking for targets. By November 1982, they began their attacks in groups of three or four, with more and more people jumping in for the fun.[34] The all-white jury convicted six of the eight defendants, the first convictions against known Klansmen in North Carolina in the decade.[35]

Suits's remarks to the media sounded oddly like something Reverend Lee might say. "I wish I hadn't involved my family in it," he told television interviewers. "It seemed like the going thing. You get a great deal of nonmembers of the Klan who would like to see these acts done but didn't want to do it."[36] To the newspaper, he said, "A lot of this could have been avoided if the local authorities had took their information and moved on it. Because they had it all, but they didn't do anything with it."[37]

North Carolinians Against Racist and Religious Violence ended its active presence in Iredell County after the convictions. It was a good stopping place. We had helped a community generate a nonviolent response to violent Klan incursion. The voices of victims had emerged to counter Klan leaders' claims that the Klan was just interested in protecting white civil rights, not in depriving Blacks of their rights. An all-white jury had found white people guilty of racist attacks, and the citizens of Statesville were alerting other North Carolinians to the dangers of white-supremacist activity. The legacy of denial and fear that had followed the Greensboro massacre was crumbling.

My eighteen months working with Black and white people in Statesville taught me many things. For one thing, I learned about risk. The threat we posed to white supremacy was underscored one evening as someone followed Reverend Lee and me back to Jubilee House. And I became personally noticed by the racists: one of the White Knights' taped phone messages (an answering machine people called for a weekly diatribe) explained that I would give people AIDS. Moreover, I began to see how much white people could do to combat racism if we did not become overwhelmed by the magnitude of the task. The initial work done by Lyn Wells and Reverend Lee had been crucial in bringing about the federal prosecutions, but NCARRV's work had also been remarkably productive. Too, I was moved by the gratitude and friendship of white people like Flora and Betty Jo.

Betty Jo's summary of her experience resonated for me. After she met Flora, she said, she began to see that there were other people who felt as she did about racism. She and Rick, after the first cross burning, had often imagined seeing flames in the window of the trailer, after which they would sit up the rest of the night, the gun on Betty Jo's lap. The fear and insomnia had passed for her, she said. "Now the Klan could kill me. But they couldn't ever scare me like that again."

Reverend Wilson Lee had a massive stroke on Christmas morning in 1987 as he knelt for his prayers. Alice left a message on our office answering machine: "Pray for him. The doctors say it looks very bad."

I planned to ride over to see him in the hospital in Salisbury, but a Carolina snowstorm intervened, the kind that Yankees laugh about, when four inches of snow immobilize life because there are no snowplows and a sheet of ice waits slick beneath the dangerously innocent surface.

Wilson died on January 9, 1988. Leah, Christina, and I drove over for the funeral at St. John, the lovely church he had pastored for so long. "Wilson Lee's Homegoing," the program read. After the service, I reached through the window of the car to touch Alice's hand.

I loved Wilson Lee, and I miss him. He was my friend. But I also recognize the time he took with me as an investment, and I try to give him just returns.

4

Coming Out

Three years after I escaped in 1971 from Alabama to Duke's graduate school, I found the woman lover for whom I was unconsciously
searching. After two years at Duke and my first relationships with
men, I tried to remember being happy. I thought of summers at girls'
camp. I had loved the scent of girls' bodies, the dawn walks to the
bathhouse when the lake was a sheet of light. We'd paddle to sleep on
slim islands. I hadn't wanted to go home. So off I went that summer
of 1973 to be program director at a Girl Scout camp outside New
York City. Intense relationships with other counselors in all-women
environments had filled my summers in Alabama Girl Scout camps,
at the end of which came depressing goodbyes. In New York, the atmosphere was considerably more open, and outlaw love had begun
to speak its name. Among the Puerto Rican junior counselors were
several open young dykes. Their presence surfaced for me previously
subterranean issues of sexual identity. I was also increasingly drawn
to Pat, one of the seemingly heterosexual head counselors, a funny
and fiery young woman from "the city." She was also drawn to me. In
June on the camp's black lake, we paddled a boat in the stillness. I saw
the full moon tremble on my blade. We docked the canoe in silence,
but now I knew what had not been said. Alone on the rocks beneath
the willow, I practiced it out loud: "Lesbian." My whisper joined the
night sounds.

Pat was nineteen, I was twenty-four. After camp I went home to

Durham and she to New York, and we wrote daily. If I expected my usual Alabama routine of intense letters that gradually petered out, I was wrong. One letter described her dreams of kissing me. "Nothing sexual, of course," she explained, as the drumbeat in my clitoris sent me the final confirmation I was queer. Then Pat's mother (a bright, angry woman who tried to bind Pat close) sat her down and explained how there are only three kinds of love and two of those are homosexual. Whether or not we were ready to admit it, her mother argued, most certainly we would end up lovers, potentially the first of many disastrous homosexual affairs for Pat. She asked Pat to break off seeing me. Pat went upstairs and wrote to me: "I can't cope knowing that I love a woman. It will be easier if we terminate the relationship now before it's too late." But she wrote a second letter, asking that we make the decision together. "All I'm asking from you is to think about our relationship, honestly, from a feeling point of view—are we in danger of entering a homosexual relationship? If you think we are—what do we do about it? I'll do the same from my standpoint."

I knew that Pat's mother was right, that I was a lesbian and that I loved Pat. I wandered around Durham that afternoon, ending up under a cedar trying to decide whether I should kill myself. I got up from beneath the tree resigned to a lonely and tragic life, but committed to living.

I wrote Pat to break off the relationship:

> I've got to stop running sometime. I am sorely afraid, my friend, that your mother is right. I am in love with you. It's becoming hard for me to explain the situation any other way. The implications and consequences shake me to the core. . . . It astounds me how much of my thought processes for a terribly long time have been devoted to avoiding the realization of my lesbian tendencies (note that, still evading, I cannot say lesbianism). . . . Quoth Goneril (or is it Regan) in *King Lear,* "He hath ever but slenderly known himself." Amazing. And, altho my *feelings* at this moment are a tremendous sense of disorientation and dismay, I also feel a weird sense of relief. Like after this, no other [revelation] can compare. Previously—when I was hiding—I had thought

that . . . whatever I was fighting was inherent in existence and that I would wrestle with it until I couldn't stand it anymore. This fear was fear that I'd have to face what I'm trying to face now. But even now I'm backing away from it. But if I can face it and work through it—accept myself and find some way/place to be accepted as myself—*then* I'll be free.

I urged her not to let the fact of our lesbian love humiliate her or make her doubt her worth, finding myself, as I recognized, "in the difficult position of trying to assure you of your loveableness which my very love for you might make you question."

I found this letter again last summer stuffed with others into the familiar manila envelope Pat gave me five years later when she left. I sat down on the bed and read the correspondence through. The passage above stood out amid pages of self-conscious literary allusion and emotional evasion as an articulation of very old (or young) feelings. *There is something wrong (with me). I do not belong.* These feelings had provided my empathy with the Black kids on the breezeway the day they integrated my school, an emotion that had shifted my relationship to my culture. I look back on that young woman two decades ago, in the moment I conceived the possibility of my freedom, with compassion and gratitude.

My mood of scared, sad resolve lasted until the next day's mail, which brought Pat's next letter, with no mention of the previous day's correspondence. In the first two weeks after she defied her parents and moved down to live with me, I discovered passion, that coming together of the body's and the spirit's longings in the plane where two bodies meet, like the sky and the land. For weeks it was as if I were floating. Our first kisses were spaced at thirty-minute intervals. It took me that long to recover. After two days she said, "Mab, at some point we have to take our clothes off." We slept curled together each night, me increasingly awake. When I finally found the courage to tell her of my desire, she protested that sex was not what she wanted. A little while later, she kissed me.

I said, "If you don't want me to make love to you, don't kiss me like that." After thirty minutes, she rolled over and kissed me again.

I rolled toward her and we began making love. We made it up as we went along. When we fell away from each other, she said, "My mother was right. I knew you had done that with other women." I had to laugh, given my inexperience. I felt both proud and hurt. I knew she was voicing her mother's fantasies of me as lesbian vampire, older woman seducing girls away from Scout camp. (Looking back on it, she did as much seducing as I did, and her mother, misjudging the depths of my Alabama repression, also speeded things along.)

That fall, Pat and I got married one night on the picnic tables outside our apartments between washing and drying a load of clothes. We swapped rings and vows with only a striped kitten for company, and it made me nervous when she forgot the part about "as long as we both shall live." I made the incredible promises because I knew feelings that intense must last forever. We spent most of our years together hoping we were bisexual. Five years later, she left me for a man. I amused myself with fantasies of Mack trucks running him down. Years later, I recognized that—however pissed I was when she left me—she was the first woman brave enough to love me openly and accept my love. I also saw that she and her new partner were more suited to each other than she and I were.

When I had written her years before in New York to break up, I had just conceived of a place where I could accept myself and find some way to be accepted. When Pat left, I discovered the lesbian community that had developed in Durham in the early 1970s. The "political dykes" in Durham may have been the horror of less open and less opinionated "gay women" in the area, but they were home to me. Their feminism was the language of my freedom, the necessary antidote to all my years of loneliness, self-hatred, and fear. The lesbian-feminist manifestos of the early 1970s reversed the familiar homophobic field: if traditional psychological theory claimed that lesbian "inverts" were not real women, lesbian-feminists responded by claiming we were the most authentic women. I was electrified to read:

What is a lesbian? A lesbian is the rage of all women condensed to the point of explosion. She is the woman who, often begin-ning at an extremely early age, acts in accordance with her inner compulsion to be a more complete and freer human being than her society—perhaps then, but certainly later—cares to allow her. . . . To the extent that she cannot expel the heavy socialization that goes with being female, she can never truly find peace with herself. . . . Those of us who work that through find ourselves on the other side of a tortuous journey through a night that may have been decades long. The perspective gained from that journey, the liberation of self, the inner peace, the real love of self and of all women, is something to be shared with all women— because we are all women.[1]

I "came out" with an energy that gave everything an intense charge. I discovered rooms full, magazines full, a movement full of lesbians, and they became the most important thing in my life. Fury came up through my feet when I suddenly saw all the evidence of woman hatred in the world around me and in the culture I had studied—the rape, battery, violence, and suppression of creativity.

For a year, I grieved and raged over Pat's leaving, seeking out solace with my new friend Barbara. Her lover had walked out on her six months before Pat left me. We decided to move into a "heartbreak hotel" with a gay male friend who had also been jilted. Barbara and I were on-again/off-again lovers for the next two years while we grounded the relationship in a steady friendship. It took a while to admit that we had fallen in love.

Folks told me these changes were just my "Saturn cycle," the astrological interval every twenty-eight to thirty years when the planets turn your life around. In 1976 I attended the Modern Language Association convention in Chicago. Instead of buttonholing department heads in hotel elevators to beg for jobs, I listened raptly to every lesbian panel. "The transformation of silence into language and action" was the theme, and I sat in rooms full of other lesbians and wept.

I came home from Chicago and, as a member of a collective that edited *Feminary*, helped to turn that journal into one for southern lesbians. The collective drew a core of wonderful women: Eleanor Holland and Helen Langa, graphic artists; Minnie Bruce Pratt, a lesbian poet who first drove up from Fayetteville, then moved to Durham; Cris

South, a poet and novelist who moved from Charlotte to Durham; Deborah Giddens, who commuted to our meetings from Greensboro; and Aida Wakil and Raymina Mays.[2] Lesbian-feminism was my door into the possibility of belonging and self-acceptance. Once there, it was not long before the other issue basic to my identity—race—began to surface.

What does it mean to be lesbians in the South? we Feminarians asked ourselves and our readers. The query brought us face to face with a potent mixture: the racism of a former slave system, the capitalism that generated it, and the misogyny and homophobia that also held it in place. *What does it mean to be white in this culture?* we asked again and again, and *What difference do other differences make—working class/middle class; Christian/Jew; northern/southern . . . ?*

With brave and brilliant women, I learned rapidly that history had everything to do with it. I knew that I could not accept a "sisterhood" as segregated as that of my Alabama girlhood, where it had been enforced by police dogs, fire hoses, firebombs, and the deaths of children. The more I read of history, the more I saw the bitter legacy from the splits in the women's rights movement in the late nineteenth century, in which white women leaders such as Susan B. Anthony attacked Black men in racist ways because they had been given the vote and white women had not.

In part because of those splits, "second wave" feminism, which emerged in the 1960s and 1970s again riding the energy of Black freedom struggles, emerged in a predominantly white context. Its most acknowledged representations tended to emphasize gender discrimination and minimize race and class. Lesbian-feminism also acted out these limits but was increasingly called into accountability by lesbians of color, working-class lesbians, and Jewish lesbians.

There emerged what the Black feminist Combahee River Collective Statement called a "politics of identity," for which the *Feminary* collective was a microcosm. I attended feminist workshops on racism, hearing their truisms with new ears: white people need to learn to love ourselves; white people should work with other whites against racism, and middle-class whites need to deal with our own class biases to do so. The larger, vibrant lesbian writers' movement (the "clitterati," one friend joked) gave me a diverse, expanded circle of friends, people like Barbara Smith at Kitchen Table: Women of Color Press; Cherríe Moraga, Dorothy Allison, and Elly Bulkin at *Conditions*, a New York lesbian magazine; and Lou Blackdykewoman from South Carolina. Black, working-class white, Jewish, Chicana—they were my new queer cousins, with whom I was determined to keep faith.

Right-wingers overly enthusiastic about a handful of the wrong Bible verses make a lot of money by promoting the idea that gay people are antithetical to family. In 1976 Anita Bryant fronted the first religious campaign against gay rights in Dade County, Florida, with the slogan "Save Our Children!" to which gay organizers replied, "We *are* your children!" We were born from our mothers, just like they were; we grew up fighting with and loving our sisters and brothers, like they did. But we also had to deal with this other fear: would our parents (on whose love we had depended for our lives) and our brothers and sisters (who were our first and closest playmates) love us if they found out we were gay? Would they allow us to stay home or come home? Most of us have kept working it out with our blood kin. But very early on we also began forming alternative families out of networks of friends. *Feminary* was like that, like I had a bunch of sisters.

Carl and Allan were like that, too, gay brothers.

Carl Wittman was tall and graceful with his strawberry blond hair and beard. Allan Troxler is shorter, his brown hair in tight curls, his head often cocked quizzically to one side as he arrives at unexpected perspectives. They had lived in rural Oregon for years in a lesbian and gay collective until Allan got homesick and came back to North Carolina. He was interested in southern queer perspectives, including what we were doing with *Feminary*. He and Carl brought a grounded feminism to the gay men's community in Durham that opened space for alliances and friendships. Carl's aunt Elizabeth had followed them from Oregon to Durham, along with her lover Elana.

In 1980, Barb and I moved in with them. Carl and Allan had bought adjacent old wood-frame houses on Vale Street, which they were interested in turning into a collective. Barb and I teamed up with Carl, who set to work immediately on his dwelling, while Allan typically procrastinated. Having lived in separate counties for a couple of years,

Barb and I were ready to live together. I was teaching college English at the time, and I recall nights in my downstairs bedroom, me doing lesson plans for the next day's freshman comp class or working on an article for *Feminary* while Carl was on the staircase outside, carefully painting the railings or pasting up bright wallpaper. He wanted us to help more, but we had neither his ability nor the time to work on it.

Carl's Renaissance and Baroque music filled the rooms in a year when I no longer listened to male composers, furious at the decimation of female creativity. The poster above my typewriter read, "The men say: 'Where is your Shakespeare?' She was a lesbian and you burned her books." Carl's taste usually left me feeling gauche, a short dyke barbarian to his tall faggot aesthete. He could quickly get bored with people—including, I suspected, me.

Our household was best together at the barricades, helping to organize the first gay pride march in North Carolina after homophobes beat to death a man at a gay bathing spot. "I don't want to die," Ron Antonovich had told his assailants before they beat him on the head with a large branch from the creek bed. "I have felt that knock on the skull my whole life long," I wrote in my journal.

The women's peace movement and War Resisters League also expanded my understanding. Reagan had come into office on a program of deficit reduction, but his administration immediately began to pump up the military budget with money taken from Head Start programs, schools, and health care. Thirty-five years of collective terror over nuclear war and very new alarm at the huge new military budget fueled the women's peace movement. It gave lesbians like me an expanded political context in which to understand our own oppressions and privileges.

My friend and mentor was Dannia Southerland, six feet tall with thick red hair, easy to spot in a demonstration. Raised in the seacoast town of Jacksonville, the location of the U.S. Marine Corps training facility Camp Lejeune, Dannia had been active in the GI resistance arm of the anti-war movement with her then-husband. She had just come out when she took the job in the Durham office of the War Resisters League. Dannia introduced the *Feminary* women to the work of Barbara Deming, who had participated in some of the major nonviolent campaigns of the civil rights and anti-war movements. Later, Barbara had come to terms with her lifelong lesbianism, realizing that the energy it took her and her partner, Jane, to win custody of Jane's children was not time away from "the struggle" but an experience of struggle at a deeper, more intimate level.

In 1980 and 1981, the Women's Pentagon Actions brought two thousand women from all over the country to Washington, DC, to demonstrate against militarism in emotional, participatory, and highly symbolic events that drew on women's culture, history, and spiritual traditions. Women wept and raged over cardboard tombstones with names of people killed by racism, sexism, and homophobia. Organized into small affinity groups, they blocked the entrances of the Pentagon with their bodies and wove yarn webs over the doors until the police carried them away, to be supported through the "justice" system by other women. The actions were both separatist in their composition and broad in their analysis. I went in 1981 with an affinity group from Durham. The armed guards at the Pentagon felt like the armed force that George Wallace had sent to surround my school. Its stone walls radiated the same coldness as the marble of the Alabama capitol. As I waited that night outside the jail in support of the last of our crew to emerge, I knew I was finally deciding to put my power against the power of the state.

Dannia and I did several anti-racism trainings together. Our workshop model began in the morning with written personal reflections, moved on in the afternoon to role-plays of interrupting racism, and was supposed to end with a discussion of anti-racist activism. Our most effective ploy was a role play in which a white daughter or son returned home for Thanksgiving and had to deal with the father's racist comments over turkey—a scenario guaranteed to generate collective meltdown. We found that participants became so absorbed in the interpersonal issues that we never got to the activism. Were we starting at the wrong end of the process?

These politics will be recognizable to many lesbians who lived through those years. We had an ideological unity then that did not survive the 1980s, for better or for worse. Class and race divisions did not dissolve so easily in the solvent of our sisterhood. "Sex radicals" raised questions about the nature of lesbian and female sexuality that many feminists, straight and lesbian, had no tolerance to hear, and the "sex wars" tore through the community. AIDS soon began to impact all of our lives. There were deeper schisms among women, and new alliances with gay men. A younger lesbian generation began to shape a different politics in the space that we had worked to open for them. Many of us old-timers took the anger and determination in those Women's Pentagon Action demonstrations off in different directions, including the massive civil disobedience at the Second National March on Washington for Lesbian and Gay Rights in 1987. One event from the fall of 1983 presaged my own later redirection.

I was at the Savannah River Plant in lower South Carolina, which produced most of the plutonium for nuclear weapons, at a peace camp planning a civil disobedience action with activists from around the South. I had come with War Resisters League Southeast, and I camped with lesbian friends in the "Women's Camp," one of two camps pitched in the South Carolina woods during deer season. The other camp we disparagingly called the "boys' camp," although it was both men and women. Women's Campers had strung a rope around pine trees to mark off "women's space," no men allowed. Mandy Carter, who had recently joined Dannia at the War Resisters League, objected. "It's like nationalism, one of the forces that causes wars," I overheard her say to the rope. But the boundary stayed.

Representatives from the Women's Camp and the "boys' camp" met tensely several times to work out strategies for the next day's civil disobedience. We were to block the road around the perimeter of the plant. The boys' camp delegation explained plans for their people to move out into their intersection in waves, lying in the road so that the police would have to carry them off on stretchers. Our camp came up with a much less militaristic, patriarchal strategy. We would begin in a circle near the highway, humming. Then those who chose civil disobedience would spiral out into the intersection to disrupt the traffic. We chose the spiral as a mystical, feminine form. That night, plans laid, the Women's Camp went to sleep with no guards, while Vietnam vets patrolled the perimeters of the boys' camp. Neither strategy made me feel very safe.

The next morning, the Women's Camp contingent clustered before dawn in a circle near our intersection, huddled against the cold blasts of air that came from the huge trucks that kept whizzing past on the highway. Humming anxiously to myself, I realized that nobody had checked out the intersection. We all stood there—humming—for a very long time, before the women peeled off into the street. The police arrested them immediately. Our protest lasted from 7:00 to 7:05 a.m. The "boys" stopped traffic for a full hour.

I resolved then and there that, spirituality notwithstanding, I wanted to be more grounded in the material reality of the intersection.

If the earth had shifted beneath my feet when I came out in the mid-1970s, the ground opened once more in 1983. I finally left my closeted teaching job the year that *Feminary* busted up from a potent mix of identity struggles and changing primary relationships. The magazine collective had been my version of lesbian sisterhood, and I found its disintegration acutely painful as, one by one, most members departed to other cities.

Lesbian-feminism in the 1970s taught that you should not work with straight women because they "gave all their [and therefore your] energy to men." After *Feminary* imploded, I figured, *Shit, nothing could be worse than this*. That's when I went to a meeting in Durham of the National Anti-Klan Network to hear from Leah Wise, Lauren Martin, and Reverend Wilson Lee that North Carolina had the worst Klan/Nazi movement in the country and they were looking for local people to organize. It was 1983 and I was ready to take the plunge. In this border crossing between the lesbian and feminist and the anti-racist movement, I began to realize how such movements separate people as much as bring them together. I found a compelling and complicated reality that neither race theory and organizing, nor class theory and organizing, nor feminist theory and organizing is capable of handling.

Lesbian-feminism had given me a clear analysis of how power operates among people and in a culture's institutions. But it gave me few of the specific skills I needed: how to put on a press conference, build up a computer database, interact with community agencies, organize

white and Black people in small towns and cities, or monitor and call
to accountability the criminal justice system. With *Feminary*, our battle had been largely interior, a psychic confrontation with the lethal
forces of the culture as we had internalized them. It was an intense,
revealing, but sometimes insular process. The "politics of identity"
could easily slip into a politics of victimhood and guilt, its focus more
purity of consciousness than effectiveness of social change. By 1983,
I had hit the limits of this internal work. (I was not the only dyke to
think that lesbian-feminism was dangerously over-literary and under-
strategic.) Guided by the people who eventually incorporated North
Carolinians Against Racist and Religious Violence, I set to work to
learn to organize.

I had previously done political work in an exclusively lesbian context, mostly white, and Barb and I lived in a white queer household.
When I began anti-Klan work, I was one of the few out gay people in
organizations whose majorities were African American. I was working on trust: of myself as a white person, of straight people, of all
other human beings and the world we inhabited. "I am continually
surprised that a chickenshit like me does this work," I would remark
when asked to speak. "I'm just more afraid not to do it."

"Cover your back," I would hear from my new companions, and
I would think, *From whom?* They urged me to acquire a gun, and I
eventually did, although I never loaded it. I felt repeatedly compelled
to apologize to my pacifist friend Barbara Deming, who died in 1984
and whom I felt watching me from the nearest cloud, gently shaking
her head. More than a pistol, my co-workers' sharpened understanding of homophobia would protect me from Klan retaliation, because
isolated people are more easily harmed.

The shit hit the fan about a year after NCARRV had begun our
work in Statesville. A woman involved in the national work suddenly
brought up gay issues across Flora's kitchen table. Flora and I were
friends by that time. I had come out to her the evening she had asked
whether my interest in the Statesville work came because I also had
a Black lover. She was on the right track, I had explained, telling her
of my different outcast status. "We still love you," she had said, and
reached across the table to take my hand.

Okay, I thought when the woman confronted me. *You want this discussion, you'll get it.*

Soon everybody had fled the room except my opponent, Flora, and me, as I heard how being gay was like being on heroin, and how this particular woman was raising her daughter to be heterosexual, and how she wouldn't want her organization to take a stand on homophobia because it might promote homosexuality.

"If I ever have a child," I countered, "the main thing I will teach her about relationships is that she deserves love and intimacy and should never let herself be abused. What this is all about—gay rights and these cross burnings to which Flora and Joe have been subjected—is the right of human beings to love."

Flora stayed beside me, nodding agreement.

When I got back to Durham, I called Leah Wise to report. Whenever an emergency arose, I could count on her to let me sit down near her desk for five or ten minutes to think it through. It was natural that I take the incident at Flora's back to her. She responded immediately, "This homophobia is like racism; it's got to be opposed." We arranged a further discussion with the woman in question, and Leah came with me for support. On the way back, Leah took the time to share with me all the things she saw me doing right.

I was intensely grateful. "Shit, Leah," I replied, wedged in the seat adjacent to hers on the plane. "I feel like I do not know what I am doing most of the time. All you folks have all this political history, and here I am flying by the seat of my pants."

"Actually, it's better that way," she said. "A lot of times, that other more sectarian stuff just gets in the way."

Her ready support in challenging homophobia and her affirmation of my work marked a major turning point for me. If I knew my enemies, I also knew my friends. Perhaps I could stop looking over my shoulder.

Leah affirmed my instincts to build not just coalitions but movements grounded in relationships. I figured I was doing work on racism and anti-Semitism because it was the right thing to do, and once I laid out the case about homophobia, the people I was working with would do the same for me and mine. I was not disappointed. The result was friendships that come among people who catalyze changes in each other. Our work carried a lot of risk, but the risk gave us occasions to develop substantial trust. I was scared shitless a lot of the time, but I never regretted what I was doing.

After thirty-five years, my life was no longer segregated.

Somewhere in my metamorphosis, I realized that I could no longer settle for "lesbian space" as just one room, or camp, or building, although I was, and am, still grateful for those gathering places. The Reagan era made it clear: there is no separate safety. "Lesbian space" had better be a world where everyone belongs.

5

Bad Blood

Nineteen seventy-nine was an ominous, fatal year. The Greensboro massacre opened North Carolina to a wave of white supremacist organizing and hate violence. In 1979 also, a gay man in New York City with a rash and enlarged lymph nodes went to his doctor for blood studies. He was diagnosed with a rare skin cancer, Kaposi's sarcoma, the first man in the United States showing symptoms of what later came to be known as acquired immunodeficiency syndrome (AIDS). The same year, a mother brought a sick baby with a weak immune system in to another New York doctor. This was one of the first children born to mothers infected with HIV, the virus believed to cause AIDS.

AIDS was a lousy epidemic to incubate the year before Ronald Reagan was elected president. The Republicans regained the White House with the strong support of the religious right, a movement of fundamentalists that, early on, targeted gays and lesbians. Reagan's Office of Management and Budget wanted to chop Carter's recommendation of $327 million to the Centers for Disease Control in half.[1] In the early years of the AIDS epidemic, the alarms of a small band of doctors and the first gay men to suffer and die from the complex of diseases fell on deaf ears. As Randy Shilts shows in *And the Band Played On: Politics, People and the AIDS Epidemic*, public institutions including the National Cancer Institute withheld money for the most basic kinds of research to identify the cause, for educating people about routes of transmission, and for beginning to find a cure. Concerned doctors could have used media attention to leverage funds, but reporters did not figure their public really cared what happened to faggots. The National Institutes of Health in 1982 spent $36,100 per death on toxic shock syndrome and $34,841 per death on Legionnaires' disease, but only $8,991 per death from AIDS.[2] Massive denial in the first several years let the infection spread.

Shilts talks about the "before" and "after" of AIDS: the moment when the disease comes into people's lives forever. I had a harbinger of that moment in a front-steps conversation with Allan Troxler after Barb and I moved out of the Vale Street household we had shared with Allan's lover Carl Wittman. I had not seen Allan in a while, and he told me that eight of his friends had died. *Eight!* "We who had been the jesters have become the tragic chorus," he lamented. How far away I was from this world. But not for long.

The moment between my "before" and "after" came on the day before winter solstice, 1985, when Barb said to me, "Carl has AIDS." It was like a kick in the stomach. I was standing in front of the open refrigerator wondering what to have for supper. I should not have been surprised, but I was in my own denial. Carl came down with AIDS the same year Rock Hudson died, drawing national attention, finally, to the epidemic. By that time, over twelve thousand people in the United States had been diagnosed, half of them had died, and hundreds of thousands had been infected.[3]

Carl had been ailing for over a year, feeling weak, getting one sickness or another. That December, the big infections kicked in. I'd known Carl had meningitis when we'd visited him the Sunday before in his room on Vale Street. He'd been doubled over, throwing up. I'd felt helpless. I was too well aware that *I* wanted to be taken care of, because of *my* fears about his illness, and he was in no shape to give care to anyone. He couldn't stop vomiting.

He had looked up at Allan between spasms and said, "I don't think this is a good sign."

Allan had followed us out of the room, worried, especially about Carl's stamina. "He doesn't appreciate pain."

A month and a day later, Carl was dead. Again I was in his room, helping his friends at Vale Street lift his body into the body bag and carry him down the stairs. We laid him for the night, surrounded by candles, on a stretcher Barb had helped to make that afternoon in the greenhouse he himself had built.

All of this happened in the house that Barb, Carl, and I had shared for nine months just after he and Allan had moved to town from their farm in Oregon. Landing in San Francisco in the late 1960s after college years organizing for Students for a Democratic Society (SDS), Carl rapidly "came out." He knew how to sew his own clothes, build his own house, fix his own car, and grow his own food, and the man had little tolerance for a forty-hour workweek. More than most people I know, he and Allan left time in their lives for friends.

One of Carl's lovers had killed himself, and one of my friends made an attempt that year. Carl and I talked a lot about suicide the summer we lived together. One afternoon we were in the kitchen chopping vegetables from his garden (in which I worked too little). Carl said, "How easy that seemed when he did it, and how appealing." He was a man with his own emotional riptides, and whatever currents he and Allan were riding carried him past us that summer. Carl's was a house we laughed and played in but increasingly fought over. There got to be too many house meetings about compost, steaming off the wallpaper, insulation, tofu versus barbequed chicken. Carl also wanted a gay men's community on Vale Street. He wanted us to leave. Carl finally told us to move out, and he gave us five weeks. We went looking for our own house, scrambling to get a decent deal in the time we had. When we closed on a small mill house four days late, he had a fit, warning histrionically that we might be responsible for his suicide. In the years after, we reestablished a relationship, Barbara closer and more forgiving than I. In the month it took Carl to die, I lived to regret the anger and mistrust underneath the patched friendship, feelings that I had neither the ability nor the will to resolve. Now he was dying; I had thought I had more time to make up.

People all over town responded to Carl's diagnosis. Friends catered every meal at the hospital—he went in to have a tube inserted into his chest so he could be medicated at home—and brought over meals once he got back to Vale Street. I was scheduled for lunch in mid-January and carefully prepared noodle soup in broth with miso, water chestnuts, and spring onions. I added strawberries and Fig Newtons for dessert, although Carl had lost his prodigious appetite. He was tall and skinny but had always been as interested in food as I was. In one of our fights he'd gotten mad at me for starting to eat a dinner he had cooked without waiting for the proper amenities; this from a man who drank out of milk containers standing in front of the refrigerator. He ate this lunch with pleasure, however, as we talked in what turned out to be our final conversation.

I wanted to do an oral history of his early involvement in SDS. Doing anti-Klan organizing, I was working with former SDS and SNCC people, and I didn't understand their ideological histories. Born in 1943, Carl was six years older than I was. He started college at Swarthmore in 1960, on the cusp of a new political era and in the vanguard of a generation that would create a New Left, "the first really *homegrown* left in America, taking its impulses not from European ideologies and practices (at least not until the end), but from dissatisfactions and distortions in the American experience."[4] Carl's parents were also leftists, and he arrived at Swarthmore alive to all the things he found "cooking" on campus in the year that Black students in Greensboro initiated the student revolt at Woolworth's lunch counter.

In 1962, Carl joined white students who traveled south, joining an American Friends Service Committee project in Jackson, Tennessee. He wrote his aunt Elizabeth, "Lots is going on in the south, especially in voter registration, and although there are really fantastic problems in utilizing the vote once you get it, the thing has some real potential also." By 1963, he was president of the Swarthmore Political Action Club, a local affiliate of SDS. The Black freedom movement was no longer exclusively a southern movement, he wrote, because it was beginning to realize "that access to 'civil rights' gets the Negro in the South no more than a Harlem."[5] During the summer of 1963, Swarthmore students supported their Black counterparts in SNCC's integration campaigns in Cambridge, Maryland, which crescendoed to near-riot conditions and martial law.[6]

When Swarthmore students went back to school that fall, the Swarthmore Political Action Club joined a Black mobilization in nearby Chester, Pennsylvania (where Wilson Lee had graduated from seminary six years before), pressuring the local government on a range of issues. According to Kirkpatrick Sale's history of SDS, the Chester campaign was "the first large-scale violent action by any white campus-based group in the North." Three community-based groups emerged.[7] Carl became a National Council representative to SDS.

The Chester campaign, to which Carl provided brilliant student leadership, was the first place that SDS's Economic Research and Action Project (ERAP) bore fruit. That fall, Carl visited national SDS leader Tom Hayden, then a graduate student at Ann Arbor. Together, they became leaders of the SDS faction that argued that student radicals should move beyond the campus in "new organizational forms which permit . . . a people-centered, instead of a student-centered movement. . . . It is striking to observe that almost no attempts are being made to organize the poor for social change—and no verdict can be reached until a long-term attempt is made."[8] Racism posed difficulties to such a movement: "Part of our whole crisis so far is that the white person has nothing specific to point towards when the Negro asks for *proof* that an interracial movement is possible."[9]

Carl and Tom Hayden moved on to Newark together on another multi-issue project in what they thought would be a mixed-race community, but which turned out to be a Black ghetto. Their tactics of rent strikes and actions at the homes of slumlords spread to other parts of the city. With other radical friends Carl opened a print shop for movement activity and to generate a minimal income.

By early 1966, Carl was drawing discouraging conclusions about community organizing by middle-class white students among the poor. He circulated a letter to his SDS friends (two days before Marvin Segrest killed Sammy Younge in Tuskegee):

We've (regretfully) found that a strategy of organizing people is extraordinarily difficult here, for whatever ends. Virtually every attempt not only to organize, but even to br[oa]ch the concept or enthuse someone we've met in such attempts, has led into frustration. . . . It's not any basic thing in their abstract values that stops [people]. It is fear, fear of being rejected by the institutions that make up every day life. . . . For all our unwillingness to "organize people," what little we've done has resulted in almost catastrophic consequences for those involved.

To ask people to "make such a sharp juncture with their roots" is an enormous request, Carl continued, but not one to be avoided, since "most anything we want to do does threaten authoritarian job, family and personal relations, for it is precisely that which is bad about life for people here." There must be alternative institutions to offer people, he concluded, institutions "better than the ones they may have to break with" and which "disrupt the authority of the system." There must also be some way of making a living that avoids "being stepped on or stepping on others." Some might see this as "deserting the movement," he said, acknowledging a departure from SNCC and ERAP "direct-action volunteer projects." However, other strategies might broaden the movement, help people to gain control over their own destinies, and provide a more stable personal life without selling out.[10]

At the end of 1966, Carl married Mimi Feingold, a friend and comrade since Swarthmore days. They had decided "not to become full-time employees of anybody or any institution." He was moving away from ideologies that were centralized or demanding national solutions, and he was less inclined to a "movement of everyone going in the same direction, with slogans, a program, and eventually an organization."[11] Instead he was inclined toward more anarchistic strategies and building locally based alternative community institutions.

In the summer of 1967, Newark Blacks joined the rebellions sweeping U.S. cities. With other white radicals, Carl left the inner cities.[12] He and Mimi went to San Francisco, where a more laid-back, hippie movement was blossoming. They bought land with other friends in Oregon to use as a retreat. His letters to his aunt Elizabeth mention a fascination with San Francisco's emerging movement for gay liberation and Mimi's increasing involvement in women's liberation. Feminist accounts of early women's liberation record Mimi's parallel realizations of how male-centered the New Jersey organizing and other SDS projects had been.[13] In March 1969, he wrote Elizabeth that he and Mimi had separated:

In the last year or so, I've realized more and more that some of my desire to get married was a way of telling the world that I wasn't homosexual—I had rationalized by saying that homosexuality could be a sick thing—but at least at this point I have to find out what was really my motive in getting married vis-a-vis this, and get straight in my head how much I've been inhibited and intimidated by what everyone has always been telling me—that I have to be married to a girl in order to be happy and normal. . . . I'm also excited by the political and social implications of homosexuals becoming accepting of themselves and challenging the order which made them feel they weren't as good as other people. In some better times, people will be sexual, not hetero- or homo-sexual, and relationships will be measured by their human importance, not how much they follow the prescribed rules. But right now I have too much to learn about how to make homosexual relationships decent and human and unstereotyped.

Coming out was like resisting the draft for Carl—a determination to be "at the frontier of my mind all the time." In the absence of a marriage, he felt himself gravitating toward "an extended family or tribe."[14] Carl's "Gay Manifesto," written before the Stonewall uprising put gay liberation on the map, was one of the formulations of the emerging movement.[15]

Throughout his metamorphosis from socialist/community organizer to anarchist/queer, Carl was a practitioner and teacher of English country dance, amid genteel company and heterosexual pairs. Carl reformulated the dances in feminist ways that avoided "male" and "female" dance roles. He understood them as rising from more egalitarian and socially responsible human interactions, signifiers of social harmony that people were attempting or had in English culture. Dance became emblematic of the cooperative community he worked all his life to create.[16]

Carl once explained his disillusionment with the community organizing he had done, the ways some organizers would "manipulate people into taking certain steps" without risking the repercussions themselves. I commented that he also "manipulated people into taking certain steps" in his teaching English country dance, but with much different consequences. He laughed and agreed.

Now I wanted to get his history on tape: SDS; the early gay liberation movement in San Francisco; the "back to the land" movement in Oregon, where he and Allan joined militant environmental actions to protect the forests from clear-cutting; then organizing against toxic dumping in his poor Durham neighborhood. Carl was a founding member of the North Carolina Lesbian and Gay Health Project, begun in the early 1980s, when there was little talk of AIDS.

"You want to tape me because I'm going to croak?" he asked.

Because I counted on your being there, I thought, *on your memory bank and your experience, and now you're leaving.* Over soup and strawberries he was running out of strength.

"I really don't think I have the breath to do the interviews," he said as I hugged him goodbye. He was trying to tell me something I wasn't ready to hear. What might I have said differently had I known? It was the last time I saw Carl alive.

Later, looking for how to explain the remarkable last month, when people streamed in and out of Vale Street carrying food or music or bringing and taking work on his book on English country dance, I found among his aunt Elizabeth's old letters the one he wrote to friends and family in 1968, asking them to support his decision to inform the draft board that he would never fight in Vietnam. "Unfortunately, in these difficult times, we aren't completely free to follow our own impulses to build and create," he wrote. "Events interpose themselves on our lives. When difficult choices loom imminent, the need to feel part of a community becomes particularly strong. At such turning points, a sacrament is necessary to keep the hope of community alive."

It was just such a sacrament that he and Allan created for those of us he left behind. "I have the easy part," he had said, slurping miso soup.

I was not, as Carl pointed out in our last conversation, a regular at his country dance class, but I counted on its being there, that on a Thursday I'd have the option of moving through intricate, shifting dance patterns that perhaps have their origins in pre-Christian, Celtic rites: folks skipping, heying, reeling, sliding, and siding, a little like planets must circle, or seasons shift, or plants lean to follow the course of the sun. Coming in from trips to Klan territory, I would be comforted by this different Celtic *kuklos* (the origin of KuKlux) or circle.

Carl's dancing was also nothing like my adolescent humiliation on high school dance floors, waiting for boring guys to ask me to dance, wondering what was the matter with me as the huddle of my girlfriends would peel away to do the twist or the dirty dog, leaving me standing alone before I would retreat to the ladies' room to cake my cheeks with another layer of face powder as I choked back the tears. At home, I would sit on my mother's bed and sob to her my humiliation. There seemed to be something wrong with me, with my body, my feelings. I defined myself increasingly in terms of my mind.

"We will dance as an ever-changing stream of faces, and groups will come together as a community rather than breaking up into cliques. No wall-flowers, no most-populars, no competitions," Carl wrote in his manual on country dance. And it worked, mixing up dykes and fags and straights, men and women, in constantly shifting patterns, and it didn't really matter who was what. And there was often the moment for me, as the pattern shifted and flung me into an outer loop, when I knew I was lost out there and would never return and there was no sense or meaning to any of the motions of my heart or feet; then I would remember the step, feel the beat, and suddenly find myself knit again into the figure, back with my neighbor at "home." This was something I meditated on in the week of Carl's death.

Carl's last month was a kind of longways dance, with his calling the steps for as many dancers as he could. In his last days, the set was more prescribed, the progression equally sure. "Now there is no fear, no doubt. I am calling the shots," he had written decades earlier to his draft board, removing his former uneasiness about refusing the draft. I guess he felt that way after refusing further medication and leaving the hospital again when the fatal diagnosis of pneumonia left him three magical days to do final work on the dance book and to say the most essential goodbyes.

Weeping, Elizabeth called me at the office on a Friday in

mid-January to say that he was coming home from the hospital. She asked me to come. My co-worker Christina hugged me.

"I don't see how you do the things you do," she told me.

"What choice is there?" I wondered.

I drove to Elizabeth's to be with her. How could Carl do this, take his life finally into his own hands? Could I give Elizabeth any comfort? Was there some chasm that could suck us both in? We embraced at the door.

That night, as we sorted through things, Elizabeth took as much care of me as I did of her. She helped me to see that Carl, as usual, knew what he was doing. She had respected him all of his life, throughout the childhood in the small New Jersey town where she helped to raise him and supported the coming out and the gay politics his parents could not understand. It was something Elizabeth knew and gave to Carl, and he gave it back to her, urging his aunt to retire early from her career as a high school guidance counselor and join him in Oregon, where she came out, too, as he knew she would. She respected his life, and she would respect his death, this woman who had been a "lesbian mother" to her "Charlie" before any of us younger dykes thought we invented the relationship.

Barb joined us at some point, as I listened and followed Elizabeth from room to room as she raged and wailed and remembered. I didn't need to say or do anything so much as be there.

The next day, Saturday, was the annual Nazi march in Raleigh. I had organized eight lesbians from Durham to join some of the monitors from the National Anti-Klan Network. As we expected, 350 neo-Nazis came. Shaken to the core by Carl's decision, I did not want to have to enter the neo-Nazi force field carrying such grief, but I went. I waited at the National Organization for Women office, three blocks from the capitol, while our monitors fanned out, getting license-tag numbers and tapes of the speeches and photos of faces, including two white supremacists who two years later would be indicted for murdering three men because they were thought to be gay.

"White power!" echoed off the granite buildings, a muffled roar in the distance, answered by a rumble in my gut, anger at so many dying from AIDS.

Allan met with thirty of us that night to tell us, gently, that the collective part of Carl's life was over: we would not see him again. Carl figured to survive only a couple of days off the medication, and he was saving that time to spend with his own parents, Allan's family, Elizabeth, and Allan. We went around the circle and talked about how we knew him (versions, when Allan related them to Carl, that brought the caustic comment, "No more Saint Carl!"). When my turn came, I surprised myself by weeping bitterly. I wanted to be sure the straight people in the circle, for whom Carl's dance classes had meant so much, knew it was fairy dancing that had changed their lives.

When we finished sharing our memories, I joked, "Now let's trash him." Carl was a complex and sometimes difficult man, but as death withdrew him, how were we to sort through that complexity?

Sunday, Carl's parents—old-time leftists—came and left. During their last visit, Allan reported, Carl thanked them for his own materialist philosophy, saying he was glad he did not have to be afraid of hell. Several years later I appreciated Carl's unfathomable equanimity toward death even more: I was standing at the memorial service of another gay man as a companion described the dead man's frantic search for peace through Rolfing, rebirthing, transcendental meditation, and therapy, concluding: "He hated his mother too much to die."

It was the years before AZT (the drug that sometimes prolongs the lives of people with AIDS), and Carl did not want to squander his self-respect grasping at straws. He had rapidly assessed his situation and come to terms with it.

"Death, I don't mind so much," he told me. "Pain, I do."

The Sunday before his death, Elizabeth's friend Elana came down from Maine, where she had recently moved. She brought some green elixir in a Mason jar, hoping that it might improve Carl's health. He rose to his emaciated but still imperious height and banished her from the room, promising to die immediately if she offered it again.

Monday, Carl still felt strong. There was more time than they had figured, and Allan and I joked about sending the "second string" in to see him. I wanted Carl to put me on the list, but he didn't; I resisted the impulse to run by Allan up the stairs to yell at him for kicking me out of the house, then to ask him what it felt like to die.

Instead, I searched for the final gesture. I flipped through the postcards at the book shop. I found one of the clown Emmett Kelly, melancholy smile grease-painted on his face, lifting his hat from the circus ring in a wistful farewell. "Carl, you are dying translucent. Bon voyage, with my love," I wrote, and sealed it in an envelope.

By Tuesday, his breathing was labored. David, a mutual friend and one of the Vale Street men, came over, saying he didn't think Carl would last much longer.

That night nine of us gathered for a potluck dinner at six o'clock, to keep watch in the other of the big, twin wood-frame houses on Vale Street that were by now the gay men's community Carl had envisioned.

Allan and Carl were up in Carl's room together, as Allan finished reading aloud all but the last chapter of *Barchester Towers*. They listened together for the last time to Bach's *Goldberg Variations*. The rest of us walked and talked quietly outside below the window, in a soft January night that did feel like spring. In ones and twos, we stepped in and out of the light from Carl's window that spilled on the grass and paving stones, the window framing spring flowers Allan had put there, translucent now before the light.

Word came that Carl had begun the final process. Elizabeth and Elana went into Carl's house to wait downstairs. Carl died with Allan; I imagine Allan sat with him for a while afterward.

I was standing outside, arm in arm with a friend, and through the window we saw Allan enter the room and speak to Elizabeth and Elana, holding one in each arm as they wept together. I saw that grief from a distance, them framed by the window, in their immediate loss—"Charlie's gone! Charlie's gone!"—saw them as a triptych, faggot lover, dyke aunt, and her friend, an image of gay and lesbian family in our love and grief. The image echoed in the winter/spring evening, like a dog's bark heard out an open window, the fact of a generation of gay men dying from AIDS, the cries of their lovers and friends: "Gone! Gone!"

Later, Allan and I embraced. "Thank you for the card," he said. Carl had opened it in the hour before he died. "It was perfect."

There was an exquisite tenderness on Allan's face when we went back up to Carl's room to carry his body down. Allan wrapped Carl in his crimson sheets and quilt and, in an act so intimate I should have turned my head, tucked his quilted pillow under Carl's head, his last act of physical love. Then we put Carl's body in the black body bag and zipped it up to his chin. As we carried his body down the steps, I took the heft of his feet, thinking as we went, *These brothers should not have to bear this weight alone.*

By one in the morning, I was home. I stripped off my clothes and sat in a tub of water, sobbing. Years later, I more fully understood my grief: not just from Carl's death but from my own inability fully to tell him goodbye because I had held on to old slights.

The next day, we reassembled. The guys at Vale Street took Carl's body to be cremated. My assignment was to help write the obituary. I scanned the paper to get the hang of the genre: cause of death, surviving relatives, organizations, accomplishments, publications, funeral home.

Let's see: Carl died of AIDS; his "club" was SDS; his publication, "A Gay Manifesto"; his surviving spouse, Allan; his work, on Citizens for a Safer East Durham against the Armageddon Chemical Company right around the block, on the Durham Food Co-op, on the Lesbian and Gay Health Project, and on his country dance history. I wasn't sure the *Durham Morning Herald* was ready for this, so I walked the piece over to their offices.

The receptionist was a bit nervous when I delivered it. Steve Schewel, my partner in the assignment and the publisher of a local alternative newspaper, had called to say that we were coming, and that we wanted a story and a picture. I explained that it was very important to say that Carl died of AIDS and that Allan was his closest survivor.

She immediately got flummoxed. "The only time they put the cause of death is for suicide," she informed me. Actually, the only time they don't put the cause of death is suicide.

"We can only use 'husband' or 'wife' for surviving spouse."

"Well, then, say Allan was his wife," I replied. She was getting distraught, so I asked to see her boss. He was surprisingly open, and I was proud to read the obituary next day: "Carl Peter Wittman, 43, a community leader and a dancer, died of AIDS Wednesday at his home on Vale Street . . . survived by his friend Allan." It was the best coverage the local media had ever given to an openly gay person.

Carl was my first friend to die of AIDS. He was also my closest friend to die. There have been too many since then, and it doesn't seem to stop. It's been almost eight years since his death, but I seem to stand there at the end of the bed, in his room at last, my hand on his foot. It is still warm, although his body has the look of sculpture (as Allan had told us it would, some carved pietà or saint in ecstasy), and I see Carl's head, thrust back as if he were listening to music or the presence in the room—and I notice the gray in his beard. Those things (his warm and ropelike body under my hand, an aging I had not noticed, the palpable stillness in the room) come together for me, and I realize that I too have passed some crucial marker in my own life, that I will not leave that room the same woman. Here is a man who did not fear death and who helped teach me about dying. I thank him silently. Then six of us carry Carl's body down the stairs I did not help him paint, into the greenhouse I never helped build. Allan carefully lays the body out, candlelight refracting off the panes like fallen stars in the still winter night.

Ten months after Carl's death, Barb gave birth to our daughter, Annie, to the cheers and tears of me and her father, David, one of the men from the Vale Street household. Elizabeth, Annie's "goddessmother," waited in the lobby. Annie did not replace Carl, of course, but I imagine a place where their spirits, going and coming, crossed.

The journey upstream, in the narrative of the body, the turbulent blood from atrium and ventricle, gushing through the arteries that divide like rivers: in the pulsing plasma, red and white cells like tiny boats are joined by infection-fighting lymphocytes that flow from the Missouri to the Mississippi, carrying their cargo of T cells like tiny barges; or at the belly, the juncture of Big Swamp and the Lumber, they flow into the Little PeeDee, then fan out into capillary beds like marshes. Except, of course, rivers run the other way, starting off in little creeks, finally opening into the great flatness of the sea. On the continent of the body, in the pulsing bloodstream, the killer waits.

Carl died of "bad blood."

"Thou shalt keep thy blood pure," early German Nazi propaganda decreed. In *Mein Kampf*, Hitler elaborated, "Blood sin and desecration of the race are the original sin in this world." This metaphoric use of blood to denote racial purity had been a staple of the racist thinking widespread in Europe and the United States. In Hitler's mind, not only miscegenation but venereal disease polluted the Aryans' "pure blood," which he called the "syphilization" of the German people.[17] In the Nazi mind, germs, bacteria, and viruses did not cause disease. Jews caused disease because they were, inherently, diseased.

In the United States, African Americans have suffered from a similar identification with disease. As one white physician articulated in the *Medical and Surgical Reporter* in 1888:

The weakest members of the social body are always the ones to become contaminated, and sooner or later succumb to the devitalizing forces of intemperance, disease, and crime and death. The Negro is peculiarly unfortunate, he has not only the inherent frailties of his nature to war against—instincts, passions and appetites; but also those nocuous, seductive, destroying influences that emanate from free institutions in a country of civil liberty.[18]

Such assumptions have tremendous ramifications for a people's health and survival. Take the Tuskegee syphilis study, for example, which lasted for forty years in the country where Osceola was born and I grew up.

In 1932, the United States Public Health Service began a study of the effects of untreated syphilis on Black men in Macon County, Alabama. It involved 399 men who were in advanced stages of syphilis. Over the years, they received a variety of tests and medical examinations and, upon death, autopsies. No one was told he had syphilis; rather, the explanation for their symptoms was "bad blood." They were deliberately denied treatment, even after penicillin was known to be a cure. Public health officials knowingly allowed the men to infect their women (or men) partners and their children. This experiment, which had no scientific value, continued until an Associated Press reporter broke the story in 1972.[19] Less than a decade later, the same Centers for Disease Control that had overseen the Tuskegee experiment would fail to deal with AIDS. In fact, David Sencer was director of the CDC both when the Tuskegee story broke in 1972 and when AIDS first came to his agency's attention in 1979. Sencer went on to become New York City health commissioner in 1982, where he and Mayor Ed Koch were grossly negligent in their response to the epidemic.[20]

In syphilis, spirochetes enter the body through skin or mucous membranes, multiplying rapidly in the lymph glands before flowing into the bloodstream, where they are transported throughout the body. They enter a "latent" period, boring into organs, glands, and the central nervous system. Syphilis finally erupts in lesions or tumors on internal organs and on the skin. Syphilis, like AIDS, is sexually transmitted and can infect children in the womb. Like AIDS, the most destructive phase occurs years after the initial infection. Neither syphilis nor AIDS gives its sufferers a kind death. For both the Black men infected with syphilis in the Tuskegee experiment and the gay men infected with AIDS years later, the tendency to identify the sufferer's race or sexual orientation, rather than a spirochete or a virus, as the *cause* of the disease severely hampered any medical and scientific response, allowing more people to become infected and, eventually, to die.

In the background lurks Dr. Frederick Weedon, Osceola's attending physician, in the moment his surgeon's saw cuts through the Creek man's flesh and bites into the vertebrae of his neck: scientific curiosity conflated with, and justifying, the rawest dehumanization.

I do not believe that the medical and scientific establishments would have responded so disastrously slowly to AIDS in gay men and intravenous drug users if racist ideology had not already permeated those institutions, engendering thought processes and bureaucratic procedures that allowed whole groups to become expendable. (I am also certain that homophobic violence would not have erupted with the force it did if there had not already been a high cultural tolerance for racist and sexist violence, both personal and institutionalized.)

Nor would AIDS now be hitting communities of color with such intensity if homophobia had not allowed the "gay disease" in its early years to rage unchecked. In 1985, the year that Carl was diagnosed with AIDS, for the first time a majority of the people with AIDS in New York City (54 percent) were Latino or African American. The disease was becoming endemic to the East Coast poor.[21] Today AIDS is spreading faster in women than in men, and I know that that means, predominantly, women of color. Today's newspaper carries a story that a federal judge has ordered the immediate release of 158 HIV-positive Haitians from the U.S. Navy base in Cuba. "The detained Haitians are neither criminals nor national security risks," Judge Sterling Johnson wrote. "Some are pregnant mothers and others are children. Simply put, they are merely the unfortunate victims of a fatal disease. They live in camps surrounded by razor barbed wire. They tie plastic garbage bags to the sides of the building to keep the rain out. . . . The Haitian detainees have been subjected to predawn military sweeps as they sleep by as many as 400 soldiers. . . . They are confined like prisoners."[22]

The severed head of Osceola floats singing in the river; the head of Osceola stares from the foot of the white child's bed.

There are a lot of us out here who have "bad blood," whether or not we are currently infected with any disease. We have been mapped by the cartographers of the body onto similar, deadly terrain. This need for solidarity among us, I am trying to tell you, is a matter of physical necessity, of our blood and bones. What goes around comes around, and any one of us can break the cycle. Nor, as AIDS has shown, will those who think that they are innocent because their blood is "good" remain immune. We are all humans, all swimming upstream in our mortality, in the common redness of our blood.

6

The White Patriot Party

"I have a question for Miz Segrest." I was the radio guest for a night-time call-in show in the seacoast city of Wilmington, in a highly conservative and repressive part of North Carolina, four hours from home. I had given my opening rap on the dangers of the Klan and neo-Nazi movement in the state, citing the failure of juries to convict the Greensboro killers as part of the reason for the Klan resurgence. The first caller was Glenn Miller, the number one neo-Nazi in the state. "Mizzz Segrest, are you a communist? Don't you know those Klanspeople were just defending themselves?" His voice alarmed me, and I searched for an answer, overcome by the feeling that most of his white listeners would be more sympathetic with him than with me.

Then another caller railed about "nigger crime." I heard snickers in the background. I could imagine the scene: Glenn Miller and his local supporters gathered in a living room somewhere in Wilmington, handing each other the phone.

"The police information network doesn't keep statistics on crime perpetrators by race," I explained, sounding weak even to myself. How could I talk about white crime to this invisible white audience—not just the escalating incidents by white supremacists (lynchings, bomb-ings, attacks) but also the systemic violence on which this country is founded: millions dead from the Middle Passage or the genocide of Native Americans to reap huge profits for a few at the top and a mod-icum of privilege for the rest? The mass violence that white people do is seldom considered violence, much less crime. And how to link that massive violence to the Holocaust, the terrible fruit of Nazism? I tried to imagine a listener to a car radio, driving in the dark.

"You people listening out there better take this seriously," commented the show's host, a local Black activist, as he leaned into his microphone, increasingly angry. "These racists are here and they are organized."

Every time the phone rang, I prayed it was somebody with a decent question. Not one sympathetic person called. I had clearly been out-organized, a lesson I tried to remember for later call-in shows. I knew only one person in Wilmington, and Leo was waiting to drive me to his home for the night. I breathed a sigh of relief when the program was over. I felt awful.

Glenn Miller was my personal nemesis. Even before I began work at NCARRV, I had set out to find out as much about him as possible. He enlisted in the army out of high school (probably around 1960, the year that Carl Wittman enrolled at Swarthmore). He was trained as a paratrooper and served two tours in Vietnam. In the early 1970s he read Hitler's *Mein Kampf*, and in 1973 he joined the National States' Rights Party.[1] In 1979 he was distributing neo-Nazi periodicals on base at Fort Bragg, the largest army base in the United States. He happened to give a copy of *The Thunderbolt* to a military intelligence officer. He was discharged as a result, but apparently allowed to keep his pension. In December 1980 he formed his own group, the Carolina Knights of the Ku Klux Klan. "People are not receptive to the swastika," he explained to a reporter. "The white people have been brainwashed for the last thirty-five years that the Nazis were somehow related to communism." His goal was to establish the Carolina Free State, "an all-white nation within the bounds of North and South Carolina."[2] He lived with his wife and four children on a twenty-seven-acre farm in the little town of Angier, thirty minutes south of Durham. Most of the state's other far right leadership was tied up in court for the Greensboro killings or, like National Socialist Party of America leader Harold Covington, had skipped the country. So Glenn became the number one neo-Nazi in North Carolina. Beginning in 1982, Miller ran for public office every two years—state legislator,

U.S. senator, governor. One of his favorite organizing techniques was a publicized Klan phone number with a taped message, such as the one in which he imitated a Black man being lynched:

> We Blacks gon' stick together. We always gon' stick together, you know that. What y'all putting them sheets and them hoods on for, man? What you doing with that rope? Y'all better get away from me with that rope! I'm goin' to call the NAACP! Get away from me with that rope! [*Increasingly hysterical voice*] I'm going to call Jesse Jackson. Y'all better get away from me. Help, help . . . [*Screams*].[3]

I got a fuller sense of Miller's fusion of old-style Klan and new neo-Nazi ideologies when NCARRV and the Durham–Chapel Hill Jewish Federation brought Lenny Zeskind of the Center for Democratic Renewal (CDR) to town in late 1985 for a presentation at Durham's Temple Beth El. (The old National Anti-Klan Network had changed its name to the Center for Democratic Renewal to reflect the widening scope of far right activity in the 1980s.) Lenny had supported himself with a print shop and had built up his files and contacts on North American fascism. He published *The Hammer*, an anti-racist and anti-fascist magazine. "We read the Nazi publications so you don't have to," its banner explained. Lenny joined the Center for Democratic Renewal as research director. He set about to strengthen national Black-Jewish coalitions against the far right, and he was remarkably effective.

At Beth El that night, Lenny explained the complexity of the far right in the 1980s. "If there are familiar Klansmen—and women—in white robes, there are also the rank-and-file farmers or workers who are increasingly being recruited by groups like Identity, a neo-Nazi theology wrapped in the trappings of Christianity; or by electoral strategies of Lyndon LaRouche's organization or the Populist Party using racist rhetoric about taxes and welfare mothers. Then there are the academics working to make fascism intellectually respectable through organizations such as the Institute for Historical Review, which dedicates itself to proving that the Holocaust never happened." Lenny stressed the insurgent nature of much of the most volatile far right organizing. The most militant neo-Nazis target what they refer to as "ZOG," the "Zionist Occupational Government" of the United States, he explained. Amazingly enough, the most radical neo-Nazis thought the Reagan administration was a Jewish/communist conspiracy. The neo-Nazis were actively seeking to overthrow the state. He explained how the White Patriots in North Carolina were pursuing a double strategy: working aboveground to build a mass white movement, and underground to build a paramilitary army.

He also explained the dangers of Christian Identity, a quasi-theological movement of small churches, tape and book distribution houses, and radio ministries that seeks to broaden the influence of the white supremacist movement under the guise of Christianity. "Identity binds the most extreme forms of the movement across the country," he explained. "It teaches that people of color are pre-Adamic, that is, not fully human and without souls. Identity followers believe that Jews are children of Satan and that the white people of northern Europe are the Lost Tribes of the House of Israel."[4]

Lenny, as well as Leah Wise and other African American members of the CDR board, became an ally in figuring out the role homophobia plays in fascism. I had first raised with Leah my desire to include issues of homophobic violence in our North Carolina work. "Document it," she had replied, and I accepted the assignment. I had plenty of materials at hand, since North Carolina was reporting more incidents of homophobic violence to the National Gay and Lesbian Task Force than any other state in the country. I worked this material into documentation for NCARRV, and it didn't take long for people to get the point.[5]

Lenny and I prepared a position paper on homophobic violence to present to the CDR's board, with me working on broader issues of homophobia and anti-gay and -lesbian violence, and Lenny working on fascist groups and ideologies. As a result, the board embraced work against homophobia and printed our paper as a pamphlet, *Quarantines and Death: The Far Right's Homophobic Agenda*. In the pamphlet, Lenny explained:

Klan and neo-Nazi groups . . . believe that white (Aryan) races represent the healthy development of civilization. Conversely, they believe that people of color are the repository of uneugenic (unhealthy) barbarism and savagery. . . . Within this racial world view, other forms of bigotry have a specific role. Anti-Semitism manifests itself as the fear of an all-powerful Jewish conspiracy to dominate the world and to end Aryan civilization through the forced integration (and miscegenation) of the races. Anti-communism manifests itself as a fear of lower forms of civilization, equated with "lower" classes and the belief that communism is the actual agent of mongrelization and barbarism. In similar fashion within white supremacist ideology, homophobia manifests itself as a fear of sexual differences that Aryans believe undermine white reproductive capabilities.[6]

Lenny and I wrangled for several months over the pamphlet. I wanted it framed as broadly as possible, giving readers background information on homophobia; Lenny wanted to keep the focus on the far right. I would write sections in, and he would write them out. The CDR's new executive director, Lynora Williams, eventually stepped in to edit both our contributions into the final version. I interpreted Lenny's editorial efforts as sexist—not to his face, to my eventual embarrassment, but to one of his adversaries. My comments got back to Lenny rapidly, as I should have anticipated. Eventually Lynora called me to tell me how hurt Lenny was. I wrote immediately to apologize not for my opinions but for my indirection, and to appreciate his friendship.[7]

Lenny takes all varieties of Nazis and Klan totally seriously, although if you listen to him, you hear a tone more glancing, ironic, heavy on ridicule. There was one evening, though, after we had known each other for a couple of years, when I heard something very different. We were in Seattle in the living room of friends of his. We were both there for "Hands Off My Neighbor," a conference on opposing the far right. Three hundred fifty people had attended that day, and we were all relieved that it was over and pleased with its success. That evening, I was lying on the sofa talking on the phone with an old friend. In the background, I heard Lenny begin to rant like a Nazi, pulling out every anti-Semitic phrase he had ever read, from *The Protocols of the Elders of Zion*, from *Instauration*, from White Aryan Resistance, from the tapes of Identity preachers played on country radio stations: *Jew parasites . . . control the money, control the media . . . Jew doctors killing white babies.*[8] He was spoofing them, but he built up to rage—*Jew, Jew, Jew!*—that I had not heard from him before, then he subsided. It's hard to explain, but I was touched by something about anti-Semitism then that I hadn't felt before—its velocity? its furious irrationality?—as I overheard my friend Lenny channeling these raving voices. I have run with a lot of very analytical people, but I continue to be hopelessly subjective. It's the way I learn most of my lessons, I guess—through friends.

I also had lessons closer to home about the dangers of anti-Semitism, when Glenn Miller called me at home to inquire about my "Jewish ancestry" ("Is it from Miami or New York?"). He was responding to a press conference in which I had called for his arrest. His questions were getting more specific. The year before, he had called my home to ask if I were a communist Jew, but I hadn't been there to respond.

"I was raised Methodist in Alabama," I explained this time, and hung up the phone.

With Lenny's help, my co-worker Christina and I began to look for links between Miller and the Order, a white supremacist group on the West Coast. We didn't know at the time but later learned of how a tight group of less than two dozen men had tired of waiting for the "race war" to begin. On April 23, 1984, they robbed an armored car in Seattle, netting half a million dollars. In June in Denver, Order members machine-gunned Alan Berg, a Jewish talk-radio host who challenged white supremacists on the air. In July, seventeen Order members robbed a Brinks truck in Ukiah, California, making off with $3.5 million. Agents found the Berg murder weapon in the Idaho house of Gary Yarbrough, an Order member who fired on FBI agents approaching his home. In late November, Yarbrough was captured in a shootout with two FBI agents in a motel in Portland. In December, Order leader Robert J. Mathews was blown to pieces in his Puget Sound hideout when a flare sent up by the FBI ignited his store of ammunition.[9] The propensity of these West Coast revolutionaries to target law enforcement, federal judges, and even potentially the president undoubtedly contributed to the seriousness of the federal and local campaign against them. I figured that Order money would eventually show up in North Carolina, and I was right.

"I can't tell you the details," Randall Williams of the Southern Poverty Law Center's Klanwatch program warned us at about this time, "but I need to caution you all to be especially careful these days. And be sure you know where your families are." We soon learned that it was the Order he was worried about. We began to worry, too, when closer links to North Carolina began to emerge.

The Carolina Knights got even more ominous during the fall of the year of Mathews's death. In November 1984, they rallied in Robeson County, in the southeastern part of the state. It was the first Klan rally in Robeson since the late 1950s, when Lumbee Indians attacked a Klan rally and chased the Klansmen out. Miller drew 250 uniformed participants down a winding dirt road to a field beside a cinder-block house. Pictures revealed heavily armed guards glowering from behind signs: "KKK Rally: No Jews Allowed."[10]

By December, the Confederate Knights (Miller changed the name from Carolina Knights, to reflect his expanding ambitions) had computer links with the Aryan Nations.

In January 1985, Miller planned a large neo-Nazi rally at the state capitol in Raleigh during my first month on the job as paid staff. I warned the Human Relations Council to expect a much larger crowd than the fifty white supremacists who had attended the year before. The Friday before the march, NCARRV pulled together a press conference of the city's religious leaders to protest the event. That weekend, I went skiing in the mountains with friends. On the drive back, as our car slipped and skidded down the mountain road in the snow, I heard reports of the rally, and the cries of 350 Nazis—*White power! White power!*—booming eerily over the car radio.

The week of the rally, a U.S. federal judge issued an injunction that would eventually lead to the demise of Miller and his organization. It resulted from a suit on behalf of Bobby Person, one of the Black prison guards in Moore County who had spoken out about racist job discrimination. Klanwatch had taken Bobby's case and filed suit against Miller and the Carolina Knights, seeking an injunction and damages. Miller agreed to the court order, on the condition that Person drop his monetary claims. The injunction said that the Confederate Knights would not "harass, intimidate, threaten or harm" Black people in the state. It also forbade the White Patriots to violate state statutes against organizing a military company or drilling or parading under arms as a military body without holding a commission from the governor.

As far as I could tell, Miller never let the court order or state laws slow him down. In early February, he threatened to sit in at the state NAACP office as his own counterprotest to the twenty-fifth anniversary of the Greensboro sit-ins.

Later in February, he held a second large rally in Raleigh, encouraged by the success of the first. Urged by the CDR to monitor the event, I put together my first monitoring team, lesbians who had been active at various Women's Pentagon Actions and friends from the local New Jewish Agenda chapter, recently revived into a strong organization. They brought back pictures of 350 men in military fatigues marching in formation and carrying new Confederate flags; tag numbers of their cars; and copies of the latest *Confederate Leader*, which praised Robert J. Mathews, the Order leader killed by the FBI, as a martyr of the movement.[11] "The Order Lives" read a sign carried by the marchers. One speaker railed, "When it comes to Jews, the only clear solution to the problem is not evacuation but extermination." I put out a press release explaining the links between North Carolina Klans and the Order and calling for an investigation of the source of Miller's money. I suspected that some of it came from Order heists.[12]

On March 19, Miller announced to the press that he had changed his organization's name to the White Patriot Party. "We want to reach the hearts and minds of Our People, and we cannot do that under the name KU KLUX KLAN," he fulminated, because of the "subversive and unAmerican JEWISH CONTROLLED liberal media." He warned that if the government tried to frame and imprison him, his men would have no other choice "but to resort to UNDERGROUND REVOLUTIONARY TACTICS . . . with the armed resources at our disposal."[13]

On March 31, I opened the newspaper to read that Order member David Lane had been captured in nearby Winston-Salem. He was wanted for counterfeiting, for the California armored car robbery, and for the murder of Alan Berg. In his shack, agents found two police scanners, survival gear, instructions on making and using bombs, a computer printout naming people who would harbor fugitives, and a "Declaration of War" signed by twelve members of the Order on November 25, 1984.

It explained how whites were "outnumbered by a coalition of blacks, browns, yellows, communists, queers, race mixing, religious zealots, traitors, preachers, teachers and judges under total control of organized jewry." Its signers declared war on those forces promoting "the destruction of our faith and race": the ZOG. Lane also had a handwritten Order manual that explained how to organize small autonomous fighting units, maintain communications in code, create diversions (by bombing porn shops or bookstores), and disguise physical appearance.[14]

Lane was arrested in Winston-Salem during the civil trial there against Klansmen and neo-Nazis and the City of Greensboro, brought by the families and survivors of the Greensboro massacre. In fact, Lane was driving the car of a member of the Aryan Crusade for Christ, a "church" pastored by Roland Wayne Wood, one of the defendants. Wood showed up in court with T-shirts reading "Kill a Commie for Mommie" and "Eat Lead You Lousy Red." His testimony included the jingle

> Oh what fun it is to have
> the Nazis back in town
> Rat-a-tat-tat
> Rat-a-tat-tat
> Shooting all the kikes.[15]

I drove over to the federal building for a press conference sponsored by the Greensboro Justice Fund, the advocacy group pursuing legal action in the killings. I urged again that law enforcement look for links between the Order money and North Carolina Klan organizing.[16]

The next month, the jury in Winston-Salem found five of the white supremacists and two police liable in three of the injuries. The settlement of $395,000 was disappointingly small to the families and friends who had sued for $48 million and had pursued the case for five years. But at least the jury had held the Greensboro Police Department partially responsible.[17]

The more I learned about the growing virulence of the neo-Nazi movement, the more urgent I felt about NCCARV's work. A clock was ticking toward some midnight disaster. Lenny sent me clippings from Rulo, Nebraska, where in August 1985 two badly decomposed bodies along with a cache of weapons, ammunition, and explosives were found on a farm. It was a compound of the Posse Comitatus, a western far right movement. The corpses belonged to five-year-old Luke Stice, who had been leashed like a dog until his neck was broken, and James Thimm, a man in his twenties, who had been skinned alive. Luke's father, Rick Stice, had run a hog farm until, like many other midwestern farmers, he got into debt and was almost bankrupt. He started listening to the anti-tax rhetoric of the Posse, to tales of Jewish banking conspiracies, and to Identity ministers preaching that white people were the Lost Tribe of Israel, that people of color were "pre-Adamic," and that Jews were the children of Satan. Stice had allowed Michael Ryan, a Posse/survivalist, to set up a compound on the farm. Ryan saw himself as an archangel of God. When Rick Stice began to question Ryan's authority, his son, Luke, was probably killed to keep the father in line. Thimm, likewise, was probably tortured and then killed for questioning Ryan's authority.[18]

Four months later, on Christmas Eve in Seattle, a white supremacist "prophet" in the form of an unemployed steelworker visited the Goldmark family. He tied up the Goldmark parents and their two children, then beat them all to death with an iron for being communist Jews. They were neither.[19]

Lenny was giving me extensive security lectures. I should check my car every morning for plastic explosives under the gas tank, under the seat, and in the motor. My God, I was doing well in the morning if I got on my brassiere and shoes. What would the neighbors think of me crawling around my car? Romley, the National Anti-Klan Network organizer who was working with the Statesville families, instructed me further. If there was ever gunfire, drop flat, don't run. He suggested that Barb and I sandbag an inner room of our house, but we could not bring ourselves up to the necessary fortress mentality. One night when I was away, Barb woke to two large explosions. She was about to hit the floor when a neighbor called to say a drunk driver had plowed into one of our cars, propelling it into the other car, totaling both our vehicles. At least it wasn't a Nazi attack.

Then Marty Nathan, whose husband had been killed in Greensboro, gave us her German shepherd, Bruno, when she went to Africa for several months. Bruno was more wolf than dog. Each morning he dragged us around the neighborhood at the other end of his leash, pausing only to piss on trees, shit in neighbors' yards, and accost passersby. We chained him to the pecan tree, and he dug up the backyard, so pecan roots were exposed in the barren ground. Our backyard looked like the impact site of at least a fallen planet. Marty came back to town, and we returned Bruno, feeling we were much safer without him. It was then that I accepted Marty's gun. I had a fantasy of finding some White Patriot on my porch late at night and blowing his face off.

The isolation cut very close to home. Barb wanted to talk about the effects of my work. I recalled how I would come in late at night, the stories rushing out compulsively, filling up all the space. She often reacted with an angry silence that made me talk even faster, or withdraw.

"I was angry at you for putting yourself and us in so much danger for so long, without caring," she began.

"Without seeming to care," I corrected

"Without stopping, taking us out of danger," Barb replied. "You might have cared, but you didn't stop. Something was worth more than our well-being. You were a driven woman, Mab."

"You never asked me to stop, either," I countered.

"It was too important to you. You asked me not to. Don't you know that? So I understood and didn't say anything. I was just pissed at you the whole time."

"I bet Glenn Miller's wife felt the same way," I laughed. "You weren't proud of me at all? Do you understand that I was instrumental in braking a fascist movement in this state?"

"I was aware of being proud of you when you worked in Durham, when I was seeing you in a context or could hear you make speeches. When Mike and Sarah and Kathleen from Jubilee House came to visit us, they gave me another context to understand that you weren't some crazy person liking danger."

I *was* driven. The white supremacists had already had too much time to grow. I was drawn to people who felt the same urgency. Marty Nathan, widow of Mike Nathan and director of the Greensboro Justice Fund, became a close friend.

Marty and Dale Sampson, Bill Sampson's widow, traveled all over the country representing the Greensboro Justice Fund. The tactics of the "widows" had mellowed considerably from the disruptions they staged in the courtroom during the state murder trials. They were winning broader support; people across the country had reacted in outrage at the acquittals of Klan members and Nazis in their state and federal trials. There was safety in the attention. Marty, like her deceased husband, Mike, was a doctor, but she put aside medicine until the case worked its way through all three courts. Marty supported me publicly and privately as a lesbian activist. She was also willing to explore the emotional dimensions of organizing, the fear and the risk, which she had learned the hard way. She had to work out great grief in such a public way, and she handled herself with courage and grace. I respected the palpable love for their living and their dead among the Communist Workers Party circle. There was a determination to keep faith. They called to mind W.B. Yeats's description of the Irishmen executed by the British for their role in the Easter Uprising of 1916. Yeats meditated on their death in his poem "Easter 1916":

Too long a sacrifice
Can make a stone of the heart.
O when may it suffice?
That is Heaven's part, our part
To murmur name upon name,

As a mother names her child
When sleep at last has come
On limbs that had run wild.
   . . . . All
is changed, changed utterly.
A terrible beauty is born.

Through the summer of 1985, White Patriot organizing continued seemingly unchecked. Our countermoves seemed futile. The Patriots were expanding from their base in the central Piedmont into the western part of the state. That summer they marched through several western counties, with Miller bragging openly that he was building a "white Christian army to take back the South." In Cleveland County, an active unit emerged and fielded a candidate for school board. Christina, Romley, and I drove over from Statesville to talk to Cleveland County ministers about the dangers we saw in Patriot activities. A reporter from the *Shelby Star* ran a sympathetic story on our meeting, and local Patriots responded with a volley of letters, one of them directed at "Mab Segrest and her lackeys."[20]

A month or so later, I spent the better part of a day on a trip to Jacksonville, in the east, trying to no avail to locate a Black Marine whom Miller had kicked in the groin during a Patriot march. Miller had commented to a reporter, "I kicked him—three times, as a matter of fact. But I was not charged with anything, so anything you say is pure conjecture."[21]

On Halloween eve, Lauren Martin, now a member of NCARRV's board, called. "Turn on the TV," she said. "It looks like a bad one."

I flipped on the local news and saw a reporter standing in front of yellow tape marking off the scene of a crime. The body of a thirty-five-year-old Black woman, Joyce Sinclair, had been found raped and stabbed to death, her body dumped on land where the Carolina Knights/White Patriots had held their huge Robeson rally one year before. I recognized the winding road and the cinder-block house behind where the "No Jews Allowed" sign had stood. Joyce Sinclair, the reporter explained, had just been promoted to a supervisory job in the plant where she worked, a job formerly reserved for white people. She had been kidnapped from her home, according to her four-year-old daughter, by a "white man wearing white," who had led her off down the highway in her bathrobe and curlers. Was there Klan involvement in the murder? Was it economic retaliation?

Two weeks later, I drove down to a meeting of citizens concerned to respond to Sinclair's death. I stopped by Moore County to pick up Jimmy Pratt and Bobby Person, NCCRV board members who had brought the Klanwatch suit against the White Patriots. I was not eager to travel these back roads by myself at night. The church was full, the audience mostly Black. Jimmy and Bobby spent most of the meeting outside, standing guard. When I was introduced, I explained what I knew about the extensive Klan activity in the area and offered NCARRV's help. In the months following this meeting, however, community response dissipated. Local law enforcement kept saying they had a "prime suspect," but they never arrested anyone for the murder.

In March 1986, I answered a call from a security officer at Shearon Harris, a nuclear power plant under construction near Durham, who told me that White Patriot Party members were recruiting there. One young construction worker who pulled out of the group had had his life threatened.

Where were the police, the State Bureau of Investigation? Wasn't Glenn Miller violating the court order and the state's paramilitary laws? If so, it was happening across the jurisdictions of several district attorneys. Neither the attorney general nor the State Bureau of Investigation was taking him seriously enough to launch a coordinated effort. Many reporters, too, seemed to think that he was a joke. Why didn't Klanwatch come back in?

Frustrated, I worked with a lawyer friend on a report to Governor James Martin, citing the part of the state constitution that held him responsible for upholding the law. We laid out the various laws we thought White Patriots were violating. We had no eyewitnesses, no "smoking guns," but enough smoke to warrant looking for several fires. We took it to a meeting with an assistant from the governor's office. Then we stopped by to see Morris Dees, who had called the day before from the Raleigh Holiday Inn. We walked into a press conference at which Dees announced that Klanwatch was bringing Glenn Miller and his second-in-command, Stephen Miller (no relation), into court for contempt. It was about time! Why the fuck hadn't he told us he was doing this? I cursed Dees and all lawyers.

I had begun to feel pretty irregularly white. Klan folks had a term for it: *race traitor.* Driving in and out of counties with heavy Klan activity, I kept my eye on the rearview mirror, and any time a truck with a Confederate flag license plate passed me, the hair on the back of my neck would rise. My reaction was more like the reactions of the Black people I was working with than of a white woman with three great-grandfathers in the Confederate Army. In restaurants with mostly white customers, I usually sat with my back to the wall so I could see who came in the door, and I viewed white strangers who entered with suspicion.

I was in daily, intimate exposure to the cruel, killing effects of racism, which my Black friends spoke of in the same way that they commented on the weather, an equally constant factor in their lives. I often found myself hating all white people, including myself. As I took on racism, I also found its effects could be turned on me. The possibility of overt violence or the reality of subtle ostracism gave me a sense of shared risk, not the same as the dangers faced by my friends of color, but close enough. I began to feel more uneasy around other whites and more at ease around people of color. I knew my role was working with other white people, and self-hatred was a bad place from which to start. Could I find ways to share and appreciate other cultures without mimicking or appropriating them, without denying my continuing white privilege? Sooner or later, would the contradictions loosen?

Maybe whiteness was more about consciousness than color? That scared me, too, the possibility of being caught between the worlds of race, white people kicking me out, people of color not letting me in. I was careful when I traveled to let people at the office and at home know my plans, but often on these trips I felt I had slipped through some heavily guarded border. Sometimes, driving down

North Carolina back roads, I would think: *Nobody knows where I am now, where I have come from, or where I am going.* I resonated with white South African writer Nadine Gordimer about this condition in what she called "the interregnum":

> The black knows he will be at home, at last, in the future. The white who has declared him or herself for that future, who belongs in the white segment that was never at home in white supremacy, does not know where he will find his home at last.[22]

In this disquiet I heard the echo of my mother's voice: "When people have to choose, they will go with their own race."

She had reached this conclusion after great soul-searching. My mother was a woman deeply torn by the racism into which she was born. She shared her sorrow with me, often telling me stories of how she and a friend had stopped a Klan rally on the courthouse steps by protesting to the mayor. She had been disgusted at the transparently racist voter registration in town in the 1940s, when registration, she said, was sometimes held in the bank vault and when whites would register illiterate white voters but fail Black PhDs. Then she was nominated as registrar and searched her conscience for an adequate response. If she accepted, she would feel honor-bound to register educated voters, whatever the color. My mother was a great believer in the power of education, and she had a class solidarity across race lines. She was between a rock and a hard place: between what she knew was right and what most of her white neighbors would want. What to do? She consulted Myrtle Preer, her mother's closest friend. "Taking the job would destroy your family in this town," Miss Myrtle admonished her. Mama turned the job down.

Lillian Smith, a southern white woman and outspoken critic of segregation, wrote in 1962:

> Freud said once that woman is not well acculturated; she is, he stressed, retarded as a civilized person. I think what he mistook for her lack of civilization is woman's lack of *loyalty* to civilization.

Southern women have never been as loyal to the ideology of race and segregation as have southern men. The southern woman has always put the welfare of one individual above the collective welfare or collective values. Many of them have been betraying White Supremacy for two hundred years but most who have done so could not reason with you as to why. Instinctively woman chooses life, wherever life is, and avoids death, and she has smelled the death in the word *segregation*.[23]

This describes my mother—up to a point. Later, she and my father made the decision together to organize white private schools. When forced to choose, she did not betray her own race. Other white women and men, who were outside the town's class structure, made the choice to work for integrated schools.

I had inherited from my mother an awareness of the deep schisms in our culture, and I suspected that it was her attempts to negotiate them that eventually destroyed her. When push came to shove, could I make a different choice?

Driving around North Carolina, Sammy Younge was also with me in the car, and in more ways than I realized. So was my other long-dead homeboy, Marvin Segrest, a gas station attendant like North Carolina Klan leader Virgil Griffin, both poor white southern men manipulated by white men far richer and more powerful, but both still responsible for their deeds.[24] I kept meeting Marvin and Sammy in the towns I visited, in the courtrooms where the mysterious moment the gun crashed was argued and reargued, clarified and confused in the defense's and the prosecution's versions of who hurt whom, a single plot with infinite variations. What it comes down to, I saw, is what a person believes. We are all on the jury, and history spreads out around us vast and intimate, with a crack down the middle that can't be straddled.

I was in the Raleigh federal courtroom in July 1985, when both Glenn Miller and Stephen Miller went to trial for contempt of court. U.S. attorney Sam Currin joined Klanwatch counsel Morris Dees at the prosecution table. Klanwatch had done all the investigation that both state and federal agencies had failed to do, turning up two former Klan members willing to testify.

I listened with great satisfaction as Robert Norman Jones and James Holder testified that the White Patriots had trained "Special Forces" units to "unite and organize the masses of white people to rise up, train, cache weapons and overthrow the U.S. government" by 1991. Holder explained how active-duty military personnel from Camp Lejeune's Marine base and the U.S. Army base at Fort Bragg had trained Klansmen in hand-to-hand combat, escape and evasion, ambush, river crossing, and search-and-destroy, using AR-15 and Mini-14 rifles, shotguns, pistols, and artillery simulators.

Jones testified that White Patriot members paid him $50,000 for weapons ranging from dynamite and claymore mines to plastic explosives and lightweight anti-tank rockets. Jones had stolen these from military bases or from a National Guard armory. The Patriots had buried these weapons in sealed containers in wooded areas in the Piedmont.

I spent an intense week in a courtroom filled with White Patriots. It was clear theirs was no ragtag operation. Glenn Miller was their media man, Stephen Miller their "chaplain" and military tactician, Richard Pounder their computer techie, Gordon Ipock their intellectual. At one recess, Ipock sidled over to where I was talking to a reporter.

"Miss Segrest, are you a l—"

Here it comes, I thought, bracing myself.

"—liberal?" he completed.

"Are you a fascist?" I asked, then walked away.

Glenn Miller had accepted a court-appointed attorney; Stephen Miller opted to defend himself (although the judge insisted that he have a lawyer at his table). Glenn was a tall, wiry man with a whimsy that sometimes undercut his sickening pronouncements; Stephen, like a handful of his cohorts, radiated evil. While Glenn had a pragmatic bent, Stephen was the zealot. As the White Patriot chaplain defended himself, the dangers of neo-Nazi Identity theology became clear: when faced with a choice of making an ideological point or making a point with the jury, Stephen tended to dig his own grave.

My favorite part of this trial was Stephen Miller's cross-examination of Robert Norman Jones:

Stephen Miller: "When you were in prison, you wrote me a letter?"

Jones: "Sure did."

Miller: "I wrote you a letter back and they read it in court today?"

Jones nodded.

Miller: "And I stated at the end of my letter, 'death to the enemy.' Where is that quoted in the Bible?"

Jones: "I don't know. Not exactly positive."

Miller: "You say you read the Bible three times?"

Jones: "I sure have, Mr. Miller, and I remember a lot of the other things, like man being created equal in the sight of God. Besides all the rhetoric you used to talk about killing and slaying the enemy and that kind of stuff, I think you missed quite a bit of it."

Miller: "Your honor, I'm not quite certain on this. Can I talk to my counsel?"

Judge: "I would suggest you do."

After a short pause, Stephen Miller asked the court's permission to have the witness read two scriptures.

Miller: "Would you please read to the ladies and gentlemen of the jury out of Deuteronomy, chapter 33, verses 27 and 28?"

He handed the Bible to Jones, who read: "Yahweh Elohim is thy refuge, and underneath are the everlasting arms; and he shall thrust out the enemy from before thee; and shall say, destroy them."

Miller: "Thank you. Now I would like you to read Luke 19:27."

Jones: "Bible class?"

Miller: "Refresher."

Jones read: "But those mine enemies, which would not that I should reign over them, bring hither, and slay them before me."

Miller: "Does that not validate my sign-off on that letter?"

Jones: "Mr. Miller, I don't know exactly what you had in mind by coming up here and having me read out of the Bible other than show-ing some of the specific things you used to point out about it. Again, as I said, you missed quite a bit of it. You pick out certain pieces of the Bible and you fail to see the rest. . . . I think when you wrote 'death to the enemy,' you meant specifically and exactly what you told me on numerous occasions, which is kill all the Jews you can. And I believe it was discussed many times, bombing synagogues. Is that in the Bible? No sir, I don't think so. I think you need to read it again."

Miller: "Your honor, I move that that all be stricken from the record as nonresponse."

Judge: "Motion denied."[25]

The jury convicted Glenn Miller on two counts of contempt and Stephen Miller on one. Both men were sentenced to six months for violating a federal court order not to violate state paramilitary laws that themselves carried far stiffer sentences, an indication of the malign neglect of the state of North Carolina in countering this danger. They immediately appealed and were put on probation with instructions to disassociate themselves from the white supremacist movement. Cecil Cox and Gordon Ipock took over the White Patriot Party, promptly disbanding it. They immediately began another organization, the Southern National Front, which disbanded a year later.

Conviction in federal court did not deter Stephen Miller. Even during the trial, he discussed with his closest lieutenants killing Klanwatch counselor Morris Dees. After the trial, an inner circle quit the White Patriot Party in order to maintain their association with Steve Miller. By August they were plotting ways to raise money for the cause and to finance a hit on Dees. Steve Miller's first bright idea was to rob and kill drug dealers on Interstate 95. He and his men decided to resort to smaller theft, and Wendell Lee Lane, Simeon Davis, and John Michael Vick made plans to rob a Pizza Hut in Fayetteville. It was to be their initiation into the Order, they believed. The Fayetteville police, who did the best job of any local or state law enforcement in countering white supremacy, had an informer inside and arrested the men on September 27, 1986.[26] These guys did not let up!

U.S. attorney Sam Currin, a Jesse Helms Republican who had assisted Morris Dees's prosecution, issued a statement criticizing the state's lack of response to the White Patriots. It sounded strangely like what we had been saying for several years:

A year ago when the White Patriot Party was marching through cities and towns of North Carolina, conducting paramilitary

training in the countryside, nothing was being done about it—
not much condemnation of their activity and no prosecution. A
mentality developed among the White Patriot Party members
that they could do anything they wanted to do. They just felt
that they were immune from the law, that nothing would ever be
done to them. They operated basically at will, and they rose to
prominence very quickly.[27]

Glenn Miller appealed his conviction and moved to Virginia, where
he jumped bail eight months later, heading out to Oklahoma to find
his henchmen. Nobody knew it then, least of all me. I'd spent the
week before in Alabama for my mother's funeral.

7

Mama

Like the Muskogees on whose land she grew up, my mother was pulled in opposite directions. The Muskogees knew an Upper World of sun and moon and thunder, marking time, releasing powers of perfection, order, and clarity. They also knew a Lower World of madness, creation, upset, and chaos. The great antlered snake, the Tie-Snake, lurked in the river bottoms making humans sick or crazy. Its scales shone like mirrors; in its head was a crystal. In the Lower World traveled restless ghosts who could also bring sickness or trouble, haunting homes until their deaths were avenged. These ghosts in their changing forms (man, woman, owl, or bear) consumed human souls. *Stí:kinni*, as the Muskogees called them, might come upon the hunter or herb gatherer alone in the forest, or upon the aged or the newborn. Holding these worlds together and restoring balance was the Creator, Hesákádum Esée, the Holder of Breath.

When English settlers appeared on the trails, on the rivers, and in the forests, they challenged and changed tribal ways. In the late 1700s, U.S. agents worked to lure Muskogees and other indigenous peoples from hunting to agriculture, from active to sedentary life, and from economies of reciprocity and generosity to private ownership and debt. Over the centuries, there were cultural mixing and accommodation with whites. Muskogees acquired manufactured tools, learned to farm, and intermarried (though more with Africans than with English). They also incorporated Shawnees, Tuasis, Taskigis, Napochies,

Guales, Apalachees, Stonos, Yuchis, Tuscaroras, and Timacuas. These refugee tribes helped the Muskogees to see that the white settlers intended their destruction.

In the face of encroachment, a new consciousness emerged. The Pan-Indian movement had new prophets like the Shawnee Tecumseh, who traveled to central Alabama with his message of resistance. In 1811 and 1812 the largest series of quakes in North America in several centuries shook the earth. The ground opened. The Mississippi River flowed backward. Europeans, Africans, and indigenous people all read divine messages in natural events. Across the Muskogee territory rose a new urgency. Prophets like Osceola's uncle Peter McQueen warned of the need for purity and renewal in the face of cultural chaos. They burned the fields of Indians who collaborated with white settlers, and they assassinated collaborating chiefs. The U.S. government intervened in the "Redstick" civil war, seeing it as an opportunity to break the tribes and claim their territory. After the Battle of Horseshoe Bend, the United States claimed fourteen million acres. When Peter McQueen fled south with survivors to join the Seminoles, and when the remaining Muskogees were forcibly marched to the western territory in 1835–36, they must have left many ghosts behind.[1]

Maybe it was one of these *stí:kinni*—or maybe the Tie-Snake—who troubled my mother's spirit.

It was a Monday morning in March, and I was trying to get the NCARRV books ready for the auditors. The office phone rang. It was Effie Jean Corbitt, my old piano teacher. I brightened. What was she doing in town? Then I heard the tone of her voice, remembered that she was married to the undertaker.

"Mab, this is bad news. Let me let you talk to your daddy."

There was Daddy's voice heavy on the line. "Your mama died this morning."

I put my head down on my desk and burst into tears. "Mama, oh, Mama." I went upstairs crying. "My mama just died," I told Leah. She embraced me.

My mother's funeral was on Wednesday, and by Thursday morning everyone else—my brother and sister and their families, cousins, uncles—had cleared out. I put Barb and our daughter, Annie, on a plane back to Durham and stayed around for the rest of the week to be with my father and to absorb as much as I could of Mama's presence, which was hanging in the house and yard, as perceptible as the scent of banana shrub. In strange and familiar ways I felt myself becoming her.

On Wednesday, I started calling myself "Honey."

On Thursday, after Daddy went to bed, I stayed up in her bedroom and went through her desk, looking for a message. It was cold, and I could almost hear her voice: "Honey, now, you light the heater in this chilled room." I found three calendars, checkbook sized, with her notations, the closest she had to a diary. In the October margins in the month before Annie's birth—which had shocked her far more than she ever thought she let me know—I read, "Whatever you are, you will be, and we should cherish it." And the next month: "Believe the best about people, and if you are wrong, it will be on the side of love." These were affirmations, I realized, ways to focus her thoughts as she lay in bed day after day, looking out at the clouds through the pecan limbs.

I looked for the fall of 1985, when I had sent her the galleys of my book of essays, *My Mama's Dead Squirrel: Lesbian Essays on Southern Culture*, all the writing I had done about her during my *Feminary* years and never showed her, including a long essay about race and class and her and her mother and the Black women who were their maids: an interrogation of the love white women claim for the Black women to whom they paid subsistence wages to clean their homes.

I had dedicated the book to Mother "for all she taught me, and all she left for me to learn," its origins in my mid-adolescent realization that something at home was very wrong and that I could not take the world as my mother taught it to me. Something was hurting her that seemed to implicate me, too. Growing disagreement with my mother over race after my epiphany under the bushes when Tuskegee High was integrated coincided with my panic over what I feared might be a common sickness, and the result of both was the beginning of an emotional separation that left me lonely still. My mother's epidermis erupted with allergies and all the white folks in Alabama went crazy

in the 1960s, bombs going off in churches killing Black children my
age, police dogs set loose, fire hoses slamming bodies against brick
walls, beatings.

By the time I wrote the book, in my early thirties, I'd been trying
to sort through what being a white woman in southern culture—what
misogyny and race and class—had done to her and us, and how, as
a lesbian, I had more in common, in an eerie way, with Black people
than with my own family, entrenched Republicans, as most of them
seemed to be, while I was having dreams of storm troopers disappearing my queer friends.

I had thought that whatever it was that killed her began when she
turned forty, and when she died I was thirty-eight. But after her death
Daddy said it had always been there—allergies, asthma, some propen-
sity for sickness, and an increasing need for steroids and other drugs
whose side effects were deadly.

From childhood, memories. Out the kitchen window pecan pollen
would fall. "It's raining death," Mama would say as she started itching.
Then I would hear conversations with my father behind the door: "I
can't take it any more." Through the doorway I would see her sobbing,
then the blue suitcase would appear on the stairs. She would send me
cards from oceans with beaches, and I would look at them and think,
I won't love you anymore.

She often showed me her poems:

Dear God,
What shall I do with a heart
Always crying after lost desires?
Ever striving to become a part
Of unremembered scenes, undiscovered fires,
Mist over mountains I never saw
All beauty not yet chilled by law?

When I was in my teens, a friend of mother's told me that she
thought Mama raised me to leave, and my younger sister to stay. She
quoted Tennyson to me: "To sail beyond the sunset and the baths of

stars." She raised my sister for the small town and the sandbox, for grandchildren to fill the picture frames. I remember an August night at the Gulf of Mexico. Mama took us both down to the beach, where there was foxfire in the water. She swam naked. On the beach my sister was crying, while I watched limbs in a rush of light. But back home it was three kids and a husband, washing sheets, cooking beans, making beds, filling Daddy's quiet with too much feeling. To get out of the house in the summers she'd take us to the county swimming hole, tadpoles in the cold water and the dive from the trestle into a creek with a bottom of dark.

My father had flown off to fight in World War II, like many men of his generation who would be blown out of foxholes or bombers or steel ships and see buddies dismembered beside them, drowned in a crimson oily sea or falling away in smoking planes, screaming over the intercom. The lucky ones returned home as heroes and married the women, like my mother, who had waited with their own terrors and dreams. They had children as soon as they could, no doubt desperate for life, contending—in the amazing tiny new bodies—with all their own mute fears. They stuffed it all into a myth of domesticity that they had dreamed out in the long war years and now saw refracted back from the new television screens.

Growing up, my siblings and I knew that our mother was a Cobb like her father, and to her that meant being wild and adventurous. Our neighbor Carribec would sit on her front porch and tell stories of when my mother and my uncles were in their teens riding up and down the dirt streets of town on their new "motor sickle." My grandfather Ben Cobb was a natural musician, Mama would explain, who picked out tunes by ear on his mandolin. In a portrait among our family pictures, he stands before a mirror, laughing, a nimbus of bent morning light caught round his head. He is dressed in soldier blue, off to fight in Cuba.

"He was underage and underweight," my mother told the story, "but he had to go to war. He got as far as Miami and spent the entire Spanish-American War in the swamp in a tent. All he got was malaria." He died in the influenza epidemic of 1918, when my mother was three. When my mother would leave town on one of her cures, I got the feeling that she left for places that she knew her father had been or would have liked to go.

In the top drawer of Mama's desk, I found what must have been the last telegram he had sent home, with a note at the bottom to tell his little girl he would see her soon. He never did.

Between my sister and me there was the constant ripple of what I came to recognize as anger. I was ten when my father, attempting to explain Mother's illnesses, the growing crisis he could not manage or understand, told me that it had been when my sister was born that Mama started getting sick. So I explained to my sister how it was her fault. I told her there was no Santa Claus. In the swimming pool, I would ask her to play shark, then bite her. But it was never her fault.

Back in Mama's bedroom, the moon was rising through new pecan leaves. I found at the top of another page of her calendar, written in her sprawling hand: "Tough times never last. Tough people do." And at the bottom that September 1985, "Would God I had died for thee, David—Absolam."

I remembered how I had "come out" to Mama in the 1970s, when I finally found the words to say what she had known far longer than I had. I had taken Pat home soon after we fell in love. When I thought everyone had gone to bed, we started making love in my bedroom in the upstairs far corner of the drafty house. Without warning, Mama knocked, then swept into the room. As we scrambled to pull up the covers, she marched toward the fireplace. "Is there a match? Do y'all have any matches up here?"

"Yessum," I'd said as I reached for the panties near my feet. She picked up the box of matches from my mantelpiece and swept back out of the room, "goodnight" wafting behind her. Pat and I pretended that she hadn't seen anything because of her cataracts. But several years later when I finally went down to her bedroom on another visit and told her I was a lesbian, she reminded me of that evening.

"I'm not blind and I'm not a fool," she said. "I've known since you were five."

It took me several more years to finally ask her how. She explained,

"The way when you were five you bossed everybody around, strode across the floor with a pistol on your hip, and cried when you had to wear a dress to school."

She asked me, "Mab, should I try to talk you out of this?"

"No, Mama," I answered. "It would be the worst thing you could do."

A couple of years later, in the face of my own procrastinations, she told my father the news, then called me with his reaction: "You are my own flesh and blood."

But it was hard for her: my anger over homophobia, my determination to fight it. She wanted me to adjust more, not thinking the world could or would change. *Would God I had died for thee, David.*

There were times as well when I wished I could die for her.

By the time I was eight, Mama had so many pills in her dresser, they rattled in bottles when she opened the drawer. She got them from numerous doctors, so when one stopped supplying her she always had another. It has taken me thirty years to realize how much by then I wanted to make her well, how much I still stand at the foot of her bed with an eight-year-old's mind, feeling furiously responsible for her pain. One night when I was in my teens I came downstairs to the refrigerator. I couldn't sleep and I wanted some food. In her room I heard her crying. The sheets were laced with her blood where she had scratched herself raw. I couldn't go in. I just stood there and thought, *My mama lives in hell.* And I was leaving her for years.

And I left my sister, too, over twenty years later, after I finally said it. I used the shortest words: "I'm gay." We were at a Georgia beach for a summer vacation, the last we would all take together: me and Barb, my sister and her kids, Mama, my brother's wife and their boys. I had opened my mouth so often for the words to explain to my sister what we both knew, words that never came out. Finally, there they were, hanging between us like a dragonfly. And her mouth ate them.

"I know," she said. "It's a problem. I'm sure you will understand. My children"—she had four kids then—"they are gifts from God. I can't let them think it's not a sin." She'd been born again, perhaps needing some place of origin other than Mama's body—but from that place, we seemed no longer kin.

And me, I thought, *whose gift am I?*

Then I heard my sister say, "There may come a day you can't see them. Or maybe just by yourself. It doesn't show so when you are alone." I started crying then, and when we got to the cottage I left her to carry the groceries and walked on the beach for hours, watching strange things wash up on the shore. I walked the beach and remembered the years.

At her wedding, I was her maid of honor. I wore a long blue dress. She invited Pat to the wedding. Then came the breakup with Pat and falling in love with Barbara, after Barb and I were firmly friends and could talk to each other about anything. Now my sister didn't like to see me with Barb and didn't want us near her children.

To the Georgia seagulls: "I have worked ten years to love and be loved, and for that she would make me ashamed?" Then I turned around. Black rocks rode out to the breakers, and I saw in the spit and the foam that I had wanted my sister to give me a child, slip me an extra one, like a lateral pass at a football game, and I would clutch it close and run.

Walking back up the Georgia beach took many fewer years. I thought of all those drives to see my sister and her family, past crape myrtle trees leaning with blossoms and boards sagging on cantaloupe-laden porches. *That road runs both ways,* I thought. But I didn't think she would come to see me, and she never has. At her house, I slipped into a life that was familiar to both of us because we had grown up in it. I think she was afraid to enter my world. I remembered one of my visits, when I was bringing her and her husband a loan of half my savings to keep their family going. We had played parlor games with her in-laws, pulling books out of the bookcase to guess them. And there one of them was on the floor, one of those fundamentalist tracts, its title *The Gay Invaders,* with double male and female symbols marching, like off a spaceship. I left the room and went to sit on the front porch steps and watch the reassuring full moon, wishing I were indeed on some other planet.

So when Daddy told me Mama died that Monday morning, I did not know if I could take my family home for her funeral. But Barbara said, "We all go." When I pulled up in the driveway, feeling thirteen, my sister's husband met us at the door and carried Annie inside, and their children bobbed her back and forth, like a happy buoy in a sea of cousins. Later, my father told me he had instructed them, "You will treat your sister right at your mother's burying."

All afternoon the day before the funeral, old friends and family came to visit us, people I hadn't seen for years. I met my mother's friend Frances Howard at the door and introduced my "adopted baby."

"Why, I had a two-hour conversation with your mother only last week, and she never mentioned it!" Frances Howard replied, flicking her eyebrows in only the slightest show of skepticism. Then the discretion we both knew we could count on kicked in, and she brightened. "That's wonderful! Isn't she the sweetest thing!"

My Aunt Tay was franker. She took Annie in her arms, looked closely at her, and turned to me. "Mab, what's the real story about this baby? She looks exactly like your grandmother!" She had looked more like me than Barb or David for the first few months, one of the mysteries of genetics. I just grinned.

It was to Judy that I told the whole truth, gorgeous Judy, the next-door neighbor I always wanted as a big sister.

"Mab, you're lying!" she said as I introduced my adopted child. Then she turned to my sister: "She's lying, isn't she?" My sister replied archly, "Would Mab lie?" Later Judy pursued me, and I explained how Barb had birthed the daughter that we would both love and raise.

I tried to figure out how I could explain my job to all these friends and family members. "I work with a small nonprofit to encourage churches, educators, and other groups to respond to hate activity," I tried.

Daddy cut across me. "She's a rabble-rouser," he said, chuckling.

It takes one to know one, I thought, grinning as well. I glimpsed the fact that he was proud of me even when I thought I was disagreeing. He has always been more tolerant of me than I have been of him! I remembered the interest he had taken in my ideas when I was a child. He had never believed that girls should neither think nor have a claim to history.

The house was filled with flowers, including an arrangement from the NCARRV board. Among the condolence cards was one from Bobby Person.

Together once again, Mama's family, we all made the walk to the end of the world, with tea olive and wisteria blooming. On the pew where we sat in the organ's swell, I didn't know if I was eight or thirteen or forty. Then they rolled Mama past, her gray casket shining, and she was gone.

After the funeral, remembering the row of Black people on the pew to my left, I realized it was the first time I had been in that Methodist church when it wasn't segregated. They were friends of Daddy's come to pay respects. Maybe there was more going on here than I have given him credit for. They were probably Black Republicans. But maybe everything changes?

The evening after the funeral, my twelve-year-old niece came into the kitchen as we were standing around drinking coffee, all of us surprised, I think, at how much we enjoyed each other's company.

She looked her mother in the eye. "Mama, is Annie our cousin?" There was silence, into which she repeated the question: *"Mama, I said, is Annie our cousin?"* My sister looked across the kitchen table at me, and nodded.

Sitting at Mama's desk that Thursday evening, watching pecan limbs shatter the moon, I kept expecting her to rise up on her elbow from her bed and resume the conversation. I remembered her asking me, "Do you know what forbearance means?" It was the phone conversation after she had read *My Mama's Dead Squirrel.*

"Mama, it means that you could throw me away, but you have decided not to?"

"I'm just sorry I've been such a poor communicator," she had said, taking everything as usual on herself. "If I had known how you felt about the stories I told you, I would not have offended you so."

As if they had offended me. Try "haunted" or "possessed"; try that they rattled around inside me where she put them, telling them over and over on long drives to Florida or Louisiana or on hot summer nights when we sat on the front porch guessing what color the next car would be. She hadn't seen that when they came out of me, they would carry her voice but not her meanings.

"Mama, I wrote for seven years, then dumped it on you all at once.

I'm sorry. If you want to tell me how you feel about it, I want to listen."
She told me, and I did listen, agreeing with much of what she said and
arguing with none of it.

"Mab," she explained at one point, "I am very isolated here now. I
have only a few friends left—like Virginia—and you have managed to
quote me saying something ugly about each one of them."

At some point in the conversation, there was a silence.

"Mama, the next book I write, I promise it will be set on Mars," I
lied. She decided to laugh. "If I make a lot of money, I will send you
and Virginia to the Bahamas."

"We'll have to go on different boats." We both laughed. We were
coming out of the woods.

Sooner or later we hung up the phone, and I cried all the next day.
"What did you want her to say?" Barb asked, irritated.

"I wanted her to be proud of me. I wanted some sense that she
agreed with at least some of what I thought I was getting from her. I
wanted some sense that the relationship will survive."

Days later, around suppertime, the phone rang. It was Mama. "I
wanted you to know I am going to be okay," she said. "I do agree with
some of what you said. We can talk about it sometime. And I reread your introduction, the part where you said you were making your
place in the world. If that's what it took, then it was worth it. After we
talked on Thursday, I felt a great burden lifted."

I hung up, crying again, to tell Barb, "She gave me what I asked for."

And it was there in her calendar for 1985, the month of our conversation: "Forbearing one another in love—speaking the truth in love."

The Christmas before Mama died, I was visiting her in her bedroom, which she hardly ever could leave now, twenty years of cortisone eating away at her, deteriorating her spine. I was standing in
front of the gas heater. She brought up the book, began telling me
everything she felt that I had gotten wrong, ways I had misquoted her.
"You were writing fiction," she said, and I still am.

"Mama," I said, trying to lighten things, "you told me you agreed
with some of it. Why don't you explain that, too?"

"Mab, there was a sustained anger toward me in that book that I
don't understand. And I'm afraid that if you get hurt doing this work,

it will be my fault because of things I didn't do when you were little."
She was crying now.

"Mama, I am grown and whatever happens to me is because of
my own choices," I answered, realizing somewhere in the back of my
mind that she was feeling what I had wanted her to feel.

"And whatever you say about race relations here, there was never
violence like in other places," she continued.

Never violence?

I said, "But Sammy Younge—"

After a while, the crying stopped as abruptly as it had begun, and
we began another conversation as if nothing had been said.

Talking to Barb about it later, I said, "In a way, what I wrote will
never be okay with her, and I shouldn't try to make it all right. For
whatever reasons of my own, I wrote and showed her the book, and
she had to take the consequences." Why did I send her the galleys? I
couldn't remember. Mama and I never talked about it again, but she
had written in her calendar during those months, "Forgiveness is total
acceptance."

She also wrote in her calendar's margins, "Just do what comes next."
She was charting the early hours between doses of cortisone. She
was addicted to a dose of 100 milliliters every other day, but often
she couldn't make it through the night. *May 10, 4 a.m., 100 ml.* Then
the next night: *May 11, 3 a.m. 40, then 20.* "Nothing happens to any
man which he is not formed by nature to bear": my mother the stoic,
quoting Marcus Aurelius and waiting for early morning light, alone
with a pain we couldn't stand to share with her. My brother and sister
and I had all left home, I think all of us sharing both relief and guilt at
leaving her there. Throughout my twenties, I fought the gravitational
pull back to her house, that bedroom, a world increasingly constricted
by cataract operations, failing joints, a corroding spine.

It was getting late, and the desk was almost empty. In the bottom
drawer, I found a spiral-bound notebook. It began with what must
have been a Sunday school lesson, then it had what I could tell were
drafts of poems and prose pieces. It must have been the journal my
mother had used in a creative-writing course she took after she retired.

The top of one page caught my eye: "I was the baby nobody wanted." I went on to read the story of her birth, which I had never heard her tell.

I was the baby nobody wanted. I don't say this as a criticism of my parents. My birth was a disaster—the last straw in a difficult situation. My parents married late in life. Daddy had been courting mother for years. They had been playmates and neighbors as children. Mother lived in Alabama Conference Female College—the only small child in a girls' school—daughter of the president. My father, one of six children. Her only playmates were the "wild Cobbs" and their friends. All the children in the neighborhood gathered in the yard of the [Cobbs'] battered colonial house.

Daddy's courting was hampered by two things mainly—the objection of Grandfa Massey to the wildest, gayest and most handsome of the two wild Cobb boys—and mother's feeling that her parents needed her. She had been running the housekeeping end of the college since my grandmother became an invalid.

In 1890 Grandfa retired from the presidency of the college and built a house in Tuskegee. Mother took over the running of this large home with the help of the negroes who came with them.

Daddy was an engineer. He had worked for three years on the Panama Canal. He and several friends quit their jobs, bought equipment, hired an Indian guide, and began an expedition up the Chagras River in search of gold.

> Beyond the Chagras River
> Tis said of stories old
> Are paths that lead to mountains
> Of purest virgin gold.
> But tis my firm conviction
> Whatever tales they tell.
> Beyond the Chagras River
> All paths lead straight to hell.

So it proved to my father. His only prize was a killing bout of malaria. His friends left him to die. The Indian guide stayed and brought him back, raving with fever, to Colon in the canoe left by his "friends."

When he got back from Panama, he got a job designing gun parts in a Prattville factory. He carried on his courtship [of Mother] from Prattville with no greater success. One day, Daddy's landlady wrote my mother, "If you want Ben Cobb, you had better marry him. A good many Prattville girls have their eyes on him and he is tired of waiting."

Mother took her advice, and my parents were married shortly thereafter. After a year in Prattville my parents came to live with Grandfa. Big Minner [his wife] having died. Here conflict between Grandfa and Daddy was inevitable. Grandfa was a dignified patriarch in his eighties—deeply religious, conservative, set in his ways, used to respect that was almost idolatry from family and town folks. How could he understand this handsome, reckless young man? Daddy was an inveterate sportsman. His money went for guns, dogs, fishing gear. Grandfa had never played a day in his life.

To add to the confusion, my brothers were born 15 months apart. The household might have adjusted to these problems had it not been for me. I came along 15 months after Ben. I was 2 months premature, weighing 4 lbs and almost killing my mother, who had been badly torn with the birth of my brothers. Apesiotomies [sic] were unknown at the time—at least to the ill equipped, badly educated doctor who delivered all her babies in her home.

Mother almost died at my birth. I would have died, too, had it not been for a good friend and neighbor—Mrs. Oscar Lewis, who took me to nurse alongside her newly born boy. When I asked Mother years later why there are no pictures of me or what I did at certain ages or why I wasn't baptized in the Christening dress, she burst into tears. "Nobody knows anything about your first year. We put you in the sleeping porch upstairs and forgot you. I was so sick, honey. Carrie Echols looked after you."

Here the entry ends, the unwanted white child in the arms and care of Carrie Echols, the invisible Black woman whose generous love and attention surely kept my mother alive. Carrie is kin, I can see, to the unnamed Indian guide who brought the raving Ben Cobb back to Colon after his white friends deserted him.

"I'm on the horns of a dilemma," Mama had told me in our last phone conversation, the day before her death. Daddy told me it had been a week of racking pain, slivers of spine piercing her spinal column. She was heavily sedated. It was in the midst of the congressional investigation of Contragate, and she was sickened by the hearings. The only news she liked to follow was about Oral Roberts: he was up in his prayer tower asking God to take him if he didn't raise $9 million, and he was nearing his deadline far short of his goal. She'd been following his story closely. "He's on the horns of a dilemma, too," she laughed. "If he can get off the horns of his, maybe I can get off mine."

The horns of your dilemma, Mama: pain and death, the devil and the deep blue sea.

"I wish she could die," I told Barb after hanging up the phone, and I dreamed that night of smothering my mother with a pillow. The next day, Mama, you slipped, gored by death, into the arms of the sea.

Sitting there with the calendars, the spare record of her pain that evening, I thought I knew then why I had written and sent her the first book: out of my old and desperate need to separate myself from the forces I saw destroying her, the parts of her to which I could not be loyal without going under. "Forgiveness is total acceptance," she might have written me. But how could I love her and accept her pain? I wrote many parts of the book in a furious attempt to understand, hoping it would save us both. And then I sent her what I had written, to say, "This is how I am and am not you," and to know what parts of her to keep alive in me and what I had to bury.

The afternoon of her funeral, her casket hung suspended above the orange gash in the earth in the new part of the white folks' cemetery, its population of the dead beginning to outstrip what was left alive in the white town. The spray of red carnations was vivid against the green imitation grass over the upturned dirt, and the day was suffused with my sense of my mother's presence. I watched the hole that would take what was left of her failing body. Could it also take my fear and despair while leaving me her courage and her love?

In Mama's papers, I turned up a portrait of my great-grandfather's family. Judge Cobb sits on the front steps of the family home, his wife and children surrounding him. I am struck by how sad they all look, how uncomposed, despite the photographer's obvious attempts to arrange them. The picture confounds me. Because their eyes are all askew, it is as if they don't know where the camera is, and neither do I don't know where I stand in relation to these people. There is an easel with a frame standing behind my great-grandmother Caroline as if it were a person. I learn from a note on the back that it contained a picture of a deceased son. But because of the camera's angle, the tintype is white, blank. That void captures some sense of emptiness that permeates the photo. There is no pretense to unity or happiness.

My great-grandfather sits inside, rigid and austere. This is the supremacist, the judge who threw Black and white Republicans onto chain gangs after Reconstruction, the congressman who stole elections from interracial Populist insurgencies, the Alabama legislator who helped to write Jim Crow segregation laws. This is the father who beat his children. I recognize Dr. Weedon in my great-grandfather Cobb. His father, William, fought Osceola in Florida in the Seminole Wars. Judge Cobb's youngest son, dressed in Sunday clothes but barefooted, sits uneasily near the edge of the picture. In 1918, he will run for Alabama secretary of state. By then his older brother, my grandfather Ben, will be dead. Ben, on the other edge, seems resolute. He and my great-aunt Carrie have arranged themselves around the column. They are the most handsome—I can see my mother was right—with something romantic about their sadness, a sense that Ben is already gone, off to the wars and the colonial adventures that in two decades will kill him, leaving behind a three-year-old daughter. This is the man my mother—who also, come to think of it, always seemed focused somewhere beyond the family frame—searched for her whole life. The wild son flees the rigid, dominating father into the arms of a racist war. There is a cost to white supremacy. Is this the picture's message? I finally notice the youngest daughter, sitting between the judge's legs, the only one who even tries to look directly at the camera, although her eyes are slightly crossed. I do not know her name, but I catch one eye and nod.

There's a truth that I am desperate to make you understand: race is not the same as family. In fact, "race" betrays family, if family does not betray "race."

8

Robeson, Bloody Robeson

In my dreams each night, a cosmic hand would deal me the Death card, skeleton on horseback riding across a field of bodies, sun setting (or rising) between columns on the horizon. Then the Tower card fell from the bony hand: lightning blast dislodging bricks, jolt of current through the cells, bodies in free fall.

Now I reach the most difficult part, the hardest place to match with words, as we push upriver toward the story's heart. At this bend in the narrative the focus scatters, the violence quickens, dangers pile up beneath the surface. The river here is the Lumber, flowing through Robeson County, and it was our undoing.

Juries helped to anchor the Statesville chapter and the earlier parts of the White Patriot story in court-anointed "fact": White Knights convicted by their own people's words, the Millers' versions of the tale turned away in the moment of the foreman's verdict. I have sat through too many trials now not to know the formula: "good fact makes good law," the lawyers say. They lay out the pieces one by one, give them numbers, log them into evidence. But the real battle comes at the open and close, each lawyer arguing the syntax in which to fit the cold metal barrel of the gun, the soft, almost invisible fibers of a glove, the slick paper of the autopsy report. Context, interpretation, is all. Then court documents and testimony enter the public domain. In Robeson, though, we could not get our stories through the courtroom door. One problem is that a large part of this story calls the question on the law itself: a white deputy on a back road, a jail in which a Black man died, a "death penalty DA," and a dead Indian who wanted to be a different kind of judge.

"The key to writing a good crime story," a journalist once instructed me, "is in the gaps." The reading, here, also is in the gaps.

Robeson County is Osceola's kind of place. In fact, I think I met some of his distant cousins there. Algonquians, Sioux, Tuscaroras, and Cherokees had inhabited the land before the English settlers came. In 1700, European settlers, moving inland from the coast, bypassed the swampy land along the Lumber River.[1] In 1713, the Tuscarora fortress Nohoroco fell to the English, breaking the back of Indian resistance in the Carolinas. Most Tuscaroras withdrew north; others fled farther south to join the Muskogee and then the Seminole resistance; fewer settled along the Lumber River. It became a refuge for what Europeans called "a mixt crew, a lawless people," remnants of Indian nations joined by escaped slaves. In 1835, the state legislature stripped the region's Indians of the rights to vote and bear arms. At the beginning of the Civil War, the Confederate Army conscripted these "free citizens of color" to work with slaves building forts around Wilmington. Three decades after Osceola's death and decapitation, Henry Berry Lowry, like Osceola in Florida, took his Indian kin to the swamps, where they were joined by fugitive slaves, to fight Confederates during the Civil War and the "home guard" during Reconstruction. The gang murdered the local sheriff in retaliation for his violence against Indians. Lowry was caught once but escaped, and today an outdoor drama, *Strike at the Wind*, keeps his legacy alive.[2]

In the 1930s Miles Horton, founder of the Highlander Center in Tennessee and its director for five decades, went to Robeson County to organize a textile strike. Eventually the company sent four hired guns to kill him. He saw them coming through the hotel window and leaned out with his own revolver, warning them to get organized: "You've got to vote on who's going to die. Are you people in the front seat going to die, or are you two in the back seat going to be the ones?" The men left without firing a shot.[3]

Commented historian McKee Evans of Robeson County, "This was a place in which to a special extent no tide of history had ever swept quite clean, where relics of the past persisted to confront the present."[4] Relics, for instance, like Osceola's head?

In late 1986, Christina and I went back into Robeson County to work again on the murder of Joyce Sinclair, who, if you remember, had been kidnapped from her home in 1985 by a "white man wearing white." Her murder, like many others in the county, remained unsolved. People were recalling her name because of another death, a year after Joyce's body had been spotted behind the cinder-block house.

Joyce was killed the day before Halloween, and Jimmy Earl Cummings died after being shot through the head by Deputy Kevin Stone, son of Sheriff Hubert Stone, on November 1, 1986, the night after Halloween. All Hallows' Eve, so conquered Celtic culture says, is the night on which the passage thins between worlds of the living and of the dead, the evening on which that other world is caricatured in the little costumed ghosts and goblins tricking after candy. Joyce's abductor, the man redundantly white, visits like a Klansman, like a ghost, like a deadly apparition flitting through the story.

I warned you about the Death card. Well, here it falls, and falls, and falls.

Everyone agrees that Kevin Stone, twenty-three at the time of Cummings's death, was a county narcotics agent. Everyone agrees he is the sheriff's son. Everyone agrees that he had stopped Cummings and Darlene Hunt on a search for drugs. After that point, the stories proliferate. I will tell you this part of the story like you'd read it in your morning paper. In fact, let me quote to you an editorial in the *Robesonian* about the multiple accounts of that November night:

> The first report, from the Sheriff's Department, was that Stone accidentally killed Cummings during a scuffle as they struggled for Stone's gun, indicating, we believe, that Cummings had his hands on Stone. The next report, from the SBI [State Bureau of Investigation], was that the two were scuffling and Stone shot Cummings in self defense, because Stone feared for his own life.

Then, a coroner's jury ruled Thursday that the shooting was "accidental and in self-defense" after testimony by Stone was read at a coroner's inquest, stating that Stone slipped and his pistol accidentally discharged. Those, essentially, are three different stories.[5]

The inquest into Jimmy Earl's death was held on November 13 at 5:30 p.m., only hours before the first community meeting to protest his killing. Page Hudson, the state medical examiner, later commented to the media about the lack of standard procedures. For example, the Cummings family had only four hours' notice, insufficient time to get a lawyer. North Carolina law gives family members the right to have counsel to ask questions and present evidence, and standard notification time is ten days to two weeks. At the inquest, Junior Cummings, Jimmy Earl's brother, asked the coroner, Chalmers Biggs, for a delay, but Biggs deferred the decision to District Attorney Joe Freeman Britt. Britt appeared to question witnesses, another procedure Hudson found highly unusual. "It's putting investigating, prosecution and judging in the hands of one person," he explained to reporters.[6]

The stories that sheriff's deputies and SBI agents recounted during the inquest also disagreed with the explanation of events that Cummings's companion, Darlene Hunt, later gave to reporters. Britt called neither Hunt nor Stone to testify, although both were in the courtroom. (Hunt was under indictment for drug charges related to items Kevin Stone found in her car.) Mike Stogner, a county narcotics agent who had arrived first on the scene, testified at the inquest that Stone said he stopped Cummings's car because it was weaving, but he did not recognize him until looking at his license.[7] According to Darlene's statements to reporters, Stone called out, "Hold, Jimmy," as he approached the car, and he did not ask to see identification.[8] SBI agent Kevin McGinnis testified that Kevin Stone told him he had ridden by Cummings's house twice, pulling into a grocery store parking lot, then following Darlene's Pinto when Cummings and Hunt left the driveway.[9] Family members' statements indicated that Cummings knew Stone was watching him and was afraid. One explained to a *News and*

Observer reporter, "Our brother was upset . . . he had earlier told us he was fearing for his life."[10]

According to SBI agent McGinnis's account of Stone's story, when the deputy opened the trunk of Darlene's car, the unarmed Cummings grabbed a plastic bucket later said to contain four pounds of marijuana and ran off into the darkness. Stone, according to McGinnis's statement, first fired a warning shot.[11]

Later, Darlene disagreed: "His gun was pointed right in front." Then, she said, the two men ran off into the night and she heard another shot. "I knew the second shot hit," Darlene told a reporter, remembering the thud of the slug hitting a human skull, "because it did not sound like the first shot." She stood in the middle of the road, holding her face.[12]

The *Robesonian* editorial went on to ask other questions. Why would Stone fear for his life when he was carrying a pistol and Cummings had only a plastic bucket? If he did fear, why did he follow Cummings off into the darkness when he knew where he lived and had confiscated the evidence? Why was Darlene Hunt ordered not to discuss the case?[13]

The coroner's jury combined the different versions of the shooting in a highly unusual verdict: "It was an accident or in self defense."[14] Commented an official from the North Carolina affiliate of the American Civil Liberties Union, "You can't have it both ways." The state ACLU announced it was entering the case out of concern with due process: upon being apprehended by a law enforcement officer, a person is to be taken safely to a place where he or she will have a hearing. With the ACLU's help, the Cummings family initiated a civil suit against Stone and the Sheriff's Department.[15]

It was not only Joe Freeman Britt's six-foot-six-inch frame that gave him a commanding presence in the county. Britt was well known as the "death penalty DA." At the time of the inquest his thirty-three death penalty convictions gave him a place in the *Guinness Book of World Records*. The March before the Cummings shooting, he had been the subject of an admiring piece in *Southern Magazine*, featured as a small-town Hemingway who plotted his murder convictions like short stories, then swayed juries with his oratory. "The oratorical traditions of the South are a real way of molding perceptions," he explained. "Today's Southern lawyers are imaginative and flexible, like artists." He waxed passionate over his death penalty cases. "In every prospective juror's breast there beats the flame that whispers, 'Preserve human life.' It's my job to extinguish that flame." He explained: "A court is the essence of order. It's well lighted, there are rules of procedure, the judge is there. And then, slowly, you bring that disordered act, the murder, into the ordered structure of society."[16]

Others have a less benign assessment of Robeson courtrooms. Maurice Geiger, director of the Rural Justice Center and former staff attorney to the U.S. Department of Justice, collaborated with the staff of the Center for Community Action (formerly Robeson Clergy and Laity Concerned) on Robeson research. The New Hampshire–based center picked Robeson County because statistics for dismissal there were so low—6 percent, compared to 30 percent nationally and 25 percent in North Carolina—indicating either that police efficiently screened cases or that the prosecutor's office was forcing an inordinate number of guilty pleas.[17] Geiger and his Robeson counterparts spent over 150 days in Robeson County during a five-year period documenting statistical evidence of inequities there. They examined approximately 1,270 closed criminal cases and observed in the courtroom for over four hundred hours. They also interviewed judges, judicial officers, probation officers, prosecutors, defendants, victims, witnesses, and so on. On the basis of their disturbing findings, the Rural Justice Center sent a report to the chief justice of North Carolina in December 1983. Geiger later summarized his opinion:

> In all of my experience in criminal justice I have never seen a jurisdiction in the United States with such a consistent disregard for fundamental due process, a prosecutor's office so pervasive in its abusive practices, or a judicial attitude that so condones those practices.[18]

In 1987, the North Carolina Commission on Indian Affairs released its *Report on the Treatment of Indians by the Criminal Justice System*. It found that court procedures in Robeson placed hardships on defendants and witnesses, that bonds were excessive, that indigent representation was poor, and that Indians served more time for the same sentences than whites do. Another study showed that defense lawyers made no motions in 65 percent of the felony cases studied.[19]

I recognized Britt's type. He reminded me of my great-granddaddy Judge James Cobb. After Reconstruction, Judge Cobb had helped to restore white rule to the county by using the bench to throw Republicans in jail or onto the chain gang. Then he was elected to Congress in 1884 and stayed there for a decade until he was thrown out for stealing the election from the candidate of an interracial Populist slate. His electoral fraud must have been pretty blatant for the 1894 Congress to kick him out, since by that time white northern and southern legislators had closed ranks. Sure, Britt with his wavy silver hair and his big cigar did not physically resemble my uptight great-granddaddy, sitting straight for his portrait like he had a corncob up his ass. But I had a feeling they were cut from the same cloth.

If Britt stood at the top of the ladder in Robeson County, Jimmy Earl Cummings was at the bottom. He was a Lumbee Indian in and out of trouble with the law, a poor man whose main income came from small-time drug dealing. His killing was the last straw for many poor people in the county.

Thirty-five percent of Robeson's population are Lumbee Indians, one-fourth of all the Native Americans in the United States east of the Mississippi. It is one of the poorest counties in the state, its unemployment rate one of the highest. Poverty and its location on Interstate 95 about halfway between New York and Miami give it a heavy drug trade. According to U.S. attorney Sam Currin's office, in 1986 the county had a cocaine trade that involved tens of millions of dollars and "four to five major drug organizations."[20] Currin observed, "I suppose for a rural county, the drug problem in Robeson is about as serious as any we have seen." He reported that drugs were being bought and sold openly on the street, with dealers operating at will.[21] Between 1975 and 1986, there had been fourteen unsolved murders in the county, many of them execution-style killings. Bodies shot in the head were found in cars on the side of the highway or floating in the Lumber River. Many of these killings were believed to be drug related.[22]

The level of money and organization Currin reported made the Klan seem like small potatoes. Yet this poor community began to take all these forces on. In fact, it was links between alleged law enforcement complicity in the drug trade and Kevin Stone's killing of Jimmy Earl Cummings that ignited Robeson residents.

Jimmy Earl's family began organizing to find out what happened. John Godwin, a Lumbee and a professional opera and gospel singer who had come home to retire, called the first public meeting, which apparently precipitated the November 13 inquest. Mac Legerton, a white United Church of Christ minister and director of the Center for Community Action, facilitated. The Cummings family came straight to this meeting from the inquest. "From my heart I feel the true story was not told," Junior Cummings told the group. Godwin commented, "I'm just a citizen who would like to see things done in a way that is acceptable to everyone. . . . Our effort is to see that justice is done, that people in the workforce are treated as human beings."[23]

Other meetings quickly followed, drawing over five hundred people. Concerned Citizens for Better Government emerged, a tri-racial coalition unusual in North Carolina—or anywhere. The Friend in Court Project (a Robeson project of the Rural Advancement Fund) joined, as did Black and Indian leaders from the county's churches. NCARRV joined the coalition the January after the Cummings shooting. These organizations provided staff and some leaders. They included people like Joy Johnson, a minister and former pioneering Black state legislator who edited the county's Black weekly newspaper; Sidney Locks, a Black minister and state legislator; Donna Chavis, a Lumbee activist married to Mac Legerton; and Reverend Franklin Reeves, another African American minister and director of Operation HELP from nearby Mullins, South Carolina. John Godwin was elected chair.

But, first and foremost, it was poor people in the county, white, Black, and Red, who were the driving force, who were finally more pissed off than they were scared or apathetic. The Cummings family formed the core around which the protest organized. Jimmy Earl's brother and sisters, Junior, Darlis, and Quessie, were outspoken in their outrage. Hundreds came to weekly meetings, spilling out into the corridors from high school cafeterias. "Dear God, give Robeson County a conscience," they implored. "Help us stop our people from going before executioners."

This kind of pressure from fed-up people can bring quick responses at many levels, not all of them benign. Cummings's murder brought several months of intense media scrutiny of the county's drug trade. Reporters began to fill in some gaps. Kevin Stone was one of two sons of the sheriff working in the Robeson Sheriff's Department. He was also one of two deputies who had access to a department locker from which $50,000 in drugs and cash had been stolen and for which a former deputy, Mitchell Stevens, and two other men were indicted. (When Stevens was tried six months later, Kevin Stone was mentioned as possibly having allowed the defendants access to the locker.)[24] The *Raleigh News and Observer* reported that Cummings family members were saying that Jimmy had told them he had bought drugs out of this cache and intended to buy $11,000 more the week he was killed.[25] Family members refused to be identified out of fear for their lives. Because no one would come forward publicly, the U.S. attorney's office discounted their claims.[26] The issue of protection for witnesses would continue to be crucial.

In another revelation, the *Raleigh News and Observer* reported that Sheriff Stone had written a character reference for a Pembroke resident convicted on drug charges in Florida, a move that Florida assistant state prosecutor Teresa Clark found "strange" and "highly unusual." Clark told a reporter, "I've never seen a letter like that in a presentencing before."[27]

The coalition that came together the day of the inquest put together a collective agenda. One thrust was voter registration. With 25 percent Blacks and 35 percent Indians in the county, people of color formed a potential majority. But feuds, mistrust, and divide-and-conquer tactics had allowed the white elite in Lumberton to elect people like Stone and Britt. The county was also divided into five school districts, with the best schools reserved for predominantly white Lumberton. The coalition endorsed a movement for merger. It also joined the Friend

in Court Project's call for a public defender to replace the private attorneys assigned to indigent clients by the court. Investigation of the
unsolved murders and of drug trafficking in the county were coalition
issues as well. Still, this agenda for reform left obvious gaps. Would
a public defender do much good with Britt enshrined as district attorney? Investigation was clearly needed, but investigation by whom?
Who would investigate the investigators?

I feared that the effort was too loaded down with prior histories
of the various organizations. Tension existed between the Rural Advancement Fund and the Center for Community Action, since RAF's
Friend in Court Project emerged from Geiger's research commis-
sioned by the center. Conditions in places like Robeson get as bad
as they do because people are deeply divided. Crises, when they inevitably come, can bring people out, but often they also exacerbate
divisions, conflicts over leadership, strategy, and vision. The level of
violence in the county made the stakes even higher. Mac Legerton,
director of the Center for Community Action, assessed:

> The problem was values and philosophies and where people were
> in their lives. There were tensions over strategy, how much to
> push and how far to push, how much people were willing to risk.
> John [Godwin] and I were more zealous, pushing to take risks.
> The families were, too. As zealots we were willing to go around
> that, to do what we felt needed to be done [without consensus].
> Zealots tend to be independent decision makers.

In retrospect, putting together Concerned Citizens for Better Government was like trying to build a raft underneath ourselves in the
middle of a flood, out of the tree trunks and branches and bodies that
kept rushing by.

Meetings of Concerned Citizens drew the mother and sisters of
Joyce Sinclair. The public focus had moved away from the Sinclair
case a few months after her 1985 murder. The FBI briefly investigated, finding no racial motive, and withdrew from the case. Within
weeks of the killing, the Sheriff's Department had narrowed the case
down to one suspect and expected an arrest.[28] But no arrest occurred.

Rumors had circulated that Joyce had been having an affair with a white man, part of what a family friend would later call a "Sears Roebuck Catalogue of rumors around the case." Her sisters and mother were occasionally followed by the man the Sheriff's Department told them was the "chief suspect."

After a year of inaction, Joyce's sister Rosetta Jones remained determined that the case not be dropped. Heartened by the widespread organizing, she began speaking at rallies, raising the issue of unsolved murders in the county. NCARRV took on the Sinclair case. Plenty of questions and rumors were circulating in Sinclair's tiny hometown, St. Pauls. A white man named Johnny Parker was in jail on a kidnapping charge said to relate in some way to the Sinclair murder. Parker was a loan shark with a long record and a mean reputation.[29] In December 1985, a month after the murder, Parker had kidnapped his own cousin, Bobby Hunt, or so the rumor went, because he had been talking to the law about Joyce's murder. Sheriff Stone reassured family members that once Parker was put away for the kidnapping, other witnesses would feel safer to come forward.

In August 1986, Parker had come up on the Hunt kidnapping charges, and a jury, fairly bravely, had found him guilty. But Parker wasn't in the courtroom to hear the verdict. He had walked out and escaped.

Christina and I worked for two months to track down the documents that would substantiate the rumors, for an NCARRV report on the Sinclair murder and investigation. We read the transcript of Johnny Parker's kidnapping trial to see how it related to the Sinclair case. The kidnapping was an event of a few minutes, we saw from the transcript, when Parker tried to take Bobby Hunt and his wife's nephew Joe out of the house at gunpoint because of Hunt's statements to law enforcement about the Sinclair case. Did it imply that Hunt had made statements and that Parker had something to hide? A sheriff's deputy read a statement taken from Hunt on the day of his kidnapping:

On Wednesday night, December 11, 1985, I was at home along with my nephew, Joe Hunt, Jr. Joe and I was at home alone, because we lived alone. . . . Joe and I was setting on the kitchen floor separating nails. . . . Around 11:20 p.m., we heard someone knock at the front door. Joe went to the front door and within approximately thirty seconds, Joe came back in to the kitchen and Johnny Parker was with him with a sawed-off double barrel shotgun in his right hand. I was still setting on the floor and when Johnny walked in to the kitchen, Johnny Parker was not pointing the gun at anyone and Johnny asked me what I had told the Deputies about Joyce Sinclair. I told Johnny nothing, that the Deputies had come out and investigated me about Joyce. Johnny said you're a damn liar. I started to say something else and he would not let me talk and told me that I was a dead man. Johnny—then Johnny told me to get up and go on the outside. Then he pointed the gun at me and pulled the hammer back and told me again that I'm a dead—that I was a dead man and I told him to let me put the nails up and he said no. He said set them down on the floor, and then he told Joe to come on, he would have to go with us. I started walking to the front door. Joe was behind me and Johnny behind Joe. Johnny had the gun pointed towards both of us. I walked about fifteen feet to get to the front door. When I got to the front door, I opened the door and ran out and slammed it behind me and ran. I ran out and laid down in a field, watching the house. I watched Johnny leave and he rode down the road looking for me. Then he left the area. Then I went for help and called the Sheriff's Department.[30]

We had heard that Parker had been picked up in Los Angeles on drug charges and was in the LA jail. I called and confirmed.

I pored over the autopsy report with its intimate details (blue robe over a pink nightgown, pinkish nail polish on toenails, knife penetration of liver, stomach, and lungs). Behind the cold page was a night of terror. I kept thinking of Joyce's four-year-old daughter, left sitting on the front step waiting for a mother who would never return. I was haunted by the image of this Halloween eve, the spirits of the dead, our other selves, hovering in the night air. Surely Joyce went with the intruder without protest to protect the girl. The autopsy explained that the cause of death was five stab wounds to the back and front of the body with a large knife or knives. The killer had also slashed her throat—a shallow, four-inch-long incision on the right side. And there was evidence of sexual assault.

Somewhere a memory floats to the surface from high school. One of my girlfriends is describing her boyfriend's weekend recreation with his friends: gang-raping a Black girl. I had not objected to my friend's tone, which I remember as almost proud. I did not tell my parents or report it to the law. That passivity was my response to a culture in which I assumed such activities were considered normal, or perhaps more accurately that they were not considered at all. This time, I wanted to find the rapist, the murderer.

Christina and I went down and met with Joyce's family and supporters to read them a draft of our report. We took suggestions for revision and came back to Durham to finish the draft. A journalist on our board reviewed the draft as well.

We held the press conference to release NCARRV's "Special Report on the Murder/Investigation of Joyce Harrell Sinclair" in late April 1987 in Sinclair's church in St. Pauls. We cited Parker as a "key figure," establishing a link between his kidnapping conviction and the Sinclair murder. We reported that he was in jail in California and urged immediate extradition, and we noted the limited degree to which St. Pauls police and the Robeson Sheriff's Department had investigated the case. Joyce Sinclair's husband, Jimmy, made a statement, as did various community leaders, echoing the call for stronger action.

Many of Joyce's family members attended, and after it was over an elderly Black man with a wizened face came up to us and held out his hand, introducing himself as Joyce's uncle. "I want to thank you," he said. "This is the first thing we have been able to do and not be afraid."

Johnny Parker was eventually extradited to Robeson County. In August 1987 he was convicted of two counts of second-degree kidnapping, and in February 1988 he received two consecutive fifteen-year sentences.[31] From jail, Parker wrote to the local newspapers about the Sinclair case: "I had an officer of the law to come to my house in St. Pauls and tell me I was no longer a suspect, that they were looking for a person that dyed their hair. . . . I did not kill Joyce Sinclair."[32] To date, no one has been indicted in her murder.

In March 1987, while we were preparing the Sinclair murder report, former sheriff's deputy Mitchell Stevens went on trial in U.S. District Court in Raleigh for his alleged role in the theft of drugs from the Sheriff's Department locker. The two primary witnesses against him were Johnny Lee Jones and John Delton Locklear, the dealers from whom the drugs had originally been confiscated. They pled guilty to two counts of conspiracy, turning state's evidence and pointing the finger at Stevens. Stevens pointed it back. He testified that he had tried to "turn" Locklear and his father, James (that is, to recruit them as informants), to get information about Sheriff Stone's involvement in the drug trade. "I had information from numerous sources that the sheriff was receiving three hundred dollars per ounce of cocaine sold by this James Locklear for protection," he said.[33]

SBI agent Arthur L. Robertson testified that the Sheriff's Department had not followed the routine procedure of taping radio transmissions the night the drugs were stolen; in fact, the tapes were probably never inserted into the machine that night. Robertson said that Stevens had alerted an old SBI friend to the possibility of the problems within the department.[34] Stevens's lawyer Eddie Knox (who had just finished running for governor) told the jury in his closing remarks, "They're hell bent on putting this man in prison. . . . Kevin Stone is out on a limb. Burnis Wilkins [the other deputy with a key to the evidence lockers] is out on a limb. If this man is set free, someone's going to start asking questions. How did those drugs get out of there?"[35] The jury acquitted Stevens.

A month later, in April 1987, Concerned Citizens for Better Government held a march for justice, the first such protest march in Robeson County history. Two thousand people turned out, packing the square in front of the courthouse and spilling into side streets. It turned out to be the high point of the movement in the county.

During the summer, Christina and I were in Robeson County less frequently. That summer, Glenn Miller sat in a jail in Wilson, and the Christian Knights of the Ku Klux Klan marched through Charlotte, Greensboro, and Durham. NCARRV worked with the communities involved to organize protests and vigils. That fall, District Attorney Britt was persuaded by white supporters to run for a Superior Court judgeship newly created to ensure minority representation on the bench. Julian Pierce, a Lumbee lawyer who headed up the Lumber River Legal Services, also decided to run. Julian was a man of integrity, a people's man. If he pulled the county's Black, Indian, and poor white voters together—a tall order!—he could beat the "death penalty DA" and the white power structure.

My partnership with Christina was unraveling. The problems began early on. I was the director of the organization. Racism could give me an automatic upper hand, a dangerous assumption of superiority. On the other hand, Christina could use my white guilt to gain a limited power—a tendency in white folks that Leah called "liberalism" and to which she urged me not to succumb. At times, my consciousness around racism made me question my own motives when I should have just gotten pissed off, a tendency to hold back that also derived from family and culture. Christina was commuting back and forth from her new home in Greensboro, and we disagreed over how much time she should spend in the office. When we went into Black communities like Statesville, she clearly took the lead, and we both knew I could never do our work alone. At times, she said, she considered me Black. Other times, I was a "controlling white woman." I was vulnerable to these charges, although I knew she had her own issues, too. In these dynamics, we jacked each other around. I had no training in administration or supervision, and for the first several years the organization had few personnel policies and no real personnel committee.

Our work brought intense pressures, not the least of which was having to raise our own salaries from grants and donations. We felt pressure to create a track record, learn how to stop the Klan, support victims of racist murder, and figure out how to break through the psychosis of white denial, while developing the board, building up the membership, and diversifing the funding sources. All this with two or three staff people over a period of five years. We found ourselves in continual crisis. The board needed to take more responsibility but, as staff, we had the responsibility of making them responsible, and I did not have any time to learn how. Later, at a funders' conference, I heard an explanation of funding patterns of progressive foundations: "Three years and out." *That's it,* I thought: *fuck-you funding. Slam, bam, thank you ma'am.* In three years, we had just gotten into the issues we were pursuing. So Chris and I would take it out on each other, until it broke us both down.

Everything got personalized. On days when we could talk about the relationship, we each could take responsibility for our own parts in the conflict and see the impact of factors beyond us both. But mostly, under more and more pressure from the weight of external and internal events, we just acted out. At times, we would close the doors and windows and yell, not often, but too much. I could fight the fascists till the cows came home, but I could not stand to fight with Chris like this. Given the pressures of the work, we both needed safety back in the office, and we no longer had it.

Sometimes Leah Wise could mediate in her roles as friend and board member. Those sessions would open up months of more constructive interaction. "You are like sisters fighting," she would observe, trying to lighten the atmosphere. "Tweedledum and Tweedledee," she called us. Then the stresses of the job would return. Someone else would be killed somewhere in the state, or we would run out of money, and Chris and I were pulled back into our battles. We were trying to work something out with each other, I recognized in my more lucid moments. If we'd been in a sexual relationship, we'd have taken it to therapy. But we were in a work relationship and there did not seem to be any help. It was like a marriage going bad. For days and weeks, I got obsessed with what she was doing and what she had said, and what I was doing and what I had said.

Responding to Christina's anger, I looked more closely at my own needs to control situations, which related to questions my mother's recent death was also opening. I knew I had a tendency to grab hold and close down, but I came to realize how much job-related fears, like getting blown up by Nazis, fed into older streams of anxiety, of abandonment and guilt from when my mother would leave us. There is some kind of vacuum seal between "family" and "history." That's why I found the story of Osceola so compelling: it shows how thin the cell wall is, and one way osmosis occurs. Trying to understand my fights with Christina propelled me to a more unified understanding. She pissed me off a lot, but I also love her. At points we were both messed up, which is to say that we were human.

I am explaining this in a couple of paragraphs, but the emotional drain on us both is there beneath much of what there's left to tell about the next few years in Robeson and Shelby—death, hostages, alleged assassination.

Most Tarot decks figure death as a skeleton with a scythe, harvesting, and often the heads beneath the bony foot wear crowns. "For medieval [European] man," as the Tarot book explains it, "death was the great leveller. It was the same for kings, queens, and princes of the church as for the wretched peasant: it was the only institution of democracy."[36]

But death is hardly democratic. Power, money, and status do insulate some people against mortality for a while. A minority of humans can purchase better health care, safer neighborhoods, less likelihood of an angry physical attack or the slow drain on soul and body from years of psychological warfare. But many people have never been afforded that measure of safety.

Take the case of Billy McKellar.

On January 12, 1988, Billy, a young African American man, died of bronchial asthma in the Robeson County jail. According to the sheriff, he died because he sold his asthma medication. According to his parents, he died because of neglect by his jailers.

I got to know Billy's parents, Betty and John McKellar, when they joined Concerned Citizens for Better Government. Betty is short, lovely and intense, the county's familiar mix of African and Indian blood obvious in her face. In the weeks after Billy's death, Betty told me, she could not stop crying. Her hair, which had been long and lustrous, fell out in chunks. She was fiercely determined to win justice for her son's death, a resolution she shared with her husband, John. John is a big-framed man, lighter skinned, gentle but equally resolute. He explained to me, "I had a tendency to drink a lot on weekends. I worked hard. But since this has happened, I haven't had a drink. I have changed my life. Because this is what they expected of me, they expected me to go off half-cocked, pick up a gun and do something." [37]

Billy had been in jail since November 25 the year before on a car theft charge, waiting for his court date, one of the many people in Robeson County who Maurice Geiger had noted stay in jail without bond an inordinate amount of time. Billy suffered from chronic asthma, and on January 12 he was having trouble breathing. An investigation by a governor's task force later found that the Sheriff's Department failed to refill one of Billy's prescriptions, and he was not given a TheoDur tablet that day until 7:00 p.m., when the jailer made his rounds, two hours before Billy died. The jailer also brought him an inhaler, which was empty. Billy's inmates yelled again for help, but none came until the next regular round at 8:19, when the jailer noticed him. A deputy put him in chains to take him to the hospital, but Billy defecated on himself. The deputy refused to transport him. The duty officer called an ambulance at 8:41. By the time it arrived at 8:44, Billy was slumped over "without breath or pulse"—dead. [38]

"To know how my son died is what bothers me," John McKellar told us. "They say he died from asthma, but if he had got any relief he would not be dead. This gives me the strength to go on [fighting], to know he died with shackles on his feet, chains on his hands, couldn't stand up, two men holding him and he dead with chains on."

But these details are out of order. I didn't meet John and Betty until later, after Eddie Hatcher and Timothy Jacobs had brought questions about Billy McKellar's death to a global audience, the day they took twenty people hostage in the *Robesonian* newspaper office in Lumberton. The Tarot book also explains: "While Death takes away, he also restores; every conclusion is also a new start. The field that he reaps, with its human remains like a charnel house, is also the field where Jason sowed the dragon's teeth to grow as armed men." [39]

I first met Eddie Hatcher the day after Mac Legerton of the Center for Community Action called from his office in Lumberton, the county seat. Cryptically, he said he was sending someone up who needed help, and I would hear from the person the next morning.

Eddie had information, and I should either figure out a way to get it to the press or get him out of the state. Clearly, Mac was afraid his phones were tapped. The next morning, Eddie called. I remembered he had served a brief stint as secretary to the coalition. He finally had *it*, he explained when I met him at his hotel—evidence to prove links between the Sheriff's Department, the district attorney, and the drug trade: maps of drug drops with the names of prominent officials and a diary by a law enforcement informant. But the sheriff knew he had them, so he needed to lay low until he could release them to the media. Could we help?

Damn. My mind was filled with scenes from the *Godfather*, men with violin cases closing in. Leah was out of town. Chris had not yet come to work that day. Who the hell did I know who could figure this one out? I thought of the Christic Institute, the public-interest law firm that had litigated the Communist Workers Party civil suit after the Greensboro massacre. They had experience with law enforcement corruption. I called Christic Institute South and asked for help. Bless their hearts and busy schedules, they said I could come over immediately to their office in Carrboro, twenty miles away. I picked up Eddie at a local motel, and we drove over.

Even under ordinary circumstances Eddie is probably a bit highstrung. With the sheriff and maybe local drug suppliers on his tail, he was in the upper octaves. Eddie is light-skinned, with dark hair down to his shoulders and, at the time, a mustache. His maternal grandparents were full-blooded Indians, although his father was white. Later the prosecution would make a big deal that his birth certificate said he was Caucasian. "Not too long ago, they'd have beat me for claiming to be white," he later fumed to a reporter. "My father was white, but I am an Indian. I claim it on the bloodline of my mother and on the way I was raised, taught to think, and taught to believe."[40] He is pudgy— not your stereotypical image of a revolutionary desperado. When we got to the Carrboro office, I introduced him to Gayle Korotkin and Allan Gregory, Christic lawyers. After hearing his story, Gayle asked us to come back the next day when Lewis Pitts, Christic South's director, would be in the office.

Lewis, a lean man with a stubble of a beard, is more impatient with the failure of the law than any lawyer I have ever met, and it doesn't take judges long to detect his attitude. Raised comfortably middle class in South Carolina in the 1950s and 1960s, he was radicalized in the 1970s when he clerked in a public defender's office and observed the hand of justice fall heavily, disproportionately, on young Blacks.[41] Gayle, blond and shorter than Lewis, is as shy as she is fierce. She came to North Carolina from New York on a bus to attend the funeral of the people killed by the Klan in Greensboro and stayed to become the core of the survivors' legal team.[42] Lewis describes Christic Institute South as a "strike force to go in where movements for social justice are being blocked in the South . . . We look at each case where the legal approach is the tactical goal," he explains, "empowerment the strategic one."[43]

Eddie laid out his case, saying that he had maps that showed all the drop-off points for drugs and connected public officials with drug dealers. Lewis wanted to help, but he had to see the evidence first before we could do anything.

That night, Eddie headed back down to Robeson County. He called a woman friend, who had the maps hidden under the frozen vegetables in her deep freezer. On a dark country road, she handed them over. Eddie called me to pick him up at the Raleigh bus station the next morning. I drove him over to Christic, my eyes on the rearview mirror, thinking unpleasant thoughts about the fate of Karen Silkwood, who died in a suspicious automobile accident on the way to deliver evidence that the Kerr McGee Corp. had knowingly contaminated its nuclear power plant workers.

At the Christic office, Lewis looked at the maps and shook his head. They were rough, hand-drawn. Anyone could have done them.

"These are just not self-substantiating enough, Eddie," he said. "We can't go public with this." The diary could also be dismissed as the complaint of a disgruntled informant. Eddie was disappointed, to say the least. Lewis worked out a plan to help get the source of the maps out of jail to see if he could substantiate the story.[44] On Thursday, Eddie headed back to Robeson. We were supposed to hear from him.

I got to the office early on a Monday morning, with no word from Eddie. The phone rang, and it was Gayle.

"Have you heard from Eddie? We just got a call from him. He claims he's taken hostages at the Robeson County newspaper office."

Oh, shit.

I called down to Mac to see what was going on. Nothing, he reassured me, just the rumor mill. I called back Gayle, relieved. Then Mac called again.

"Something *is* going on. There are police cars all over downtown. Uh-oh."

Eddie had walked into the *Robesonian* newspaper office that morning with a young friend, Timothy Jacobs, and a sawed-off shotgun, and taken twenty people hostage. He later claimed that he had felt in increasing danger from the Sheriff's Department, after he saw deputies watching his apartment. He recruited Tim in a plan he hoped would save his life and bring attention to his claims. Tim was a handsome Indian teenager, chestnut hair down his back, who had traveled the powwow circuit as a dancer. At various tribal gatherings, he had connected with activists of the American Indian Movement. Back home, he had seen too many of his friends' fathers die in the drug trade or from Robeson's other violence, and, like Eddie, he was fed up. The two were demanding investigation of the drug trade in the county and of Billy McKellar's death. There were local, state, and federal law enforcement officers surrounding the building.

I felt nauseated, panicked. If anybody started shooting, there would be a lot of people dead. Had I said anything to Eddie that helped precipitate this?

Chris and I drove the two hours down I-95 to Lumberton, getting there by early evening. Cops and television vans were everywhere. The moon was full, eerily peaceful above the barricaded streets and the human commotion. We were all worried that come nightfall the Sheriff's Department might start shooting.

Eddie must have had similar concerns. At eight o'clock, word came that he had negotiated a deal with a representative from the governor's office, who agreed to the investigations he had demanded. He and Tim let the remaining hostages go (they had freed half of them already), and Eddie walked backward out of the *Robesonian* office with his hands raised, his figure casting strange shadows on the brick walls as he was caught in the glare of police searchlights.

John McKellar commented on the two young men who forced the governor to investigate his son Billy's death: "The people in Robeson County have been held hostage all their life. Timmy and Eddie were the only ones who stood up for it." Betty McKellar added, "I would have went with them myself if I had known they were going."[45]

Even though I was exhausted, the rest of the week provided no chance to let down. Coalition leaders held a press conference decrying the "Third World" conditions that had bred the takeover. Clearly, Eddie and Timmy had changed the focus of the Robeson movement permanently. Many people found the young men's resort to violence difficult to justify.

The next week, I flew out to California to do a gig on the far right at the University of California at Santa Cruz. I stopped for the weekend to visit my friend Dorothy in San Francisco. I tried to tell her about Robeson County: *cinder-block buildings, blood in sandy soil, asthma, jail houses, twenty hostages. . . .* I felt incoherent. You had to have been there. Dorothy took me for a walk around the Castro. We were looking for a restaurant, but I realized I had no stomach for food. Back at her apartment, I stayed up for a miserable night puking my guts out. How was I supposed to know what to do when people took hostages? I sure as hell hadn't learned that in graduate school. I felt like I had crawled out to the end of a long limb in a high tree, and somebody was sawing it off. By dawn I fell into an uneasy sleep. Two days later I was well, and I spent a restful several days at Santa Cruz with Ruth Frankenburg, who was teaching a class on women and racism. As I lay in the California sun and talked with her students, the events in North Carolina were far away and my work had meaning.

I went home and got sick again. Chris and I were also traveling back and forth to Shelby, a town in the western part of the state where neo-Nazis were accused of murdering three men they had perceived to be gay. I was in the motel there when I began to feel my throat close up. By the time I got home to get antibiotics, I hurt too much to swallow. I got well, and then got sick again. I had been sick a lot that year.

Everything always seemed so urgent that I never had time to recover completely. Three years into the work with NCARRV, the accumulated pressure, not to mention the impact of my mother's death, was getting to me. When I got NCARRV reports late to funders, explaining my poor health, one of them wrote me back, "Mab, your health is as important as your commitment." A novel concept.

While my health faltered, events in Robeson rushed forward. On March 8, there was a referendum on merging the county's five separate school districts into a more equitable one, a position the coalition supported. On election evening in Durham I stayed up for the late-night news to hear that we had won! It was the first time that Blacks, Indians, and poor whites had formed a voting majority. Power was shifting, and the atmosphere was electric. The victory gave added momentum to Julian Pierce's candidacy for Superior Court judge. If the electoral coalition held, Pierce could beat the deadly DA Joe Freeman Britt. Pierce was doing a great job of bringing Indians and Blacks together, and there were also whites working on his campaign who had never worked with people of color before. A friend of his later commented, "There was a hope that there had never been before."

Here comes the hardest part of this hard, hard story. I wish that we could freeze the narrative here, as if we were freezing time, as if Julian were still alive at the moment of greatest hope. Many of us, listening or reading now, long to be able to cry out to him a warning that would resonate back to that late March night or early morning when someone broke the glass at his kitchen door. *Julian, don't go to the door! Don't go!* If only we had read the signs of danger in spiders on the leaves, like the people in Cameroon, or in the way termites strip branches. But no one did, and I tell you the next scene of the story from this far distance. Julian got up in his nightshirt to answer. He opened the door, and whoever stood there pointed a shotgun and fired, point blank. Then fired again, hitting Julian in the side as he fell. And again, in the head. Julian lay dead on his kitchen floor.

A relative found Julian's body at seven-thirty the next morning. Julian's supporters, who gathered outside his home as word of his death spread through the community, insisted that the Sheriff's Department allow them to view the scene before federal and state investigators arrived. News spread rapidly to the mourners at coalition leader John Godwin's funeral Saturday morning. John had died the Tuesday before from injuries sustained in a car wreck. There was a resonance between the two deaths, a one-two punch, which made each more devastating. Late that afternoon, Robeson sheriff Hubert Stone emerged from Julian's house to ask for the crowd's cooperation, saying that the killing looked like an assassination. "You're crooked as hell!" someone yelled. As an ambulance drove the body away, an Indian woman screamed, "Oh, God, oh, God. How much longer do we have to take this? Oh, God, how much longer?" One of Pierce's campaign workers told reporters that someone had warned Julian the day before "that something like this could happen."[46]

Community leaders asked for calm. Reverend Joy Johnson, one of the coalition leaders, remarked, "Those of us who want to carry out the wishes of Mr. Godwin and Julian . . . are planning for nonviolence. We are encouraging that. But there are others who feel they have no protection, that they will have to protect themselves." Mac Legerton was worried sick that people in the county might take things into their own hands, in the footsteps of nineteenth-century guerrilla fighter Henry Berry Lowry's "strike at the wind," but he figured things would remain calm until after the funeral, out of respect for Julian. Governor James Martin asked National Guard leaders to remain accessible.[47] Eddie Hatcher's uncle Jim Hatcher, state representative and minister Sidney Locks, other coalition activists, and Joe Freeman Britt received anonymous death threats. On Monday the Robeson County Board of Commissioners asked Joe Freeman Britt to ask for a special prosecutor and take himself out of the case. Pierce's campaign asked Governor Martin to convene a special legislative session to delay the May 3 primary long enough to find another candidate.[48]

"I'll be surprised if they find their suspect alive," a friend remarked.

By Tuesday the Sheriff's Department reported that they had found a suspect, twenty-four-year-old Indian John Goins, who was indeed dead. Goins was the boyfriend of the daughter of Julian's longtime woman friend, and Pierce supposedly had kept him from seeing her. Goins had been enraged, the sheriff said. Goins and his lifelong friend Sandy Chavis became suspects after someone called the Pembroke

Police Department to say he had seen Goins upset and with blood on his clothes near Pierce's house that Saturday morning. At four o'clock Tuesday morning, Chavis confessed to driving Goins to Pierce's, but said he had no idea Goins was intent on murder. Stone said he spotted Goins early Tuesday morning and chased him, radioing for help. At dawn, an SBI airplane located Goins's Camaro in woods near his father's house. On an initial search of the small bungalow, a deputy and an SBI agent found no one. Shortly thereafter they returned to the house and found the young man's body in a closet, dead of what they said was a self-inflicted shotgun blast to the head.[49] That Tuesday morning, I was in a hotel in Robeson, again with a throat infection, for a meeting of community leaders at which we heard the news of Chavis's arrest. On Wednesday, the day of Julian's funeral, Britt asked Governor Martin for a special prosecutor; but Goins was dead and Chavis never came to trial.[50]

The fields and woods along the highway stretched out before us, deceptively peaceful, as Christina and I drove back down for the funeral on Wednesday. There was evil here; I could almost taste it like grit between my teeth from the dust the car was kicking up off the highway. I had never met Julian, but my grief was real. It was clear, even from a distance, that Julian Pierce had had integrity. He would not have sold out. Julian was the people's man. For all of us, close to him or more distant, it was also hard to untangle the grief from the fear. As one organizer later reflected, "We realized that we were up against people who would do anything to maintain power." People from all over the country flew in for Julian's memorial service. It was too late to find a new candidate, and who would want to step into a death sentence? "They said it was a domestic dispute, but I think it was power," commented John McKellar. "When the merger was passed, all people was talking about was Julian Pierce, Julian Pierce, Julian Pierce. They could see strength building. This is what triggered his death."[51] Christine Griffin, Pierce's friend and co-director of Lumber River Legal Services, commented to reporters, "I think that if Goins killed Julian, he was a pawn, a tool. It's almost like a phantom that sends fear through the community. If you could put your finger on an individual—but you can't. It's drug deals, political opposition, the

Sheriff's Department. I think it's all of them. . . . The system is the root."[52]

Sheriff Stone called it "just another murder," and reassured a reporter only minutes before the department received a bomb threat: "I've never been more popular in this county than I am now. . . . Morale is good. . . . They trust me and we're all safe here in Robeson County."

In May, Julian Pierce won the election. More folks voted for a dead man whose name remained on the ballot than for Joe Freeman Britt. But Britt was alive and Julian was gone, and Britt became Superior Court judge. So much for democracy. The legislature created a second judgeship, with the understanding it would go to an Indian.

Christina and I were staggering under the weight of the violence as we tried to build an organization to deal with it. All through the spring crisis in Robeson, I had been to a clinic every two or three weeks, seeing doctors about my various ailments. After a couple of months, my primary caregiver ran a series of tests that indicated I had had some underlying virus. I was fried. I dreaded going back to the office each day. Barb, having observed my general downward spiral, let me know that if I did not change the way I did my work, she would leave me. Finally it occurred to me that I could quit. I retreated to the beach for a weekend and realized that I did not want to leave NCARRV, but I did not want to be the director. I asked the board if I could move to part-time after taking August off. They decided that Christina would move up as director. Christina, part-time NCARRV staffer Eleanor Holland, and I spent the summer and fall making a video about Robeson County, traveling to all the murder sites and talking to the victims' families. Eleanor was a close friend. We had worked on *Feminary* together and she was one of Annie's key babysitters. She brought a keen politics and aesthetic sensibility to the task of the film. If we could just tell this story right, we thought, something would change.

During the summer, the momentum passed to Christic Institute South lawyers Lewis Pitts and Bob Warren, who were preparing for Eddie and Tim's federal trial on hostage charges. In June, the governor's task force (responding to Eddie's demands) released a report saying that it had found little evidence of corruption. Christic lawyers

countered that the task force had ignored witnesses and failed to follow up leads. More than a dozen witnesses had come to them with
testimony on the county's drug trade, they said. But they needed government promises of immunity, which were not forthcoming.[53] Warren
told the press about fifteen suspicious deaths in the county since the
siege at the *Robesonian*, and added, "Some of these people, including
Julian Pierce, had evidence that we intended to use." Someone blasted
out the windshield of Bob's car on one of his forays into Robeson.[54]

In August I was to hand my job over to Chris. But she was in the
hospital with a huge blood clot from her knee to her thigh, a condition
that had been sending her signals she had ignored. For several days,
Chris lay in the hospital, heavily sedated. We held our breath that the
anticoagulants would kick in before a clot floated up to her lungs or
heart. She pulled through, but in six months she would need surgery.
By then, doctors hoped, they would have her blood in shape so that
she could survive the operation. Beyond exhaustion, I left for my August vacation after agreeing to come back as director part-time for the
fall while the board searched for a new director.

I had become a woman haunted by the dead.

I was haunted by people like Julian Pierce, whom I had not known
personally. And the others that I knew only by their mothers, sisters,
fathers, brothers: the ones left crying in empty houses, fistfuls of hair,
and the wildness or muteness of grief. The others I knew only as absence, always looking on from photos placed carefully on the mantel
or hanging above the sofa, weddings, graduations, one looking even
from his coffin, face restructured past remembering. I heard about
their lives in speeches before crowds, or later in quiet conversations,
knew their names cried out as "Justice! Justice!" from the podiums
or mikes or into pillows salted with a parent's tears. Or, worst of all, I
knew them in the too-intimate details of autopsies: the scar above the
navel, pink curlers in dark hair, or three pair of socks on.

I had lingered too often at the moment of death, suspended like
their spirits above the broken bodies, looking down at asphalt, or lino-
leum, or sandy soil—quizzical after the terror, suddenly broken free.
Who else was there in the scene below, with knife, or gun, or bloody

tree limb? Who are those white figures lurking in every midnight, or noon, beyond my reach? Do they laugh, or moan, do they run hot or cold when the blade slides, the trigger lurches? How do they leave the roadside or the scrub brush—by foot or car? Why are they never followed, these tracks that lead everywhere?

I had driven too many nights down the snaking interstate, black and massive around the feeble blaze of headlight, or following spidery lines on maps, beside me on the seat coffee or Coke, chocolate or ham biscuits, feeding fear with poison. Listening to news or country music on a static radio, I had wondered, *What propels or pursues me?* An answer out the car window almost caught my peripheral vision, some figure in the blurring trees. I had driven with my eyes glancing to the rearview mirror, or sat with my chair against the wall in restaurants, at times too carelessly silhouetted against porch lights. Back home, I had walked into rooms or parties, uncertain how to drop death into the conversation.

I was what the murderers would call a nigger lover and what they'd call a dyke. I had called their victims' names, for justice and for money. It was time to make peace with the dead.

The story of the events in Robeson does not end at the end of this chapter, just as it did not begin at its beginning. But my part of the story does, the part I can tell from the inside. Exhausted, we at NCARRV withdrew from our active role in Robeson County that fall of 1988. The rest of the events ran on by me, like a raging river out of which I had climbed. But few of the major characters in the rest of the events got away unscathed.

Eddie Hatcher and Tim Jacobs were tried in federal court in October 1988 in front of a miracle jury of nine Black people and three whites. The trial was likely one of the most contentious in recent North Carolina history. It was a running battle between Lewis and Bob, who represented Tim, and Judge Terrence Boyle, a Reagan appointee and the son-in-law of Helms's top political strategist. Boyle refused to delay the trial to allow famed civil rights lawyer William Kunstler, busy on another case, the time to defend Eddie, a judgment that Eddie protested in court at every opportunity. Boyle then tried to appoint as Eddie's lawyers Barry Nakell, a law professor at the University of North Carolina and an old friend of Eddie's, and a young legal intern; both refused the judge's offer outright. Then Judge Boyle denied Hatcher and Jacobs the legal defense of "necessity"—the defense that legitimate fear for their lives necessitated their actions. He also refused to allow into court any testimony about government corruption or the Robeson drug trade from witnesses who had come to Christic Institute South, so that material never became part of the public record. Several witnesses did manage to get in some opinions between the prosecutor's "Objection!" and the Judge's "Sustained!" In spite of all the court's hostility, the jury found Hatcher and Jacobs not guilty on all charges, to the amazement of everyone but Lewis, who knew he had the case won as soon as he had the Black-majority jury. Like I said at the beginning, these questions of truth are pretty subjective, and many cases would turn out very differently if they had that jury that Eddie and Tim lucked out on.

Their luck, however, was short-lived. While Eddie and Christic Institute South organizers promoted a petition drive to recall Sheriff Stone, Joe Freeman Britt in his last months as district attorney brought state charges of kidnapping. The grand jury returned indictments for fourteen counts of kidnapping against Eddie and Tim in December. Tim escaped to the Onondaga Reservation in upstate New York. Eddie skipped out on a $25,000 bond put up by the National Council of Churches and joined Tim in New York. Eddie traveled from New York State to the Shoshone-Bannock Reservation in Idaho, saying that he wanted to be tried in tribal courts. Federal officials challenged his right to sanctuary, citing his birth certificate, which listed him as white. Then Eddie turned up at the Soviet consulate in San Francisco and was arrested when they refused him asylum. Tim was captured in New York in a high-speed chase after he left the reservation. The Christic Institute South lawyers battled to keep him from being extradited, but New York governor Mario Cuomo sent him home. Both Eddie and Tim plea-bargained.[55] The Christic Institute South, with Kunstler and Nakell, filed a suit in federal court against North Carolina attorney general Lacy Thornburg, Britt, SBI agents, Sheriff Stone, and others, alleging a conspiracy to intimidate Robeson residents out of their First Amendment rights and interference with the right to the counsel of Hatcher's choice

Darlene Hunt, Jimmy Earl Cummings's girlfriend, died, authorities said, of an overdose.

Bob Sheldon, who had helped Eddie escape to New York, was found murdered in the Chapel Hill bookstore he managed. The case has never been solved.

The suit in Jimmy Earl's death was settled out of court at the decision of a court-appointed guardian for his children. This was some time after the arrest of Jimmy Earl's mother, Lula Mae, a woman in her seventies, on drug charges. Sheriff's deputies took her to the jail and strip-searched her. When her family and Mac Legerton arrived on the scene, they rushed her to the hospital, fearing a heart attack. She spent several days in the women's prison in Raleigh before being released for health reasons. Lula Mae Cummings died in 1993 and was buried with an outpouring of respect from people of all races all over the county.

Sandy Chavis, represented by former U.S. attorney general Ramsey Clark, eventually plea-bargained and got time served for his alleged role in the Pierce murder.[56]

John and Betty McKellar settled out of court for $195,000 in April 1991 in their suit against the Sheriff's Department for Billy's death, explaining that they no longer had the energy for a sustained legal battle. Their family had suffered enough.

Lewis Pitts, William Kunstler, and Barry Nakell were hit by the U.S. attorney general's office with a Rule 11 motion, charging a frivolous lawsuit, for the suit they had mounted against Britt, Stone, and others. Another Reagan-appointed judge fined the three $122,834 (later reduced to $48,000). Christic Institute South, which had been renamed the Southern Justice Institute, folded from lack of funding.[57] The North Carolina bar association tried Nakell for a grievance similar to Rule 11; finally able to present evidence, he was exonerated.

Many people in the county and state say that none of the coalition's claims were ever substantiated. That is the view of Mike Mangiameli, a *Robesonian* reporter who was one of Eddie and Tim's hostages. He wrote an angry letter to the editor of another paper: "Of all the investigators sent to Robeson County since Feb. 1, not one has been able to uncover any evidence of corruption at any level of government, or any link to drugs by the sheriff's department or any local police. . . . All reports of 'corruption and fraud' were merely the repeating of unfounded rumors and gossip."[58]

Unless you consider the verdict of that majority-Black jury.

Some people point hopefully to the reforms precipitated by the county's troubles: a public defender, a human relations council, merged schools, redistricting that has led to the creation of majority Indian and African American governing bodies at the county level, and a Native American Superior Court judge appointed to a second specially created seat after Pierce's death.[59]

The poverty remains, grinding as ever, and crack has hit Robeson in a big way.

If I were writing myself a goddamned mystery novel, I would have myself some police types and some lawyer types in the same type of scummy jail where Billy died and Eddie waits. Hopeful, energetic people would be voting in candidates of integrity of all races. Law enforcement officials at every level would crack down on the drug trade and clean up the county. People would have hope and good jobs and would not feel they needed to sell or use drugs or kill each other. Corporations, brought to the table by the county's elected leadership and community pressure, would be working to turn Robeson County around economically, accepting their responsibility to the human and natural environment. We would end on a note of certainty, the moral order not so much restored, as Prosecutor Britt would have us believe, as invented. But I have to adhere to events and my interpretation of them. That other ending to the story, in Robeson and elsewhere, will take more than a mystery novel, than fingers clicking on a keyboard to achieve. It is the work of many people's lives.

I called Mac Legerton recently. He still doesn't like to think of those times a lot, but he reflected on what he learned: "There's been a major political revolution here in terms of more representative leadership. It's not just an issue of race anymore, it's economic stratification.

Further changes will depend on the values that new leadership brings, and how we hold them accountable." He went on to comment on personal changes: "For a long time, I had survivor's guilt. Zealots are necessary to movements, but there's a time when, if you want to stay alive, you have to move beyond that. Now, I'm more into learning than achieving. Miles Horton had a similar experience. He was in Robeson County in a union campaign in the 1930s and found himself with a gun to his head. He learned that he wanted to be an educator rather than an organizer."

Mac laughed. "I think I learned the same thing. I'm an educator now."

9

Take What You Need

It was a bleary-eyed two in the morning at Blue Mountain, a retreat center in upstate New York. It was the fall of 1991, and I was up way past my bedtime, hanging out with the women who had come for three days to discuss new strategies to counter violence against women. In new company I was seldom gregarious, but I loved this kind of gathering, equal parts African, Native, Latina, Anglo, and Asian American, with plenty of lesbians. Community formed quickly, enlivened by the blend of cultures, accents, rhythms, colors, and flavors. We were done dancing to salsa; I had appreciated Graciela's lessons—it was all in the hips. A crew in canoes still paddled on the lake in the moonlight. I was talking with Loretta Ross, whom I had become friends with from anti-Klan work. That afternoon I had done my usual rap on genocide, the dangers of a growing right wing. Loretta wanted me to see that genocide would not happen *if* the government went far enough to the right; it had been happening for quite a few centuries. She had not challenged me from across the room, wanting to avoid embarrassing me. I figured I could have probably taken the comments publicly; I agreed with her point once she made it, and I knew we respected each other. But I appreciated her thoughtfulness.

She moved on to the second item on her agenda.

"In the nineties, we activists are going to need the support of our families." She looked at me pointedly.

My heart sank. "But my family, you don't know what they've done. We got Klansmen, murderers—"

She interrupted me. "Look, Mab. When I was fourteen, I was raped by an uncle, and for the past twenty-two years I have raised the child, my own son, whom I have loved and hated. My family let that happen to me. I have worked that out with them, and if I can work that out with my family, you can work out whatever it is you have to with your family."

Damn. I resisted her instructions. That resistance recalled for me Alice Walker's essay on her relationship to Flannery O'Connor. The Black and the white southern women writers lived, briefly, "within miles of each other on the same Eatonton-to-Milledgeville [Georgia] road." Walker struggled with her ambivalence to her more privileged counterpart. Her bitterness came "from a deeper source than my knowledge of the difference, historically, race has made in the lives of white and black artists." What she found close to unbearable was knowing "how damaging to my own psyche such injustice is." She acknowledged, "In an unjust society the soul of the sensitive person is in danger of deformity from just such weight as this." Yet Walker appreciated O'Connor's unsentimental view of white people, especially white women. "She caused white women to look ridiculous on pedestals, and she approached her black characters—as a mature artist—with unusual humility and restraint." The essay had intrigued me because of my own love-hate relationship with O'Connor, in whose characters I had felt the heavy weight of deformity. Alice Walker's solution to *her* Flannery dilemma encouraged me:

The magic, the wit, and the mystery of Flannery O'Connor I know I will always love. I also know the meaning of the expression "Take what you can use and let the rest rot." If ever there was an expression designed to protect the health of the spirit, this is it.[1]

What were the things I had forgotten that I loved?

I began to number them. First, the endless childhood games of kick the can. Children scattering in the evening. I would find my favorite hiding place behind the steps on the yard's cool side. Settle back against the brick to watch the dusk dissolve the Studebaker, dissolve the gladiolas, dissolve the rose arbor and the scuppernong-laden well. I would watch my brother dodging in and out of shadows. I used the time not being found to listen to the evening, to move in currents of gardenia musk, hear crickets luting from the tree boles and under shuffling leaves. Then I would relax to see my brother stretch flat in shadows between tea olive and magnolia, counterpointing fragrances in the streetlight's glow. (But even now, in evening conversations, I love the forms that loosen in the dusk before the back porch light flicks on, and I lean to catch the voices in spilled kitchen glow as the screen door slams.) Then mothers from neighboring houses would begin to call us in.

When I was little, I loved for my father to take me out after Sunday school every week to watch the trains spouting cinders and black smoke. My brother and sister and I would ride out to the country in the back of his blue pickup truck, making Tarzan cries all the way as the truck bounced over rocky roads—"AAAAaaaAAAAaaaAAAAaaa."

I remembered my father sitting month by month in his reclining chair watching the news, then going off to bed with the *National Review* or *Human Events*. Every morning he would go to work at six, come home for lunch, come back from work at five-thirty, watch the news, and go to bed at eight. Once a month, he would spread the bills out on the dining room table and pay insurance on the house and car and health, grocery bills, Mother's drugstore bills and doctor bills, and income tax and car payments and payments on the washing machine. As a general rule, he made money and Mama spent it, but at a faster rate than it was coming in. I guess I lost him somewhere in there. Maybe all those years he had been as lonesome and confused as we were, and what had seemed in him the absence of love was only shyness?

I remembered Sunday morning church. The only difference from year to year was the preacher who filled in the sermon slot. But hardly anybody listened to the sermons anyway. The men would sleep, leaning on their elbows against the ends of the pews figuring everyone else would think they were praying. The children would fidget and make airplanes and cootie catchers out of the church bulletins or drop their collection nickels and giggle as the nickels rolled on the edge down the floor under shuffling feet, careening around and around before finally dropping over. Then we would have silent prayer with the organ playing on tremolo, "I come to the garden alone, while the dew is still on the roses." And the organist, Effie Jean, tried her best to keep the hymns going, but everybody was singing in separate keys until there were not enough keys to go around, so we started reinventing old modes, not only singing different keys but in different times, so that nobody was on the same word, one lady's "Jee" another lady's "Zuss," while a few gentlemen worked on the "blessed" and the choir was already to "Re-dee-mer," dividing it up, soprano, alto, and bass. There in the middle of the choir always sat Alma, her neck sticking out at a peculiar angle and her eyes blinking slow and huge behind her glasses as she peeped down at the hymnal for the next line, then rolled her eyes up to heaven to the left and right until her whole head swayed like a metronome gone slightly berserk.

Christmas brought the most elaborate festivity, the Christmas pageant to benefit the Methodist Children's Home in Selma. The director always picked the blondest, most cherubic, and skinniest girl to play Mary, with the runners-up as angels, and the mothers would make the disgusted boys put on long striped robes and carry crooked sticks to be wise men and shepherds. My sister was brunette and cried each year because she was not chosen as an angel, until finally she was. And since I did not quite fit into either angel or wise-man category but was somewhere uncomfortably between, I was always the reader. I intoned each year as the lights dimmed, "There went out a decree from Caesar Augustus that all the world should be taxed."

After it was over, our family would walk up to the square to see what E.W. Wadsworth had added this year to the manger scenes, made from plywood and painted elaborately, twice as large as life. Every year, E.W. set his shop students at the high school to work cutting out more figures until there were two mangers, then four, one for each side of the square, and more and more wise men and shepherds and staffs in the east, and then west and north and south, and a flock of sheep that proliferated until the whole square was covered with people and animals wandering amazed at whichever of the four baby Jesuses, away in their mangers, no cribs for their head. My mother and father thought it was in poor taste, but my brother and sister and I knew it was a miracle.

When I was thirty, I went back home for three weeks. Many young people in old white Tuskegee had left. As my parents' generation died off, the old houses on Main Street were boarded up. At church that morning, the oldest people were dead, the old people ancient, the people my own age looking strangest of all. They all came up and hugged me, and they still sang in multitudinous keys and rhythms, only twenty-five in the congregation now, still all white because Black people controlled the town government and were no longer interested in this dying church. I stood between my father and mother, loving them more than I had in years, Daddy on my right side making up the words he didn't know, like he always had, then thundering forth on the chorus, Mother on the left using a large magnifying glass to find the page, then singing the first verse, which she could remember, and standing in poignant dignity through the rest she could not see. I cried through the hymn, and another, and the Gloria Patri and the doxology and silent prayer and the offertory and announcements and the responsive reading.

> If I forget you, O Jerusalem
>   Let my right hand wither!
> Let my tongue cleave to the roof of my mouth
>   If I do not remember you.

I was born to a town of white folks willing itself to die, a world in which love and beauty mixed inextricably with hatred and pain. How to grieve for what should not, did not, deserve to last?

Then I remembered Alice Walker's advice.

Take what you need, Mab, take what you need.

10

The Bookstore Murders

In Robeson, death happened singly and in isolation: Joyce's kidnapping, Jimmy Earl fleeing from Kevin Stone on a dark back road, Billy handcuffed between his jailers. In Shelby, the deaths all came one terrible evening. It has taken weeks since writing the last chapter to gather myself again, to edge back into the river running red, blood on the floor of the Shelby III, an adult bookstore. There was so much blood the killers were slipping as they went out the door.

I first heard about the Shelby bookstore murders the week after Martin Luther King Jr. Day 1987. I was at home with an intestinal bug. I was also giving myself a rest. I had helped to monitor the annual white supremacist rally the weekend before, figuring it was safe to show my face. This year's event was sponsored by the Southern National Front, heir to what was left of the White Patriot Party. In early January, the U.S. Justice Department had indicted Steve Miller, Robert Jackson, Tony Wydra, Simeon Davis, and Wendell Lee Lane. The charges were conspiracy to obtain illegal weapons and explosives from the U.S. armed services "by whatever means necessary, including robbery and murder, in order to maintain, train and equip a paramilitary armed force and otherwise to further the goals of the White Supremacist Movement." Stephen Miller also was charged with two counts of possessing illegal weapons. The twelve-page indictment drew on the evidence from the Klanwatch prosecution of the Millers and the subsequent Pizza Hut robbery attempt.[1]

The past weekend, I was pleased to see, the march had been much smaller: only 85, whereas Glenn Miller had pulled 325 in 1986. Although Dave Holland was up from Georgia bragging about a white supremacist attack on civil rights marchers in Forsyth County the day before, maybe we had broken the back of the North Carolina movement. Maybe I could stop worrying.

I had been pulled from these thoughts by the voice of Cecil Cox, Southern National Front leader, haranguing from the microphone: "We have someone in the crowd I want to recognize. Mab Segrest, one of the sisters who put Glenn and Steve in jail. Let's give her a white power salute."

Instinctively, my friends closed around me, and I felt a jolt of fear as the crowd turned to find "the woman in the gold coat." Then I grinned. I'd thought Morris Dees had done it all! I stepped outside my guards to meet Cox's eye. He saw my smile and sputtered even more. "White power! White power!" his men yelled, right arms raised in the traditional Nazi salute. I took the tribute. When they finished, I found one of the cops I knew. "Would you please escort us to our car?"

Two days later, miserable with the flu, I got a call from Robert Field, a reporter at the *Shelby Star*, a small-town daily in western North Carolina.

"Did you hear about the bookstore murders here?" he asked.

My stomach contracted. "No," I said. "Tell me about it." I lay across the bed.

He explained that on Saturday, three or four men in ski masks had gone into a little adult bookstore at midnight and shot five men in the head, execution style. All the victims were white. Police were saying the attack was related to pornography or drugs or a homosexual affair gone sour. But the store had had anti-gay threats from the Klan before. Did I think it could be a Klan attack on gay people?

I felt both nauseated and heartsick. Execution-style mass murders were not the modus operandi of the gay men I knew.

"Yes," I told him. "I do think it could be Klan. Yes, I do."

I realized that something in me had expected this news.

Robert sent me news clippings. According to one of the survivors, three or four heavily armed men had entered the store and ordered the men inside to lie facedown. They had shot each in the head, some several times. They set incendiary devices (which malfunctioned) and left. Killed were Travis Melton, nineteen, Kenneth Godfrey, twenty-nine, and Paul Weston, twenty-six. Two men, badly wounded, had reached their cars, where a passerby spotted smoke and found them. Police were calling the Shelby III (the last adult bookstore in the county) "part of an international pornography network linked to organized crime and a man known as the 'Prince of Porn.'" The "complex, murky" trail leads "all over North Carolina, throughout the United States and even worldwide," one story explained ominously (and falsely, as events would show). Sheriff Buddy McKinney admitted that the store had "somewhat a reputation" as a meeting place for homosexuals, but he did not believe it was a factor in the murders.[2]

It was a factor in the coverage, which described each of the victims as single. Paul Weston planned to get married one day, his father explained, and fill up his new station wagon with children. A "powerful man," Paul had served in the Air Force. He was at the Shelby III to testify against pornography, his father asserted. "Like the average American male, it had been a part of his past and he saw how it held people in bondage."

Travis's father, Bobby, described his son as a "quiet boy" with "still . . . a lot of young'un in him. He never really grew up." Terry Godfrey described his brother Kenny, an unemployed furniture worker, as a "good boy" and a "homebody" living with his mother at the time of his death.[3]

Was this, like Joyce Sinclair's murder, the event I had feared after learning of the Posse murders in Rulo, Nebraska, and the murder of the Goldmarks in Seattle in 1985, the same year White Patriots first marched in Shelby? I'd been haunted by a sense of imminent disaster. In June 1985 I had written to North Carolina attorney general Lacy Thornburg, "If state law enforcement does not take action soon, we fear there will be people hurt, perhaps killed."[4] I was working against a clock that had indeed begun its chiming that midnight in the cinder-block store, and three more mothers awoke that Sunday morning to three sons dead. We failed you, and I'm sorry.

Have you ever gone fishing in late July and stopped at a country store a couple of miles before the pond to buy yourself a carton of worms for bait, heat shimmering off the highway? You get to the lake and open the container. A hundred worms have woven themselves together, and if you try to pick one out of the ball, it hangs on for dear life, stretches, breaks in your hand. That's what I feel like now, trying to separate out the strands of my story: worm guts on my hands. These things happened all at once. In the spring of 1985, Chris and I first went into Statesville. We drove over to Shelby that summer when the White Patriots marched around the town square. That November we were down in Robeson when Joyce Sinclair was killed. Carl died in January 1987 at the height of White Patriot power. Jimmy Earl Cummings was killed in November 1986, the month my daughter was born. NCARRV began working with Concerned Citizens of Robeson County the next January, the month of the bookstore murders, a year after Carl's death. Reverend Lee died in 1988, while Billy McKellar was in the Robeson County jail. It's the accumulated effect I am trying to get you to comprehend. What does it mean—about North Carolina and the United States—that all of these things happened in one state in so short a time? That's the shark I am fishing for with this seething mass of bait.

Also, remember that my mother died about six weeks after the bookstore murders, and read into this space that fullness and that grief.

Robert Field's question about possible far right involvement in the Shelby murders proved prophetic, but for months the investigation focused on pornography and organized crime. In the meantime, Glenn Miller pursued a path that eventually linked his organization to the bloody midnight at the Shelby III and established the motive as an attack on people perceived to be gay.

On April 6, 1987, the white supremacists indicted in January for the weapons conspiracy and Fayetteville Pizza Hut robbery attempt went to trial in U.S. district court in Elizabeth City. Defendant Robert Eugene Jackson did not show up, nor did subpoenaed witness Douglas Sheets. The prosecution outlined an inner circle of White Patriots and their associates planning a series of robberies and assassinations, including the Pizza Hut job and plot on Dees's life. The jury found Stephen Miller and Robert Jackson guilty (in absentia) of conspiracy and Miller of two more firearms charges. Tony Wydra was acquitted.[5] Glenn Miller, not implicated in this federal case, was out on bail from his paramilitary conviction. U.S. attorney Sam Currin said that the trial brought the party's activities in the state to an end.

A couple of weeks later the phone rang while I was cooking supper and listening to the news. It was Margaret from Jubilee House in Statesville. "Have you heard?" she asked. I braced myself, wondering what else had happened. "Glenn Miller skipped bail and sent out a letter declaring war on 'mud people,' queers, and the federal government. You should be careful till they catch him."[6] I got a copy of the declaration as rapidly as possible. It was vintage Miller:

I warned those SOBs. I always said that once we had 1,000 White men in uniform marching in the streets on a regular basis, that the masses of our People would flood into our ranks and join with us. The federal dogs and their Jew masters knew this too and refused to allow it. . . . All 5,000 White Patriots are now honor bound and duty bound to pick up the sword and do battle against the forces of evil. In the name of our Aryan God, through His beloved Son, I Glenn Miller now this 6th day of April, 1987, do hereby declare total war. I ask for no quarter, I will give none. I declare war against Niggers, Jews, Queers, assorted Mongrels, white Race traitors, and despicable informants. We White Patriots will now begin the Race War and it will spread gloriously thru-out the nation. . . . And, so fellow Aryan Warriors strike now.

The declaration went on for two closely typed pages: how he expected ZOG agents to kill him, ordering his three young sons "to swear upon my grave to take my place in battle, when they come of age," and asking White Patriot leaders to bury him in his family graveyard in uniform with his right arm raised in the White Power salute. (Would they just cut a hole in the coffin and let his hand stick through? I imagined Glenn's fingers poking up through the daisies in the Angier cemetery.) He even said what songs to play: "Tomorrow Belongs to Me," "The Old Rugged Cross," "Ride of the Valkyries," and "Dixie."

"The man has gone over the edge," a contact in the State Bureau of Investigation exclaimed when I finally got him on the phone. *He's been over the edge for quite a while, buddy,* I thought.

April 23 brought another bizarre communication from Miller, this one to WPTF-AM radio in Raleigh. He issued seventeen demands, including requests for $888,000 in cash, an apology, and revocation of his paramilitary conviction—or else "eight teams of freedom fighters are prepared to start a race war nationwide."[7] Three courthouses were being closely watched for bombs, including the one in Durham.[8] U.S. attorney Sam Currin was under twenty-four-hour guard. Nobody thought about guarding us except for Paul Martin, Lauren's husband, who alerted police officers on his beat to patrol past the office and the houses of several of us. Barb and I decided to sleep with friends. As we quickly packed our bags and gathered up six-month-old Annie, I thought of the Jewish families who must have moved under cover of night to escape Nazis, of mothers who feared their babies' cries might mean discovery and death. After a couple of days, we moved back home. I got out the pistol and put it on my dresser.

On April 30, Missouri police and federal agents captured Miller and his closest lieutenants, Robert Eugene Jackson, Douglas Sheets, and Jackson's younger brother, Tony Wydra, in a trailer park in the Ozarks. No shots were fired, although police confiscated a small arsenal of weapons. Within a few days, the men returned to North Carolina, where Miller was charged by the U.S. attorney with sending threats through the mail.[9] They would later face federal weapons charges in Missouri.

White Patriot crises had swept me up and away from the grief over my mother. The sweet sadness in the week after her death had passed. *Is this all there is?* I thought. I wrote in my journal:

> My grief's gone underground. For weeks, I knew exactly where it was. I made it register, required its weekly visits for parole. Then the Parole Board slipped and it skipped, and now I hear it on the wire: my grief is underground. Will the feds close in on it at dawn in a trailer park in Missouri, tear gas for morning mist? Will it resist arrest? It called in seventeen demands, but who but me can it hold hostage? It could turn up at my door in camouflage. I check the car for bombs. The dog sleeps near the bed to bark of night attack, and I await the rat-a-tat, the tongues of flame, that would split the night into a thousand stars.

That fall, I was stunned but not surprised when wire stories carried news accounts linking the White Patriots and the Shelby murders. On September 4, Sheets appeared at a Raleigh detention hearing. A law enforcement officer cited two confidential informants who linked him to the Shelby attacks. *Fayetteville Observer* reporter Pat Reese began to break the story the same day.[10] The informant who led police to Miller in April had come to Reese for help. Bob Stoner (whose name Reese did not reveal at the time) was leader of a Fayetteville White Patriot den. Glenn Miller had called him to come out to Louisiana to help mail the "Declaration of War." But what he saw and heard scared him. Miller, he said, was a changed man. The group talked of blowing up a synagogue in the Midwest and of killing fifty Blacks in Atlanta to ignite a race war. Frightened, Stoner returned to Fayetteville and asked Pat Reese for help. Reese is a cadaverous man with a voice like gravel from a bullet he took in the mouth while working on a story. He had covered the Klan for decades. He contacted the police and got Stoner limited immunity. Then Stoner gave police the information that led to Miller's arrest. As a result of this informant, the *Fayetteville Observer* reported, the Shelby III probe was shifting focus to white supremacists.[11]

I called a law enforcement contact, who gave me the names of Robert

Jackson, Doug Sheets, and two local men as the suspects Stoner named in the attack. The murder, he explained, was to "avenge Yahweh on homosexuals." I called a very helpful Pat Reese next. So far, he said, police had only circumstantial evidence to back up Stoner's story. They needed one of the four men to break to get a clear murder rap. The White Patriot Party, Pat said, was "unlike any organization that ever existed in North Carolina." He estimated that it had 150 Special Forces types—"trained killers," he called them.

In mid-September, the oddest person came forward to back up, in a way, Stoner's story. After spending the summer in prison, Glenn Miller himself became a "despicable informant," agreeing to testify against Sheets and Jackson and other local and national white supremacists in return for a plea bargain that reduced his charges to one plea of mailing a threatening communication (the Declaration of War) and one weapons charge from the Ozark trailer arsenal.[12] I was not surprised at the deal, although I was disgusted.

On November 16, a Cleveland County, North Carolina, grand jury indicted Douglas Lawrence Sheets and Robert Eugene Jackson on sixteen counts, including arson, robbery, first-degree murder, assault, and conspiracy in the bookstore attacks. District attorney Bill Young explained his strategy: "As to whether this was the first act of a war [against homosexuals], I have no idea. They are charged with state crimes of killing. I'm looking at this as murders."[13]

The next week, Jackson went on trial in Wilmington for "failure to appear" at the Elizabeth City trial on the arms conspiracy and Pizza Hut robbery charges the spring before.[14] I drove over to Wilmington to monitor the proceedings and to get as much information as I could on both Jackson and Sheets, the latter subpoenaed in this case as a witness. I soon realized they were both highly ideological zealots.

Jackson and Sheets, both Oklahoma natives, came to North Carolina in 1984 and assumed central roles in the development of the White Patriot Party (although both apparently were never official members). According to Glenn Miller's court testimony, Jackson and Sheets organized for him for six to eight months and received $7,000 to $8,000 apiece. Their salaries came from $200,000 in money stolen by the Order in armored car robberies. Jackson explained that they had merely been developing an "unorganized state militia," a far-fetched theory that originated with Posse Comitatus/Identity leader William Potter Gale. Sanctioned by the Militia Act of 1792, the "unorganized state militia" would supposedly come into effect if illegal authority seized the government, or federal officials usurped power.[15]

According to Doug Sheets's prior testimony before a grand jury, he appears to have urged Miller to standardize his ragtag Klan into a more uniform paramilitary operation, with AR-15 rifles as the weapon of choice. Sheets admitted to "unorganized" training that included target practice, woods survival training, river crossing, and working with artillery simulators, flares, and booby traps. Sheets also said that he had bought three thousand rounds of ammunition, forty to fifty pipe bombs, and C-4 plastic explosive from black-market arms merchant Robert Norman Jones, gun trafficking to which Jones had testified in the Klanwatch trial. Sheets testified that he had buried the pipe bombs in a swamp and retrieved them in 1986 on a visit back to North Carolina.[16]

Ex-Patriots Wendell Lee Lane, Robert Norman Jones, and Simeon Davis all testified that there was a feared inner circle around Stephen Miller, made up of Jackson, Sheets, Wydra, and Cox. It was these men, rather than Glenn Miller, from whom they sought federal protection.

Jackson's defense was that Glenn Miller forced him to come underground, fearing that both Jackson and Sheets would turn state's evidence. Miller threatened, he said, to have a "team of freedom fighters" kill their families. Jackson's wife sat faithfully in the courtroom, even when the prosecutor brought in two women who testified that they had had sex with Jackson on the Patriots' trek underground. The jury returned a conviction.

In January 1988, Glenn Miller was sentenced to five years out of a potential one hundred for multiple firearms charges, extortion, and receiving stolen Order money.[17] He was expected to serve only half that time. He was accepted into the federal witness protection program. Jackson was given six months for failure to appear at the Elizabeth City trial.[18]

Both Jackson and Sheets were extradited to Missouri. There the

following April (1988) they were convicted on federal weapons charges
for the armaments in the trailer. They defended themselves by arguing
that the charges were unconstitutional because they were part of the
"unorganized militia." "If they were out to cut their own throats, they
sure used a dull knife," the prosecuting attorney observed. They were
given sentences of twenty years and shipped to Leavenworth Prison.[19]

In a year and a half, the White Patriot Party had unraveled in a
series of indictments and trials: Glenn and Stephen Miller's contempt
of court trial brought by Klanwatch (July 1986), federal prosecution
in Elizabeth City on weapons charges from information uncovered in
the Klanwatch trial and the subsequent Pizza Hut robbery attempt
(April 1987), Jackson's trial for failing to appear in Elizabeth City (November 1987), and a federal conviction in Missouri for the weapons
found in the trailer (April 1988). The only pending court action was
the Shelby murder trial.

In October 1987, I first met the families of two of the men killed in
the bookstore.

"I'm trying to find the brother of Kenny Godfrey, who was killed
in the Shelby III," I spoke into the phone. There was a long silence
before Terry Godfrey indicated that it was he on the line. I explained
quickly who I was and asked to come talk.

The next day, I drove over to Terry's home in Forest City to talk with
him and his sister Dorlene. They were both younger than I—in their
late twenties or early thirties, I would guess. They served me Pepsi
and talked about Kenny. Nine months earlier, Terry had gotten the
call on Sunday morning to go down and identify his brother's body. It
was the hardest thing he ever had to do, he said. Dorlene brought out
a picture of Kenny in the coffin. She explained that the resemblance
was bad, because the mortician had had to reconstruct his face.

Dorlene was fierce in her hatred of the White Patriot Party, and
fiercely loyal to her brother's memory. She reminded me of people
from Robeson County, of Jimmy Earl's brother and sisters and Joyce
Sinclair's sister Rosetta. Dorlene was concerned that people were saying Kenny was gay. If anyone claimed that Kenny was homosexual in
court, there was no telling what she would do, she exclaimed. "The

point was he was probably killed because people thought he was gay," I offered. To be too vehemently opposed to homosexuality might play into the killers' motives. She seemed willing to think about it. They described Kenny to me, a large twenty-nine-year-old man so shy that he had a hard time holding a job. He took care of Terry's children, and he had nursed his father through terminal cancer. He was his mother's right hand, and she was devastated.

I explained that we had been following the White Patriots for years, trying to get local, state, and federal law enforcement to take them seriously. I shared some of our tactics from Statesville. We hoped to be able to generate similar community involvement in Shelby, I explained, and would appreciate their help. We called Faye Melton, the mother of Travis, the nineteen-year-old store employee also killed in the attack, and asked if I could drop by. She agreed. I promised to stay in touch.

On the road from Forest City to Shelby, I passed the building that had housed the bookstore. It was a windowless, rectangular structure set back from the road at the end of a gravel driveway, fields on all sides. Isolated, I thought as I got out of my car, perhaps to allow its patrons some discretion. I remembered the picture in the *Star*—a body covered with a sheet behind the "Sheriff's Line Do Not Cross" tape, a sign reading "ADULT BOOKSTORE • Magazines • Paperbacks • Video Tapes" over the entrance, and a fireman in the foreground reaching for a match to light the cigarette on his lips. The signs were gone, and in the sunny afternoon it was hard to imagine the terror and violence of that January midnight.

Faye Melton greeted me at her door. She had invited Cindy, a neighbor and friend who had supported her through the ordeal. A picture of Travis in his graduation gown was on the piano. He was a slight, sweet-faced kid, looking closer to sixteen than nineteen. Faye told me about how she woke up Sunday morning not knowing anything was wrong until a friend alerted her. She drove to the bookstore to find the place cordoned off and filled with police. She asked for her son, and they said he had been taken to the hospital. *Surely he's alive,* she thought with relief, *or they would have let me know.* But at the hospital, she was asked to identify his body, her own flesh and blood, marks of a violent death on the person she had carried and raised. Seemed like the Sheriff's Department could have sent someone over, she thought. A car filled with men in fatigues drove back and forth on the road past their house in the days after the funeral, and the family got strange phone calls.

"The Klan has been marching around here all of my life," Cindy remarked, "and I never thought much about it. Then this happens—a friend getting murdered. It really makes me think."

When she was growing up, Faye had thought of the Klan as a good thing, an enforcer of community morals against wife beaters and the like, not as killers. Now she knew a different story that made her afraid for her life. She wanted to see the real history of the Klan taught in school. "The Klan hates all kinds, anybody they can get to hate," she said, articulating her new knowledge. "Blacks, Jewish people . . . it just goes on and on, but there's got to be a stopping point somewhere.

"I mean, none of it made no sense. Them boys was minding their own business in that bookstore. If they had been down there beating up people or getting onto people when they came in the store, making fun of them, you might understand it. But they was bothering nobody. Folks were telling all kinds of lies. Why, they even said all them men that went there was dressed up in dresses and running up and down the highway. Well, I saw my son. He had red pants and a red sweater with these holes in it." She concluded, "If there was anything in the world I could do to stop it happening again, I'd practically give my life for it."[20]

Angry and impatient with the progress of the police, Cindy, Faye, and Bobby Melton had conducted their own investigation, focusing first on possible drug links. When White Patriot involvement and a homophobic motive emerged, they visited Terry, the man who had worked the shift before Travis, at the home where he lived with his lover. It had been a shock for them to see the gay men together. Faye noticed homey touches around the place and spotted the lover as their source. She had never thought much about homosexuals before, she said, but now in the store where she worked as cashier she could spot them. *It's not their fault,* was her conclusion. It was like being born without an arm.

"Do you think Travis was gay?" I asked.

How could she know that? she replied. How would he know? He was only nineteen.

I explained to them, too, what we hoped to do and said we would stay in touch.

As a lesbian, I had a lot personally invested in this case. If informants' allegations were true, it had been the second multiple killing by white supremacists in North Carolina in a decade (Greensboro being the first) and the most visible case of homophobic violence. As we had done in Statesville, Christina and I were traveling in and out of a small town not unlike my hometown. But, this time, the issue was not the Klan and racism; it was neo-Nazis and homophobia. My heart went out to the Godfreys and the Meltons as they sorted through the information. Were the victims, their loved ones, gay? After hearing Dorlene's vehemence and Faye's questions, I knew that was not the issue. They were killed because their attackers perceived them to be gay. The perpetrators' motive, rather than the victims' identity, was the place to focus. But I couldn't help wondering. Did the young men gathered that night at the Shelby III offer some window onto small-town life for homosexuals?

Lesbians and gay men have organized visibly in North Carolina since the early 1970s, drawn to the more liberal atmosphere of several Piedmont cities from surrounding towns and university campuses. In the 1980s the AIDS crisis brought a new surge of statewide gay/lesbian activity, as did Jesse Helms's intensely homophobic campaigns for U.S. Senate and the Second National March on Washington for Lesbian and Gay Rights. Had any of this trickled down into small towns? What was life like for the people who stayed at home? What might my life have been like had I stayed in Tuskegee? Whatever their sexual identity, I felt a kinship to the wounded and dead young men.

Christina and I soon found that there was no organized gay community or even acknowledged gay presence in Shelby. Folks at the *Star* gave Christina the name of a "gay spokesman." She called him up from our hotel, but he quickly explained that he was closing his store and moving out of town. I heard from others that homosexuals congregated in a certain parking lot at 1:00 a.m. on a weeknight. None of Shelby's churches opened their doors to the gay/lesbian groups within denominations, such as the Episcopalian group Dignity or the Catholic group Integrity. I guessed that some of the town's lesbians and gay men drove to Charlotte's gay bars. For others, Charlotte was no closer than the moon. Porn stores like the Shelby III might offer them their only gathering places.

I kept debating whether I should come out to the Godfreys and the Meltons. Partly the issue was my own safety. Partly I didn't want them to reject me—and perhaps, by implication, their dead relations. In a weird way, they were also standing in for my parents and my siblings. Terry's sister Dorlene often reminded me of my own sister, and I remembered my sister's painful reaction when I finally came out to her. Again I heard my sister say, "There may come a day you can't see [my children]. Or maybe just by yourself. It doesn't show so when you are alone." If our own family members, who have known us all our lives, reject us for their interpretation of the Bible or the propaganda of the religious right, what will strangers do? But I figured that the Meltons and the Godfreys had enough to deal with without responding to my projections. I shared as much information with them as I could about homophobia and gay people, but I decided against coming out.

The city of Shelby was founded in 1843 after an influx of European settlers during a rush for gold discovered in 1834 on nearby King's Mountain, also the site of a decisive battle during the Revolutionary War. I noted two of Shelby's native sons listed in a slick Chamber of Commerce brochure: Thomas Dixon Jr. and W.J. Cash, an ironic duo.[21] *The Birth of a Nation*, the movie based on Dixon's *The Clansman*, had helped to stir a Klan revival in the 1910s. Two decades later, Cash explained the Klan's appeal to poor whites in his own classic, *The Mind of the South*.

Stock in trade for Dixon's white supremacist novels, three of which sold over one million copies, was a depraved Black man's rape of a pure (read: white) southern female and the obligatory lynching that followed. Dixon equated Black political power with the "insolence of a class of Young Negro men" liable to commit rape:

The encroachments of Negroes upon public offices had been slow but resistless. Now there were nine hundred and fifteen Negro magistrates in the state, elected for no reason except the colour of their skin. Feeling themselves entrenched behind state and Federal power, the insolence of a class of young Negro men was becoming more and more intolerable. What would happen to these [Black] folks when once they roused that thousand-legged, thousand-eyed [white] beast with its ten thousand teeth and nails! He had looked into its face, and he shuddered to recall the hour.

He knew that this power of racial fury of the Anglo-Saxon when aroused was resistless, and that it would sweep its victims before its wrath like chaff before a whirlwind.[22]

Cash offered the best explanation of the family income figures also provided by the Chamber of Commerce. "The conservative governing bodies have guided Shelby into continued prosperity by working closely with area business and industry," the Chamber's brochure assured. Low wages were part of the bargain. The 1985 population of the town was 40,426. Per capita income was $8,900 and median family income was $28,175. The population was 72.8 percent white, 27 percent Black, and 0.2 percent "other."[23] As Cash explained, the southern mind was a product of the frontier mentality and a bargain struck between the "common white man" and the dominant white class. A modicum of white privilege brought "the almost complete disappearance of economic and social focus on the part of the masses."[24] The White Patriot Party was the latest in a long line of racist organizations to fill the political void. Black political power immediately translated in the racist's mind to sexual threat, making white savagery necessary for the survival of white civilization. Wasn't savage response to the homosexual threat only a short step away? Had Kenny, Travis, and Paul also felt this aroused "racial fury of the Anglo-Saxon"? Had they been swept before its wrath like chaff before a whirlwind?

Lillian Smith speculated about links between racism and homophobia:

I know it is not Negro women but Negro men who have seduced
white men's feelings, not knowingly, but this has happened
down here; and I know the sense of tabu has aroused deep anxiety in the white man . . . and he loathes himself. . . . [These
white men] hate themselves with a viciousness that is almost
indescribable. . . . Why do they want to mutilate? what great
master form are they trying to destroy?[25]

With no visible gay community in Shelby, Christina and I began
with Kenny's and Travis's families and with the Black community,
which had a stake in opposing far right organizing. We presented information on the White Patriot Party to the NAACP and the Black
ministerial alliance and asked for their help. We suggested a resolution similar to the one Statesville had issued condemning Klan and
neo-Nazi activity. They agreed to support it before the City Council.
Chris and I set up a meeting between the families and Black leaders
in a Black church, and it went smoothly. White leaders proved more
difficult. We had the support of a white Presbyterian minister, who let
us use his church. We called an interracial meeting of leaders in November 1988 to explain what we knew about the White Patriot Party
and to ask for their help. But we had underestimated the resistance.

Following our strategy in Statesville, we suggested possible responses to the murders and the upcoming White Patriot trial: letters
to the editor, editorials, a memorial service for the victims, townspeople attending the trial to show their concern. At one point, the
white ministers seemed poised to consider some action. Then a Black
participant disagreed with us that public response was necessary and
support evaporated. I felt the meeting slipping away from us. Not
enough had happened, it seemed, to require a response. I made an
impassioned plea about "keeping faith with the dead." I must have
sounded a little crazy. The Shelby folks said they wanted to have another meeting, without us. Perhaps it was the combination of queers,
dirty books, and Klan, but the white leaders decided to lay low. Black
leaders declined to move without them. I sorely missed Reverend
Wilson Lee, whose presence in Statesville had generated action, and
I missed a visible gay presence in the county. There would be no

organized response from citizens of Shelby during the long month of the trial.

January 1989 brought another strange development. Shelby defendant Robert Jackson's little brother Anthony Wydra was shot and killed while he was riding in a car. Ex-Patriot Cecil Cox had been driving, and a Marine named Paul D'Onofrio had fired the fatal shot. The Sheriff's Department declared it an "accident" with unseemly haste and did not press any charges. What window into neo-Nazi machinations did it reveal?[26]

Then a bizarre anonymous letter arrived in the office mail purporting to tell the "actual facts surrounding the Shelby porno bookstore shootings" based on "sources extremely close to these events." It laid out an incredible scenario in which Glenn Miller led the attack on the bookstore because he was being blackmailed with some kind of sexual pictures taken there. The U.S. Justice Department, according to the highly imaginative account, had also blackmailed Miller with the same pictures, forcing him to send his "Declaration of War" in their hopes that he would precipitate assassination of leftists— among whom I was named first—and racial uprisings. This turmoil would influence the 1988 presidential election. The letter only intensified my feeling of being caught in a bad novel. If this were a mystery, I would know how it all fit together by the final chapter. But each revelation only generated multiple uncertainties.

We soon found that the anonymous letter writer had sent the letter to many people in Shelby. Shortly before the trial, former National Socialist Party of America leader Harold Covington also showed up in Cleveland County, threatening to stage a Klan march through town that never materialized. (To my dismay, Covington had returned to the county during the summer of 1987, when Glenn Miller was in jail.) Then someone filled the town with bogus flyers, purportedly by NCARRV, titled "Racism Sucks" and claiming, among other things, that Jesus was gay. Townspeople hunkered down even further.

NCARRV sponsored a press conference in Charlotte on May 3, 1989, the day Doug Sheets's trial opened in Shelby. (Jackson's trial was scheduled for June.) Rev. C.T. Vivian, chair of the Center for Democratic Renewal's board, came to speak, as did Kevin Berrill of the National Gay and Lesbian Task Force's anti-violence project. Carolyn Coleman, state director of the NAACP (also on NCARRV's board), Rob Sikorski (who had served briefly as executive director of NCARRV), and Brother John Dolan (a Catholic priest from Charlotte) made statements as well. We held the event in Brother Dolan's church. C.T. has a long resume and much respect nationally as a civil rights leader, dating back to his role on Martin Luther King Jr.'s staff. Sheriff Jim Clark had knocked C.T. down the Dallas County Courthouse steps on national television in 1965 while C.T. lectured him on his Nazi tendencies, escalating events that led to the Selma-to-Montgomery march and the Voting Rights Act. I was grateful to C.T. for making the trip up from Atlanta, bringing history with him.

At the press conference, he spoke eloquently, both as a civil rights leader and as a Christian minister, on the need to oppose homophobic violence.[27] We then drove Kevin and C.T. to Shelby, where we had invited local leaders to discuss the case. Black clergy showed; white clergy did not. C.T. was persuasive in his arguments about the need to respond to homophobic violence. Rev. R.E. Devoe, a local Black minister, commented to the press, "If this case isn't prosecuted to the max, other hate groups will look for other vulnerable groups. It's testing parameters of society's consciousness. All people have to live without intimidation and have an open society of peace."[28]

I drove Kevin back to the Charlotte airport. He was moved by the Black ministers' support, very different from the response from Black fundamentalist clergy he had encountered in other places. He was also struck by C.T.'s clear grasp of homophobia—deeper, he felt, than that of many gay organizers. "He's grounded in four hundred years of struggle," I observed. "Gay movements do not have that history." Kevin was leaving with a broadened understanding of the possibilities of coalition. A year later, C.T. brought down the house when he gave the keynote speech at the National Gay and Lesbian Task Force's annual conference.

Back at Sheets's trial in the Cleveland County Courthouse in Shelby, a policeman in a flak jacket stood guard on the roof. There were sheriffs' cars at both sides of the building, and a metal detector framed the entrance.

"This is a case about murder, killing, robbery and burning up at a dirty bookstore involving homosexuals on January 17, 1987," District Attorney Bill Young began his brief opening arguments.[29] My heart sank. Homosexuals and dirty books, not neo-Nazis and murder. And this was the prosecution! If Young did not take on neo-Nazi politics, the jurors would have no context within which to interpret the events. The defense made it clear that they would be putting Glenn Miller on trial, claiming that he had tied Jackson and Sheets to the murders in exchange for his plea bargain. Unlike his Missouri trial, here Sheets was not defending himself. He had two local lawyers and Kirk Lyons, of Houston, Texas, familiar in right-wing circles, whom Sheets trusted as an advocate in a legal process he believed had no jurisdiction over him. Strong and handsome in a sinister way, Sheets was an ominous but restrained presence at the defense table.

The first day of testimony, Young called Terry, the first-shift clerk at the bookstore, who testified that he was homosexual and that homosexuals gathered at the bookstore on a regular basis.[30]

The second witness was James Parris, thirty-eight, one of the two survivors of the shooting, who gave a gripping account of the crime. He had arrived at the bookstore in the late afternoon to visit Travis Melton. Six hours later, after finishing their last game of Pac-Man, the men in the store were helping Travis to clean up so that they could all go out to eat after the store closed. About midnight, his life changed forever. "We heard this car come in and the door opened. Travis said, 'Oh, no.' I turned and looked, and these three men with ski masks and guns came in. They told us to lay down." Young had Parris lie down on the courtroom floor on his stomach to show the jurors what had happened. Dorlene and Faye sobbed. "After I laid down I heard some shots. Then I heard a voice I didn't recognize say, 'You don't have to do all this. Please, don't do this,' and someone said, 'Are you a g-d-faggot, too? Get down.' Then they continued to shoot all of us."[31]

Parris testified, choking back tears, "I felt him put the gun to the side of my head. I felt something, it felt like it was soft." The bullet went through his right temple and exited through his left eye socket. "And I was still knowing part of what was going on. I felt the blood running over my hand. I fell on the floor." Parris heard someone instruct, "Go in the back and light the charges." Then, "Give me your lighter. I left mine at home." After a brief time Parris came to and figured from the heat that the building was on fire.[32] "I was completely blind at that point. I felt blood running over my hands." He got up, ran into a wire book rack, and then bumped into someone wearing a sweater. It was John, the other survivor. Parris found his car key by the shape of it and opened the second car he found. He backed it away from the burning building and signaled with his headlights. A passerby found him and summoned the police. Parris showed the jury where he had been shot in the right temple and through his left eye, which was blind. He could not identify any of the gunmen.[33]

The following week I listened intently to witnesses presenting tedious "chain of evidence" testimony for materials found both in the bookstore and in the trailer in Missouri where Sheets and Miller were captured. I hoped for strong material evidence, such as a murder weapon, ballistics, or fibers—which police had hinted to me that they had—to link Sheets to the crime. After two days, it was clear that there was little such evidence. There were possible matching fibers between a glove and the bomb, not exactly similar tape on the bomb and in the trailer, similar brands of .22 and .45 shells. But none of the slugs from the bookstore matched the ballistics of guns confiscated from the Ozarks trailer where the defendant was captured.

Other white supremacists and Sheets's cellmates provided most of the prosecution's testimony. Most of the cellmates were Black, which probably affected both their credibility to the all-white jury and their safety.

One of the Black inmates who testified for the prosecution was Clifton Patterson. Patterson was a "jailhouse lawyer," a prisoner who had learned enough legal skills to file his own briefs and give advice to other inmates. He and Sheets were at the Federal Correctional Institution in Butner, North Carolina. They strung up dental floss between their cells and passed notes back and forth. Sheets asked Patterson for legal advice such as whether indictments could be procured in the absence of murder weapons and if testimony from someone who overheard a conversation about a murder would be sufficient. Patterson replied that any indictment would depend on all the evidence in the case and that hearsay evidence would have to be substantiated. Sheets replied, "We're cool," according to Patterson. "How about we say we didn't know anything about the bookstore until Bob [Stoner] told us about it?" Patterson acknowledged destroying one set of notes. He said he chose to testify because he was alarmed at Sheets's and Jackson's intent. "They said they were preparing for the war of Armageddon. . . . They were intending to kill hundreds of people."[34]

Fayetteville White Patriot den leader Robert Stoner also testified for the prosecution about Sheets's and Jackson's conversation when they were on the lam together with Glenn Miller. Jackson had said that he, Sheets, and a local man named Jeff Johnston went into the bookstore while another local man named Hugh Black stood guard. They lined up the men inside the store, and when the largest person made a threatening move, Sheets hit the man on the head. His weapon went off, blowing a hole in the man's skull. Sheets commented how good the blood spurting upward looked. Jackson turned to see someone in the door and shot him in the chest, according to Stoner.[35]

A Forest City man, Leslie Dean Watts, testified that he had been in the store earlier that evening when two men had threatened Travis Melton. One was described as a large man with sandy-colored hair and a prominent jaw, a description that fit Jackson. They had pretended to be gay, going into one of the booths together to watch a movie. Travis had tapped on the booth, saying only one person at a time was allowed inside. Fifteen minutes later, the men returned to the front room, and one of them grabbed Melton by the shirt. "You're all faggots and queers and we'll be back." He had shoved Melton, saying, "Faggot, I'll be back for your ass."[36]

Apparently local police and federal BATF agents had heard both Parris's and Watts's stories about the assailants' hostility to "faggots" at the time they were pursuing their murky leads into pornography rings all over the state, the nation, and the world.

Clear out, guys! I wanted to yell at the young men at the bookstore that evening. Were they inured to this kind of homophobic abuse? Whatever their reasons, they stayed.

During one lunch break, I invited Bruce Henderson from the *Charlotte Observer* to eat with the Meltons, Dorlene, and me. They agreed to give him an interview. The more the public understood the humanity of the victims, the better. I trusted Bruce, whom I had met during the White Knights trial in Statesville. We had both been in Raleigh for the Klanwatch prosecution of Glenn Miller and Steve Miller, then back again for Eddie and Tim's kidnapping trial.

The discussion led into issues of homosexuality. Travis's aunt Sadie ventured, "The people in this community look at people who are homosexual almost like they're criminals. I don't believe in that."

Dorlene added, "People say they were just minding their own business, and whether they were gay or not, it didn't make no difference."[37]

Bruce asked Dorlene, "Would you have loved your brother if you had known he was gay?" I held my breath while she thought about it. I imagined Kenny floating around somewhere near the ceiling, listening as intently as I was.

"Yes, of course I would have," she replied. I started breathing again.

One of the first witnesses for the defense was Pete J. Peters, an Identity preacher from Colorado. According to Identity "theology," homosexuality is a capital offense, like murder and rape, but homosexuals should be executed by the state, not by individual vigilante acts.[38] Young did not challenge the bogus "theology" of Identity, question Peters's credibility as a religious leader, or point out that Sheets would have believed that his "unorganized militia" made him part of the state.

As I reviewed all the Shelby transcripts and clippings to write this section, I was filled with old fear, jumpy about strange noises in the empty house. I dreamed that four of my lesbian friends were killed by neo-Nazis in an attack on my childhood home. I found one of their bodies in my father's room, lodged behind a big bureau that serves as the only closet. I remember the thud of her body, my shock of recognition that she was dead. Later, I met her lover in the kitchen. We burst into tears and fell into each other's arms. All day, the dream lingered. I checked to be sure the doors and windows were locked. This is the real intent of hate violence: the psychic ripple, the creeping anxiety or sudden fear. *It could have been me.*

Sheets took the stand in his own defense, and he was a strong witness. He testified that Glenn Miller was trying to frame him, that Miller had forced him to go underground by threatening his family. He said that cellmate Clifton Patterson had destroyed other notes, which included such comments as, "How could they place me at the scene when I wasn't even in the state?"[39]

Sheets attempted to pin the murders on Glenn Miller. "I knew the bookstore incident was going down before it went down, and it had me worried," Sheets said. His defense followed the narrative of the anonymous letter. Miller was being blackmailed with photographs and had already paid out $75,000. Miller tried to recruit him for the hit, he said, but Sheets got out of North Carolina, arriving at his mother's farm in Oklahoma on January 15. Unable to locate her, he was somewhere in Arkansas or Missouri on January 17, the day of the murders. Sheets said he had never been a member of the White Patriot Party but had top security clearance with them. Throughout his testimony, he referred to his "unorganized" militia and his Identity beliefs, but Young never drew him out on them or sought to put them in context.[40]

Glenn Miller appeared on rebuttal for the prosecution. He testified that Jackson and Sheets had gone with him voluntarily. He gave further details of what he said were their accounts of the killings. He quoted Sheets as saying, "Jeff Johnston zipped [one of the victims] up" with an automatic pistol. He also recalled the story about Sheets's hitting a man on the head and the pistol going off. Both men had laughed, Miller said.[41]

The lawyers during closing arguments battled out whose narrative would best capture the most "facts." Witnesses had relayed accounts of Sheets's comments that varied in many details. Did that make their testimony more or less reliable? Dorlene and Faye were optimistic about a guilty verdict, but I was depressed. It was not a bad case, but juries often err on the side of caution, prejudice, or fear in incidents of hate violence. In the war of conflicting stories, one fact was not contested: neo-Nazis had killed the guys in the Shelby III because they thought they were gay.

The jury deliberations started about 4:00 p.m. Friday, May 26. People in the courtroom heard lots of commotion and loud voices. Around 8:00 p.m. they heard sudden applause. Then the jury came back in, some in tears, to deliver a verdict of "not guilty" on all counts. "Praise the precious name of Yeshua, my King and Savior, and hail his victory," Sheets exclaimed.

Betty Godfrey, Kenny's mother, screamed, "I hope they have children and somebody murders them like he murdered my son! How can the jurors leave me like this, in a nightmare?"

Dorlene, according to the newspapers, cried and shook her head. "They know he lied on the stand, and they are stupid to believe him. That's what I don't understand. Some of the jurors even come out crying. How can they come back with not guilty?" Faye told reporters, "I think the whole thing stinks. I think if it had been in another county, it would have been first-degree murder. I just hope justice will prevail down here, although it has not so far." Sheets was heading back to Leavenworth for his Missouri weapons conviction.

I was deeply discouraged and felt especially sad for Faye and Dorlene. A guilty verdict would have brought some closure. This verdict was bound to kick up hopelessness and grief. When a reporter called me for a comment, I conveyed my disappointment that the town's leaders had not gone on record during the trial against neo-Nazi activity and violent hatred. I was especially critical of the lack of ministerial presence in the courtroom, given that Sheets justified his beliefs on biblical grounds.

The week after the acquittal, District Attorney Young dropped the case against Robert Jackson. NCARRV staffer Eleanor Holland organized a demonstration in front of the governor's office, demanding that the Human Relations Council's Task Force on Racial, Ethnic, and Religious Intimidation include homophobic violence in its mandate (which it later quietly did).

A few days later, the editor of the *Shelby Star* ran "An Open Letter to Mab Segrest," responding to my critical comments in the press. It articulated the unstated assumptions we had battled in trying to elicit a public response. Tom O'Neal, the *Star*'s editor, felt that I had linked the murder to "some inherent hate and prejudice" within the Shelby community. He protested that the kind of violence at the Shelby III was alien to the community. But people carried their beliefs "deep within" and did not need to go on record with them, any more than they needed to "proclaim our belief in the goodness of spring rains." Public proclamations were for people who felt uncertain, and local ministers' presence in the courtroom would have given legitimacy to Sheets's beliefs. Public statements should be "reserved for times when a community is heading down a dangerous path." There was no inkling that Cleveland County people had contributed to the murders.[42] It was the first editorial response to the trial since it opened. O'Neal had used my first name six times. I hadn't realized we were so familiar.

I responded with a letter of my own. I acknowledged the work of the *Star*'s reporters and of District Attorney Young and the Sheriff's Department. They had clearly wanted convictions and had taken the verdicts hard. I was interested in Tom's aversion to accepting any communal *guilt* for the attack when I had felt more their lack of accepting *responsibility* in the wake of it. They could have added their energies rather than withheld them. Nor was the clergy's passive attendance in court what I had had in mind. They could have made clear their opinions from their pulpits and in the local press. I wrote:

> The reason you do not have an active White Patriot Party in Shelby now is that many people across the state, myself included, worked very hard for much of this decade to bring that activity to an end. We did not stand around explaining we weren't complicit in their hatred—we weren't. We just saw an urgent job that needed to be done, and we set to work to do it. We have learned in this work that ignoring the Klan and Nazi groups (as you seem to suggest), that a cold shoulder, is not enough. Many members of hate groups hurt people thinking that they have the approval of the general public and of their communities. Silence, to them, implies consent.

I reminded him of how active the White Patriot Party had been in Shelby in 1985 and that over a hundred local people had voted for White Patriot candidate Jimmy Bailey. I also pointed out that, according to witnesses, at least one of the unindicted alleged assailants was from Cleveland County.

If the people of Shelby oppose such activity as vehemently as you indicate—and I don't question it—what [is the] harm in going on record in making it absolutely clear to anyone else who might have such terrible acts in mind that the community will not tolerate them? We did learn something from the Nazi extermination policies of World War II that left 12 million people dead: "The only thing it takes for evil to prevail is for good people to do nothing."

You say that you don't need to go on record with your community's stand against prejudice any more than you need to go on record for "the goodness of spring rains or the glory of an upper Cleveland autumn." But when tornadoes struck Cleveland County—an aberration to your usual climate—people responded: raised money for victims, helped clean up the damage, cared for the bereaved. In January 1987, a tornado of hate touched down at the Shelby III, the hatred of people perceived to be gay. It left homes and families shattered, just as much as if they had awakened to find the trees in their yard uprooted, their roofs flying in the wind, their loved ones dead in the rubble. Those victims of the hate tornado needed help. For one thing, they needed their neighbors sitting in court with them during the ordeal to show that they cared. . . . I am not talking about guilt here, Tom, I am talking about a failure of compassion, a need for neighborliness.

As to local clergy's response, I firmly believe that if Jesus had been in Shelby in May, he would have been sitting in the courtroom, between Dorlene Robbins, Kenny Godwin's sister, and Faye and Bobby Melton, Travis's parents. "If you have done it unto the least of these, my brethren, you have done it unto me."

I am not talking about guilt, Tom. I am talking about love.

The *Star* ran an abbreviated version of the letter, mixing the order of the paragraphs.

Would I have been as critical had the verdict been guilty? Who knows? I sure did not get to find out, which I might have if townspeople had reacted differently. Maybe Shelby native son W.J. Cash explained it better than I:

It is far easier, I know, to criticize the failure of the South [or the United States] to face and solve its problems than it is to solve them. Solution is difficult and, for all I know, may be impossible in some cases. But it is clear at least that there is no chance of solving them until there is a leadership which is willing to face them fully and in all their implications, to arouse the people to them, and to try to evolve a comprehensive and adequate means for coping with them.[43]

I left Shelby with a sense of failure, my own as much as theirs. I wondered if the white supremacist satirist who penned the "Racism Sucks" flyer had gotten it right:

During the trial, we will come to Shelby. We will come in our hundreds, our thousands, black and white, brown and yellow. We have endured so much at the hands of white male supremacy. We have endured persecution, discrimination, and AIDS. We will not endure heartless murder. We are coming to *demand* justice from the people of Shelby, North Carolina, and we *will not accept anything less*

In December 1990, I quit NCARRV altogether. My last major task was to write a report on an upsurge of white police officers killing Black men, which turned out to be a precursor to the police beating of Rodney King that set Los Angeles in flames. *No justice, no peace!* I could absorb no more stories until I wrote out the ones that already inhabited me. They were part of a context that I only glimpsed. I had hoped I could write about the work while I did it, but the inevitable adrenaline rushes disrupted reflection. I felt like a photographer in a war zone, with scores of rolls of undeveloped film, except that these images were printed on my body. Seven years before, I had deliberately set out on a journey, not unlike old stories tell, a descent with border crossings, with helpers and guides, battles with monsters at the chaotic human nadir, villains and heroes reflecting back my multiple—my fractured—self. I had touched the toxic heart of whiteness in places like Robeson and Shelby. As my next task, could I bring back a dissident knowledge, like the old magical elixirs, to help transform the world?

11

A Journey We Make Daily

"Ichi! Ni! San! Shi! Go! Roku! Shichi! Hachi! Ku! Ju!" I lay on the dojo floor with ten women, counting sit-ups in Japanese. My mind wandered. How had I let Eleanor talk me into this two years before? She said I had been sick too much, and it would help keep me healthier to work out twice a week in the dyke dojo. Besides, I needed some self-defense training. I had just cut back to half-time work at NCARRV and had begun to pay attention to my health. The first several weeks of karate, I had to fight the impulse to quit. I felt humiliated, trying to get my body to do all the simultaneous things that karate seemed to imply—knee over the toe, fist clenched in Master Shimabukaru's Number One Fist, butt tucked, shoulders straight, chin up, eyes ahead. And that was standing still! When it came time to move, I could not possibly send all the necessary signals out to my appendages. *I . . . will . . . never . . . get . . . this,* I would think through sit-ups, push-ups, and leg lifts, to the count.

But I kept at it. Carol was an excellent teacher. She had her bad days, but most of the time she brought a joy to the workouts, a gift for pushing limits and respecting them at the same time. She could break the most complex moves down into small steps, and I found that if I mastered each step, the larger moves began to come. But it was very slow. *Patience,* I would counsel. *Your mind is not used to being in your body. This requires synapses that haven't functioned in years.*

"Taikyuku shodan," Carol called, referring to the beginner's *kata.*

"*Kiotsuke. Rei.*" We moved from ready position to the bow. My hands slid along the legs of my *gi* as I leaned forward from the waist, trying to keep my upper body straight.

"*Kamaete. Hajime.*" Left into front stance, step in and punch. Pivot right into front stance, step in, and punch. Eyes forward, ninety-degree turn into front stance. My mind began to wander. *What will happen in Shelby? What about the Presbyterian grant? Fuck, where am I now in the kata? Oh, yeah, down the middle: step-punch, step-punch, step-punch. Focus, Segrest. Focus.*

Carol stepped over beside me. "Like this," she shifted my hips forward. "Hips square. Now lean that knee out over your toe." My quads protested vigorously as she nudged me forward. *Master Shimabukaru doesn't get his knee over his toe in the picture hanging in the dojo. Why am I expected to? What will I have for supper tonight? Will Chris be on time for work tomorrow? What in the world is going on with Annie's day care?*

"*Yame.*" Eyes back to the front, we all bowed. I was glad that *kata* was over.

Had I lived in another century, I would probably have headed off to the confession booth or on a pilgrimage or to a doctor who would have fastened leeches to the flesh. As a white lesbian in the late twentieth-century United States, I turned to self-help. Karate, twelve-step, co-counseling.

Dear God, give me the courage to change the things I cannot change. I could never get that goddamned prayer right. When people asked me how I coped with the work, I would laugh and say I ate a lot of bagels. I also ate ham biscuits and had even taken to buying M&Ms on solitary drives that brought me back to Durham after midnight. I had gained forty pounds, and I could feel it. So off I finally went to Overeaters Anonymous, where each Monday night we recited the Serenity Prayer: "Grant me the serenity to accept the things I cannot change, the courage to change the things I can, and the wisdom to know the difference." It spoke to the heart of my dilemma: how the hell did a person know what couldn't be changed? I was supposed to admit I was powerless and turn my difficulties over to a "Higher Power," a concept that gave me the heebie-jeebies. I remembered Reverend Lee observing me kneeling at one of his church pews as I prepared a slide carousel for a presentation on local Klan activity: "Mab, I didn't know you ever got down on your knees." I'd never seen him kneel before any man or woman either. Then I realized it wasn't humans he meant. He had died praying.

By Step Four, we were to undertake a "fearless and searching moral inventory," then admit our character flaws to God and one other person. I resisted this, too, with the view that I was generally more sinned against than sinning. Wasn't it one more way to blame myself, when I took too much responsibility as it was? But just maybe the thing I could change was my part of interactions, which I was powerless over as long as I perceived myself as acted on? Somewhere in this process, I lost twenty pounds, then gained ten back.

"Mab, Mab, please take care of me. Please, please." Tobi lay on her rug, imitating my mother. Tobi was my co-counseling partner. We had spent an hour a week counseling each other for the past year. The purpose of co-counseling (or Re-evaluation Counseling) was "discharge": crying, laughing, yawning, shaking. Co-counselors took turns giving attention to each other, provoking or coaxing discharge. It had taken me a while to get the hang of it, but it seemed to help. This afternoon Tobi was counseling me about my rage at Christina. She had shifted it to my "chronic" material, my mother's sickness. She had started off sitting herself in my lap and hanging on to me, asking me to take care of her. I had spent ten visceral minutes wrestling her out of my lap. It was sweaty work; we are both large women.

"No, that wasn't it," I explained. "It was that she had just given up, and it was somehow my fault."

"Oh, I can't go on!" Tobi began to moan, inert now on the floor. "I can't go on."

My response was immediate. I grabbed her arm and pulled, but it just flopped back to the floor.

"Get up. Get up. Get up! *Mama, get up.*"

"I can't," she moaned again. "I can't."

"Yes, you can, too, Mama, get up." Tears were on my cheeks. I pulled harder and felt a quick jolt of panic, then anger.

"Mama, get up!" I began to sob. "Get up! Get up! Get up! Get up!" I was crying harder than I could remember, an ocean of salt on my lips, the taste of very old tears. I was so angry I was shaking.

Finally Tobi sat up.

"Mab, it was not your fault. That your mama hurt so much and that she died. It was not your fault. Maybe it was nobody's fault. Maybe it just happened. Maybe you don't need to punish anyone or to fix everything."

"You are getting your power from inappropriate sources," my karate *sensei* Carol explained, frowning. The story of my life. I was as aggravated as she was. I had been practicing these two damned *kata* for months, and I thought I had them.

"The power should come from your stances, not just flailing your arms."

Back to the drawing board. I tried not to feel pitiful.

Three months later, my undershift and *gi* soaked with sweat, my green belt test was almost over and I was happily in my body. My quad muscles were stretched and strong as I moved through stances in *seisan*. Over the past months, I had strengthened my legs and stances by feeling my way tortuously through the intricacies of every move: the initial plunge-punch-block, the turn at the top of the T, the crane-like blocks back up the middle, the flurry of kicks and punches in the fighting series. I got the larger movements right, then perfected the details. Stances, hands, and eyes were sure from repetition. I knew what came next, and I knew that I knew. Two weeks before, Carol had gotten past her irritation to notice the transformation.

Lunge, back fist to the head, kamay, middle block, step-step-kick, block-punch. My foot slipped on a sweaty spot on the floor, but the recovery was immediate. At the end of the *kata*, I bowed and resumed position. I looked at Carol, and we laughed.

"What do you learn from the art of karate?" Carol asked me later, in the verbal portion of the test.

"How not to quit at something that comes very hard to me," I an-swered. "How to have a mind in the body, that can send and receive messages from fingers and knees and neck and toes. How to build from basics, not jump over them."

Then came the green belt. I had earned every stitch.

It was 1993. I was back in the NCARRV office, the familiar overflow of clippings at the Xerox machine, grant proposals in process on the desks, and Klan and anti-Klan flyers on the walls. In the last stages of writing this memoir, I had come to talk with Christina about our relationship. I needed to hear her current understanding of what had happened between us, especially since I was struggling to describe it. She responded generously.[1]

"At the time of our biggest fights," she began, "I was involved in a new marriage, trying to deal with all the issues of sharing my life with this man who is totally different in many ways than I am. I was living in Greensboro, an hour's drive from Durham, out of interest to work on the marriage, having to drive back and forth between work and home. There were real issues around whether there was trust between you and me. We sometimes voiced it, but did not always support the words by our actions when differences came up. Trust issues were even harder for me to distinguish because of the whisperings of my husband. He was coming from his place and history as an African American man, never having believed that there can be a genuine level of trust of the oppressor by the oppressed. I had my real need to know/believe that there could be trust because of the relationship that you and I had constructed, had worked to develop."

I was ready to respond. "It's become apparent to me how hard it is for me to trust anybody. Trust issues with you happened in a vacuum. And then there was this race thing, too, that made it even harder. My main anger with you was in your not being here in the Durham office enough for me. You're talking now about how you had other places that you needed to be that you couldn't explain to me."

Christina: "I wanted to believe there was this genuine relationship, I wanted to believe it was a personal relationship, too. I also believed that there's a need to keep work and home separated, or I was not really sure to what extent somebody could empathize or sympathize with what I was dealing with at home, regardless of how it's impacting work. We come from this place of believing that we need to keep those things separate, that whatever is going on at home should not stop us from being able to function in the workplace. We need to be sensitive at work about what's going on at home, especially when there's the kind of relationship you and I had, doing the kind of work we were doing, which was life-threatening, which was a place of real fear for both of us."

Mab: "But also a place of real creativity. Things were happening because of the work we were doing. People's lives were changing. We made a difference. That was what bonded us. It was almost like raising a child together: raising this organization, would it survive or not? It had elements of a marriage—we had to share money, we had to share time. It didn't have the sexual dynamic to it. But the shit that gets you in trouble in a marriage is money and time. As much as sex."

Chris: "I like the analogy of the marriage. That's the piece that wasn't working in my head, that didn't get really thought about and talked about. Even in a marriage, in a relationship that you are shaping with someone, it's a different person and you come from different cultures. There's still this real issue that this person doesn't know me, and I don't know them, I can't share with them all the things that are going on in my life. On one hand, we were working very closely together, we were having this major impact on the lives of people, our lives touched. But there was still stuff that happened individually that we didn't feel completely whole and real about sharing with each other. For me, it was very easy to pin it on the issue of race and of cultural differences when I knew that those barriers and those blocks were there."

I shared with Chris passages in this memoir, and she shared with me the story of how a white woman had betrayed her in a painful way during her college years.

Christina: "[That experience] showed me what stops me in being able to genuinely relate to white women: what I returned to, how I reacted and what the triggering mechanism was, the block or the barrier, the place that needed healing. More and more as I am seeking to do the healing, I am able to relate to the experiences that put me in this place of not relating openly."

I shifted. "I have been trying to look some at the structural conditions that made us personalize everything. There would be trust issues that meant we couldn't share everything. Then there was my being a supervisor. I didn't know for shit how to do that. I had been working in non-tenure-track academic settings where I had never really been evaluated myself, or in *Feminary*, a collective where there were power differences but it wasn't like somebody was supposed to be the boss. I really wanted to do the work with you collectively. I set our salaries the same. At some point the board said, 'No, you are the director, you get more money, you are accountable to us, Chris is accountable to you.' Good supervisors need to be direct, need to say what's on their minds immediately, stick to their guns, and go on to the next thing. But when issues came up between us I would feel them first as *personal* betrayal or *personal* fear or *personal* confusion about what was going on. It was cloudy for me: when was I personally your friend and co-worker, and when was I your supervisor? We had to put the personnel policies in place ourselves; we had to put the board in place. The board helped eventually at least to pull us apart and to get a little clarity so that we could go on. I didn't have the management skills, and sometimes I didn't even know that I didn't have them. To ask for something, you have to know what it is you need. There were times that I didn't even know what it was I needed.

"I've found it instructive to be a parent," I continued, "although supervising and parenting are clearly not the same. But in both you're supposed to maintain the rules. You need to be consistent, and I've had to work hard as a parent on being consistent, saying what I mean and sticking to it. With the Klan, I can kick ass. But with people I'm close to, I'd rather negotiate and hope it all works out. You're a much more direct kind of person than me."

Christina responded: "I tend out of that directness to be able to say right now what I'm feeling and with much more ease to ask for what I need. I didn't get that sense from you. I don't think that when I ask for help it in any way shows I'm weak or incompetent. Maybe that's the difference in being from a big family, always knowing there was somebody to ask for help if I needed help. I learned early on not to let things get so bad you're about to fall through a hole before you ask for help. That was an area of argument for us. When there were major explosions, there was a barrage and a litany of stuff that you'd been holding on to that you could have nipped in the bud if you'd said it at the time. That was another place I felt betrayal. If I care about a person, then I want to hear what's happening with you."

Mab: "Yet what would have helped me was your filling in where you had been, which you didn't have the trust to do. My style was not immediate conflict but it was listening, understanding, empathizing. It would have helped me to see, 'This is not about me, it's not even about the work, it's about something that's going on in Chris's life.'"

Chris: "It was hard to penetrate that wall of silence to say, 'I see that you're feeling this way, here's some information that might help you.' You were not in a place to hear what the fuck I had to say. You were pissed off, and that was that. In many ways, we were these sisters who saw the sibling stuff happening and sidestepped it because we didn't know how to deal with it. It's good to look back on it, to figure out what was happening."

Mab: "There are Black folks who are willing to work with white people and Black folks who are not. That was the difference between you and your husband. I am curious about what's in it for you, because the work together is clearly hard. And I guess I am asking myself the same question. What's in it for me?"

Chris: "For me, the real issue is that the hope for the world rests in us, people of goodwill, people of consciousness, working together to do the hard work of reforming, deconstructing, reworking this society. I really do believe that work must be happening on many fronts. There *is* a place for nationalism. But if we are really talking about a whole society, then we all have to get in here together. We have to roll up our sleeves. We have to be willing to grapple with the issues of distance, of distrust, the history that has provided those dynamics to be real for us, to work on them personally so that we do the universal healing, the universal work that has to happen.

"I don't think that it's light work. I don't think that it is easy, and I don't think that it's something that is going to happen in a short period of time. It's long-term. It's a journey that we start on and become committed to understanding as a journey we have to make daily."

We stood and embraced. "I love you," she said.

"I love you too."

My father looked little and scared in his hospital gown, standing in the waiting room of the Veterans Administration hospital. When I hugged him, he started to cry. I was glad I had driven the five hundred miles home to see him, after my aunt May had called to say he was in the hospital with complications from a bladder infection and severe arthritis. The doctors had said his prognosis was not good.

"You mean he could die?" I asked May.

"That's what the damned doctor said, and right in front of him. I was so mad I could spit!"

It had taken a few days to get clearer information over the phone and learn that there was nothing terminal in my father's condition. It sounded more like he was exhausted and depressed. I decided to drive down to visit.

Daddy was obviously glad that I had come. At night, I stayed out in the country with Aunt May, who had built a lovely home on the site of the old farmhouse where she and Daddy had grown up. I drove in to the hospital to visit my father every day, walking around the halls with him while we talked. On the way in, I would stop at Mama's grave to visit her as well. Neither Daddy nor May thought it was safe for me to be in the cemetery alone, but I wanted the private time. I would sit there in the late winter afternoon, quiet in Mama's company, as she was in the company of other family members buried long before. I would remember the holidays when we would bring flowers up for the gravestones, my brother and sister and I playing among the dead. Now there were times I would just say aloud, "Mama, I'm home." After visiting Daddy, I would drive by the house, walking around the yard trying to imagine what it would be like when I did not have this place to come home to—or to avoid.

When it came time to say goodbye, Daddy walked me down the flight of stairs to the door. I could tell that my visit had picked up his spirits. At the heavy door that led outside, we both began to cry.

"Daddy, I love you," I said. "I was scared to come when Mama was sick because I always felt there was nothing I could do to help. I don't feel that way about you."

"I love you, too, girl," he sobbed.

When had my "racist daddy" contracted to himself—to one aging man—from the balloon into which I had inflated him: a caricature of everything in the culture that I hated, my archetypal white person, whom I could never convert because I could never accept, the him of me? No Black friend had ever asked me not to love my daddy.

I thank Alice Walker and my dreadlocked friend at Blue Mountain, my final guide, who directed me back to my family.

Christina nailed my difficulty asking for help, reading in it an aversion to showing weakness. She was right, but wrong about the reason. In her large family, help was ready. In my family, confronted with my mother's pain, why ask when nothing helped? The times that Black friends, families, and communities welcomed me, I sensed—because I joined—their complex interdependence. Sure, racism sought to ravage them and often did, but by drawing on each other, they survived and thrived. This community became available to me at the moments it became palpable to me; at the moments I saw through the racist stereotypes about dysfunctionality to the basic health in the cultures; at the moments when I, too, assumed some of the risk and the responsibility to protect it from the racism that constantly lapped and tore at the underpinnings, threatening its young people with the new realities of drugs, violence, and urban decay. As a child of Europeans, a woman whose families have spent many generations on these shores, some of them in relative material privilege, my culture raised me to compete: for grades, for jobs, for money, for self-esteem. As my lungs breathed in competition, they breathed out the stale air of individualism, delivering the toxic message to cells and corpuscles: *You are on your own.* Being "queer" only amplified the problem. Traveling across race and class and cultural boundaries, my ear eventually became tuned to different vibrations so that I began to hear, first as a murmur, then as clearly articulated sound: *We . . . are . . . in . . . this . . . together.* My lungs relaxed some, my cells gasped the clearer air.

Lenny taught me that fascism was about isolation, about political movements deliberately breaking down the human bonds between people so that they give blind allegiance to a leader or an ideology. Reverend Lee showed me how to go after the lost, to defy the isolation imposed by denial, terror, and ideologies of hate. But I was lost myself, and I found myself, in part at least, in the acts of searching out others. It made me a different person—but not a *better* person—than either of my parents. To differentiate myself, I have had to accept the gifts they gave me, which paradoxically I could not do until I was sure I am my own person. "When people have to choose, they go with their own race," my mother had said, but she was wrong. It is not a matter of choosing one race or family and betraying another. The choice is for *justice? community? humanity? the glimpse that we are all one organism . . . ?*

After all these pages, the language for it escapes me still. But it calls me forward, and I come, with a clearer courage to change the things that we can change.

12

Epilogue

Writing autobiography, if nothing else, has deepened my appreciation for why people write fiction. As I wrote myself out of isolation, I implicated more and more people. I was able to tell much less than I originally anticipated when I set out. All writers, I suppose, write against the limits of language and genre. There are some characters, stories, and themes that just did not get developed as neatly as if I were writing fiction, or writing autobiography about something less dangerous than a white supremacist movement that still operates around the book's "characters." There are also shifts in tone between the "personal" and the "organizing" chapters that are determined, more than anything else, by libel laws and my own concerns about people's privacy and safety. I have used pseudonyms where requested. At various points I had writer friends urging me to heighten the language and lawyers urging me to flatten it. I may later use the material in more fictional or poetic form; in this book, however, I wanted to keep the documentary, and those requirements are different from the confessional requirements of the more personal parts. Laying claim to fact also involves considerable risks.

The counterpointing of personal and public, historic and familial, was basic to the structure of the book. I was driven to the organizing and the writing not only from political necessity but also to resolve personal/identity questions. As I struggled to bring coherence, if not unity, to the narratives, the personal and the historic collapsed in ways that allowed my own identity to shift and realign. At the end, I have finally come to see that the effort on one level has been a struggle for a measure of psychic integration (which came more through relationships than solitary self-analysis) in a fractured world: never complete, but also not reversible.

Individuals project onto others the characteristics they cannot accept in themselves, then control, punish, or eradicate the objects of those projections (whether female, dark-skinned, homosexual, poor, Jewish . . .). Our identities, structured as they are on what we hate, resist, or fear, are disturbingly unstable. This leads to further repression and gives us a curious interest in proliferating the things we oppose. (I think of how Jesse Helms's campaigns against gay people have generated a gay rights movement in North Carolina, or of how recently fundamentalists, supposedly opposing homoerotic passages in a high school reading list, passed out Xeroxed copies of these passages at a meeting that included high school students.) My "racist self" resists, for example, Sammy Younge, Christina, and Reverend Lee; my "anti-racist self" resists my parents and Marvin Segrest. So they all shape me (a hybrid of the slayer and the slain), and the more consciousness I have about how this process operates, the clearer I will be.

Many friends have helped me take responsibility for this narrative as both my own and many others' stories. In the last stages of this memoir, I sent portions of it to many of the people involved—members of my own family and the families with whom I worked at NCARRV—to check my memory against theirs and to give them some say about how they are represented.

In the spring of 1994 I sent a draft of the entire manuscript to my father. I prefaced it by a telephone conversation in which I apologized to him for judging him in ways that kept us apart.[1] "But that is how you felt about things," he said. "I still do," I replied. "We do think differently on many things. But there are many ways in which you are a better person than me." I explained how since Mama's death I had come to realize how much I had blamed myself and him for her sickness. This came as a surprise to him. "It was never your fault," he reassured me. (Later, he even polled my brother and sister and assured me that no one in the family thought I was to blame.) I asked him to read the manuscript. I sent it off and called a week later, my heart in my throat, remembering how much my mother had hated my first book. "Have you read it?" I asked. "I sure did!" he replied. "I found it heartrending. Mab, I think you are too hard on yourself." He explained that his memory differed from mine at critical points and promised to write his comments. He sent me a letter that began, "There is nothing in the material that I have any objection to." He shared varying recollections, some of which I have included in the notes. I invited him up to share Christmas with me and my family, and he accepted.

My sister was also generous. "Your memories are your memories, and you have a right to them in your own book," she said, "although there were times I wondered if we were in the same house." She apologized for not having responded in more detail—an opening she acknowledged I had given her. "With six kids, when will I have time to do anything?" she laughed. She caught me up on the exploits of her teenagers, the oldest of whom has taken to slipping out of the house at night to roll neighbors' yards with toilet paper. "Here we are, laughing like Mama and Granny," she said. "I like you," I said. "I like you, too," she replied.

I also sent portions of the manuscript to the families with whom Christina and I had worked. This is their story, too, and I wanted their input. I also wanted them to know, if they didn't already, that I am gay. I was happy to be touch with them again, instantly recognizing voices on my answering machine that I had not heard in several years, as they helped me with details and caught me up on their lives.

From Statesville, Flora reported that Joe died of brain cancer, and they remained friends to the end, when he would try to call her from his mother's house using the TV remote control.

On November 3, 1993, the fourteenth anniversary of the Greensboro massacre, I called Marty Nathan in Massachusetts, where she had moved with her second husband, Elliot. She had left a message on the answering machine the week before congratulating me on completing this book. Although she was getting anniversary calls from all across the country, she was more preoccupied with calls from the local hospital, where she's a country doctor.

In Robeson, Rosetta commemorates her sister Joyce's murder each year and Betty and John McKellar remember Billy, their son.

Lauren and Paul Martin have won the hearts of their community, where Lauren has cared for children at a church day care center for ten years and volunteered for the fire department on the emergency medical response team. They are raising two adopted children. One turning point for them came the evening when Lauren received an emergency call to the home of a person she suspected of having burned the cross on her lawn. She entered the kitchen to find the whole family waiting. It was a pregnant moment, as they all realized she could do something for one of their family members they were not able to do, and she was willing to respond.

In Shelby, Dorlene, Kenny Godfrey's sister, has twins who keep her and her mother busy. Faye, Travis's mom, became a nurse. She would have gone crazy otherwise, she said. I finally came out to them both when I sent each family the Shelby chapter. Faye left a message on my answering machine to give her a call, and I did, my heart again in my throat. "You did a good job," was the first thing she said, although she said it had been hard for her to read. "You know, I think Travis *was* gay," she continued. Looking back on it, she could see that he was "going through hell" trying to sort it out. She saw her other children going forward but Travis dropping behind, and she had not known what to do. "You were right, there wasn't nowhere for gay people to meet," she said. When Travis was little, he would call his brother a "faggot." Faye told him not to call people names like that, it wasn't nice.

"Looking back on it, I reckon he was testing me, to see my reaction," she realized. "He didn't have anybody to talk to about it, and I didn't either," she continued. "I would think, 'He'll never get married, and when I die he will be alone.' He was in the dark and I was in the dark, and there wasn't no help." Travis had wanted to move to Charlotte— probably to be in a gay community, she figured now—and she had advised against it, feeling that Charlotte was too dangerous. "There should be classes in school, like sex education classes, that teach that people like this may be in your family, and how to accept it," she said. "Can I quote you in my book?" I asked. "It might help." She said I could. She was still angry about the trial, feeling that the jury had not gotten to hear important evidence. "At least it quietened this whole area down, though," she concluded. "There are no Klan signs on the road or rallies. People know that those are sick-minded people."

I am back in touch with my first woman lover, Pat, who over Chinese food read my account of our getting together with visible relief. She had expected that I would remember her bitterly. We caught each other up on our respective families. I found it hard to believe that seventeen years had passed since we broke up.

Last year, Leah Wise offered me a new job with the Urban Rural Mission of the World Council of Churches, a global network of community organizers and liberation theologians, a "community of clowns" dedicated to a spiritual mission of justice, and I accepted.

Christina continues to direct NCARRV, which reports scandalous numbers of hate incidents each year—Klan and neo-Nazi rallies, mass murders, brutal mutilations. She plans to quit in the spring.

In a recent statewide poll on attitudes toward hate crimes, 61 percent of respondents thought that the media give too much attention to attacks against Blacks and lesbians and gays. Eighty-six percent said they would express sympathy toward a Black couple targeted for hate violence, and 50 percent said they would express sympathy toward a gay or lesbian couple. Sixty percent said they had no known homosexual friends or co-workers.[2]

Homophobic ballot initiatives are winning in many states across the country, playing white gay racism against the homophobia in the Black community. Powerful people deliberately sow divisions, trying to undermine all civil rights by convincing the public that "gay rights are special rights," rather than the right of people like Travis and Faye to get the help they need in their own communities.

Osceola's head mysteriously disappeared about the time of the Civil War. Weedon family papers indicate that the head was passed to Dr. Valentine Mott of the Medical College of the City of New York, who apparently had a collection of skulls. Dr. Whitehurst, a Weedon family representative, wrote Mott in 1843:

In obtaining the head of such a man, I am aware that the sen-
timents of the ultra philanthropist would be shocked . . . and
much sympathy would be expended that a child of the forest . . .
should be conveyed to the tomb, a headless corpse. But with the
scientific and intelligent, such influences are of little worth, and
in the preservation of the dead we do no violence to the feelings
of humanity or even the strongest attachments of love.[3]

Shortly after Dr. Mott died in 1865, the Mott Museum at the
Medical College burned to the ground. No one knows for sure that
Osceola's head was in the building, but I imagine a smoldering from
Dr. Mott's "cabinet of heads," then flames shooting from the sockets,
spontaneous combustion from the violated skulls finally together in
critical mass, sliding from the cabinet to the ceiling, racing the floor,
licking the walls, beams crackling, walls collapsing, shooting sparks
and flames high into the evening sky. In fact, on a clear night, I still
see the fire.

The ravishing of our country's economic, environmental, and social
structures engineered by Reagan and Bush in the 1980s cut deep in
the 1990s, as multinational corporations rearrange the economies of
nations to squeeze further profits at the price of great human suffering. What I uncovered in North Carolina in the 1980s will be our
legacy into the next century, unless we intervene. The racism, the
homophobia, the hatred of Jews and women, the greed accelerate, and
they sicken us all. But we do not have to accept it. We do not have to
accept any of it. There is a lot to be done, but how we go about it is
also important. Because all we have ever had is each other.

My friend Chrystos also admonishes me: "Mab, you need to have
more fun."

Part Two

ON BEING WHITE
AND OTHER LIES

A History of Racism in the United States

For Jacqui Alexander

Four years of full-time anti-Klan organizing and I began to get sick. First it hit my stomach, and I was up all night puking. That was the week after Eddie and Tim, Tuscarora Indians, walked into the local newspaper office in Robeson County with sawed-off shotguns and held twenty people hostage for most of the day. While I and a host of others waited outside, they finally released everyone after the governor promised to investigate racist violence, drug trafficking, and law enforcement complicity in both. I got home and got well, then it hit my throat and came and went for another three months. The first time, I was back in Robeson County, after Lumbee Indian leader Julian Pierce was killed the month before he would have beaten the white power structure in a fair election for district attorney by consolidating the votes of Blacks, Indians, and poor whites. Later it hit me in a motel in Shelby, where we were trying to build up local support for a case against neo-Nazis who murdered three young men in an adult bookstore, "to avenge Yahweh on homosexuals."

I slowed down then and started tracking another way; my road map was not the spidery backroads of North Carolina but history. I knew I needed to understand the genesis of the violence that was sickening me.

A year or so into the process, I found James Baldwin's piece "On Being White and Other Lies" on microfiche in the Duke University library. Baldwin's face watched from the opposite page, light off his features showing as whiteness on the duotone, his intelligent eye emerging from the blackness like a galaxy, Andromeda perhaps. But in his universe it was definitely I who was under observation:

America became white—the people who, as they claim, "settled" the country became white—because of the necessity of denying the Black presence and justifying the Black subjugation. No community can be based on such a principle—in other words, no community can be established on so genocidal a lie. White men—from Norway, for example, where they were Norwegians— became white by slaughtering the cattle, poisoning the wells, torching the houses, massacring Native Americans, raping Black women. This moral erosion has made it impossible for those who think of themselves as white to have any moral authority. . . . It is the Black condition, and only that, which informs the consciousness of white people. It is a terrible paradox, but those who believed that they could control and define Black people divested themselves of the power to control and define themselves.[1]

Baldwin's words resonated with my own sense of whiteness. I could see the country was going backward, and I understood instinctively from my childhood in the Jim Crow South what that meant. This knowledge had brought me to anti-Klan organizing, and it also fed my deepening sense of crisis. But I also came to suspect that these changes, the bloody effects of which I had experienced so intimately working for North Carolinians Against Racist and Religious Violence, might involve more than just the rollbacks of the civil rights movement I had lived through in my adolescence. What was the larger historical framework, and what did it mean?

I was convinced that most white progressives hugely underestimate the power of race in U.S. history as well as the degree to which racial struggles have shaped other political struggles in this country. I suspected that both feminism and the gay and lesbian organizing I had done for over a decade had been as profoundly shaped by race as by gender, but with far less acknowledgment. I had spent many of my years in these movements trying to ensure that my new women's community would not replicate the segregation of my Alabama childhood, but I often felt my head bloody from beating it up against a familiar wall of what felt like willed ignorance, or disoriented from wandering in fogs of personalization and guilt. If racism equals "power plus prejudice," as the anti-racist formula states, how do we really go about explaining this "power" to people in ways that help them to understand what a huge force it is we are up against, how inevitably we all have been shaped by it, and how much we need to do beyond "fixing" ourselves?

As I worked on these questions, the globe shifted: the Soviet bloc collapsed, the Sandinistas lost the Nicaraguan election, Nelson Mandela walked out of a South African jail, Bush went to war against

Iraq, and a hard-line coup against Soviet premier Mikhail Gorbachev brought the end of state-sanctioned communism in the Soviet Union and that union's collapse by the year's end. How did these volatile and massive international shifts relate to my sense of growing crisis at home as Los Angeles burned in the wake of Rodney King's judicial beating and the economy unraveled to the extent that Bill Clinton could defeat George Bush in the 1992 race for president?

In an attempt to answer, or at least more fully frame, some of these questions, I set out to write a history of racism as it emerged in what is now the United States. The immediate context for the project was my participation in the editorial collective of *The Third Wave: Feminist Essays on Racism*, which publisher Barbara Smith of Kitchen Table: Women of Color Press had approached me and several other women to edit in 1988. Barbara assembled a multiracial group of women: Jacqui Alexander, an African Caribbean woman living in Boston (then later in New York); Sharon Day, an Ojibwe from Minnesota; Norma Alarcón, a Chicana at Berkeley; Lisa Albrecht, a Jew relocated from New York to Minnesota; and me, a white southerner. Early in the process, we came up against the question of how anti-Semitism would be incorporated into the anthology. Was anti-Semitism a form of racism within the U.S. context, or not? To answer that question with any integrity, I realized that I needed a clearer sense of what racism is in the United States, how it has evolved. I soon learned that I would have to understand more about capitalism as well.

Putting together the anthology became a major learning experience for me. As we met in each of our home communities to discuss manuscripts and the emerging vision of the book, we also shared our lives and cultures. In the context of our continuing discussions I would hear what to me was new information and say, "You should write that up for the book." The response I often got was, "I already know that. I want to do something that is fresher for me." It occurred to me that I could take on as my part of the project some of these understandings that seemed so basic to particular cultures yet were so foreign to people outside. The bibliography for this essay emerged from those *Third Wave* discussions, as my co-editors recommended books and I read them. I began to synthesize what I was learning into very rough drafts, which I brought back to the collective for comment. Whatever strengths this essay has, they have arisen from this collective process.

I have attempted this overly ambitious project not with a scholar's time and degree of specialization but with an organizer's urgency. It is the result of a rich collective process I underwent with women who became my friends. They helped me to struggle with and against a knowledge that was coming to me through the pages of books, their usually remote and objective tone reinforcing the very white emotional denial that created the devastation in the first place.[2] This "book learning" was balanced by the passionate oral histories of communities in struggle that we shared.

My co-editors also urged me to find a way to close the distance between myself as a white person (a lesbian, a woman) and the material. Near the end of my reading, I remembered part of my mother's legacy. Before she died, she passed on to me the genealogical work done by her cousin to establish her father's lineage back to emigration to the British colonies from England in 1613. She thought that someday I or my siblings might want to belong to the United Daughters of the Confederacy, the Daughters of the American Revolution, or the Colonial Dames—all women's organizations predicated on proving European pedigree. As my mother explained it, the genealogies were designed to help me "know who I am." I got out those family papers and decided to put them to use, as a way to locate myself within this history and to frame it in more personal and immediate terms.

My goal, then, is to provide an overview of the history of racism in the United States that can be read in one (long) sitting: a place for beginning students and activists to understand the extensive and cruel history of institutional racism, as well as for others more veteran to review this history in light of the present emergency; to understand how capitalism has worked with racism to write various of us into it differently according to gender, class, sexual orientation, religion, nationality, geography, and skin color. The essay has had an additional value for me in getting a historic perspective on my own family's emotional dynamics. In that respect, it serves as a long footnote to the first, more personal section in this book, "Memoir of a Race Traitor."

1

Commerce Capitalism

*"So Great a Supply Exhausted
in So Short a Time . . ."*

My great-great-great-great-great-great-great-great-grandfather Ambrose Cobbs landed at Yorktown, Virginia, on the *Treasure* in 1613 with his brother Joseph. The Cobbses were among the earliest emigrants to America from Devonshire, Lancaster, London, and northern England. Ambrose had been born in 1590, two years after the English Navy defeated the Spanish Armada and opened up North America to British conquest. Ambrose arrived six years after the first settlement at Jamestown, only three years after the "starving time" when colonists living in cave-like holes dug up and devoured newly buried corpses, one man killing his wife, salting and eating all parts of her except her head. European settlers in such new worlds probably often found themselves in such desperate situations acting similarly savage and animal-like, responses that intensified their need to project such characteristics onto the peoples they encountered.[1]

Ambrose and Joseph came to what we now call North America as settlers. Joseph's wife and two sons came over to join him in 1624; Ambrose married Anne and settled in York County, Virginia, where they were granted 350 acres of land. These Cobbses were part of the worldwide massive burst of discovery, colonization, and conquest that catapulted Europe out of feudalism and into commerce capitalism, the first stage of capitalist expansion that would amass the huge amounts of resources needed to make the industrialization of Europe and the United States possible. Its cost I can only describe as a maniacal decimation of other peoples and resources across the globe.

Western Europe, of course, did not invent empire building, the conquest of other peoples and appropriation of their resources justified by a sense of the conqueror's superiority.[2] But capitalism and modern technology allowed these behaviors much more global and totalizing effects than they had ever had before in what we know of human history. By 1914, Europe would control 80 percent of the globe: 283 million Europeans would rule 900 million non-European peoples.[3] Racism in the United States today cannot be understood outside of this context, that is, the emergence of capitalism in its commercial, industrial, and finance stages, and the global imperial agenda that it required.

In Africa and Asia, Europeans initially conducted their business from fortifications and limited their emphasis to trade, given the geographical, political, and climatic considerations in those vast continents. But the Americas, New Zealand, Australia, and South Africa became settler colonies, to which people like Ambrose Cobbs brought their families, intending to stay and take advantage of economic and political opportunities. Of all these settler colonies, only in the Americas would European colonials import Africans for slave labor, and it is from this fusion of settler colonization and chattel slavery that the particularly vicious character of U.S. racism emerges. "There is not a country in world history," concludes historian Howard Zinn, "in which racism has been more important, for so long, as in the United States."[4]

Ambrose and Joseph landed in Virginia six years before the first shipment of "negars" to the British colonies would debark in Virginia in 1619, recent starvation having sharpened British appetites for a source of added labor. By the Cobbses' arrival, however, European enslavement of Africans was almost two centuries old and had become "a fixture of the New World" in Latin America and the Caribbean. The English got the idea of enslaving Africans from Spain and Portugal. Explorers had brought Africans to Portugal to serve as slaves in the fifteenth century.[5] Slavery did exist in the African states to which Europe turned for slaves, but with nothing like the severity or inhumanity that European slavery derived from a relentless pursuit of profits and from racial hatreds.[6]

The Spanish and Portuguese also led the way in exploration and colonization, establishing the first basic and deadly practice of racism in the Americas: the genocide of native peoples necessary to control the new lands, and the enslavement of Africans for the labor needed to tap their wealth. Spanish conquistadors rapidly destroyed the centralized states of the Aztecs and Incas, partly because of the hierarchical nature of those cultures, partly because the Spanish had the advantage of gunpowder, horses, iron, and bacteria that spread European diseases with fatal results among the indigenous population.[7] By the end of the sixteenth century, Spain had a colonial empire twenty times its own size. So vast a territory would require massive amounts of human labor to yield its riches. The Spanish first tried indigenous labor, but the Indian population was soon decimated by the brutal nature of that labor and by disease. As one Jesuit remarked casually in 1583, "No one could believe that so great a supply [of labor] could ever be exhausted, much less in so short a time."[8] Practically the entire Indian population of the Caribbean was wiped out by the end of the seventeenth century. In 1492, indigenous people in the Americas totaled at least 70 million; by 1650, they had been reduced to 3.5 million.[9]

For anyone trying to understand racism, this terrible history brings us to a crucial question: What could allow for the deaths of 66.5 million people? Or for the deaths of an estimated 50 million Africans in the beginning centuries of the slave trade?[10] The Spanish and Portuguese, like the British after them, seemed driven by a psychosis of domination. It affected kings as well as soldiers, workers as well as priests. When Columbus wrote home about his first encounter with Indians, he described their amiableness and their love toward all others in preference to themselves, and his own confusions as to whether they had any private property.[11] When Cortés's forces slaughtered the Aztecs at the fiesta of Toxcatl, it came (according to an Aztec who was present) "at this moment in the fiesta, when the dance was loveliest and when song was linked to song, [when] the Spaniards were seized with an urge to kill the celebrants."[12] When the exploring party of Cabeza de Vaca lost three of its men in an accident, the survivors were amazed when the Indians who discovered them sat down among them and expressed a loud and earnest grief, feelings that the Spanish had not been able to muster for their own people.[13] It is this failure to feel the communal bonds between humans, I think, and the punishment that undoubtedly came to those Europeans who did, that allowed the "community of the lie" to grow so genocidally in the soil of the "New World." Historian Howard Zinn has pointed to a possible source of this European malady: tribal life, with its more communal spirit and kinder rules and punishments, had been destroyed in Europe by the slave societies of Greece and Rome.[14] What took its place was an individualism that was only sharpened by the drive for private ownership as Europe emerged from feudalism. The massive denial that results from the destruction of communal bonds is the undergirding of the epistemology or the "way of knowing" of genocide: We do not feel, and thus we cannot "know."

The silver that indigenous people were forced to mine during this period of genocide fueled Europe's economy while it killed the native people and sapped the natural resources of the colonies. By 1650 silver was 99 percent of the mineral exports of Spanish America, exceeding by at least three times the total European reserve. That silver passed to Dutch, French, Genoese, English, and German bankers. This enormous capital in northern Europe fueled the spirit of enterprise and financed manufacturing, which propelled the advent of the Industrial Revolution. The concentration of global wealth in Europe prevented the accumulation of industrial capital in the lands that produced the wealth. Conquest had shattered the foundations of native civilizations, and forced labor in mines or plantations destroyed the collective farming system, further punishing the people and land from which European wealth flowed. These historically created patterns of poverty are the source of what we now call "underdevelopment."[15]

Having exhausted the native supply of labor, the Spanish needed an alternative. However, the kidnapping and importing of Africans to use as slave labor did not become a profitable alternative until European consumption of chocolate and coffee imported from the colonies made the demand for sugar skyrocket; by the end of the 1500s, sugar was the most valuable agricultural product in international trade. The profits from sugar production offset the costs of the slave trade and opened Africa up as a new supply of labor.[16] It seems no accident that two of the cash crops that would make slavery profitable—sugar and tobacco—were highly addictive substances; the physiological responses to these substances further incorporated racism into the European body, demarcating European and "Other" as consumer and consumed. No wonder that in the late twentieth century, people all across the United States flocked to a host of twelve-step programs that offer a solution (whatever their political strengths and limits) to a proliferating sense of addiction.

England did not realize the potential in overseas exploration until the reign of Queen Elizabeth. The English did not get to Africa until 1550, and their encounter there with Africans would reverberate in the American colonies. The English, hailing from a small northern island, had more limited cultural experience than the Spanish or the Portuguese, who had both been conquered by a darker-skinned, more advanced Muslim civilization during the Middle Ages. When these Englishmen met Africans for the first time, one of the most fair-skinned peoples on the globe came into contact with one of the darkest, a difference reinforced by the existing dichotomy between dark and light in British culture. It led the English to see the Africans as both "black" and "heathen" and to link them immediately with barbarity, animalistic behavior, and the devil (not a healthy combination).[17]

The English were coming from a culture in which the Protestant Reformation required of its pious aspirants self-scrutiny and internalized control at an expansive time when medieval moral restraints seemed to be disintegrating. British (and other European) explorers projected their disquieting sexual feelings onto the darker, seemingly less inhibited peoples with whom they came in contact. For example, Europeans found both apes and Africans similarly lustful ("sexuality was what one expected of savages").

They concocted stories of cross-species copulation and of apes attacking African women.[18] It was with a shock of recognition that I read of these accounts in Winthrop Jordan's *White over Black*. I had just co-written *Quarantines and Death: The Far Right's Homophobic Agenda*, which discussed the contemporary neo-Nazi "explanation" for the origins of AIDS as cross-species copulation between Africans and monkeys.[19] That such racist mythology could find resonance across four centuries (I don't think the Nazis had been reading Jordan or the writings of early explorers) is cause for alarm. I hardly believe in "racial memory," but in the absence of such biological theories we have to account for the ways in which such cultural residues are kept alive and passed on from century to century. I think in the twentieth century the presence of overtly fascist movements is one medium of transmission, which is one reason why such movements are allowed by capitalists, the state, and regular white folks to operate.

This tendency of Christian European men to project sexual desire onto an Other and then to exterminate the "polluted" was already in practice in the witch burnings in Europe in the late Middle Ages and the early modern period. Estimates of the number of women executed range from thirty thousand to nine million—in a time period that coincides with the beginnings of imperial conquest.[20] Excessive female sexuality, as church documents explained, made women susceptible to witchcraft. "From 1480 to 1700, more women were killed for witchcraft than for other crimes put together," explains historian E. William Monter.[21] The emerging nation-state also needed to assert control over its male subjects' bodies at home and overseas. In 1533 Henry VIII's Parliament made the act of sodomy a crime, the first in a series of statutes that recodified as felonies crimes that were previously under the jurisdiction of church courts.[22]

Sixteenth-century biblical justifications for slavery based on the story of Noah and Ham also show how the European mind linked sexuality with racism. In fact, the Genesis story has no mention of race or color. After the Flood, Noah's son Ham looked on his father's nakedness while he lay drunk in his tent, the violation of a patriarchal injunction. For this, Noah cursed Canaan, son of Ham, saying he would be a "servant of servants" to his brothers.[23] According to Elizabethan commentators, Ham's posterity was cursed also with becoming "so blacke and lothsome, that it might remain a spectacle of disobedience to all the worlde. And of this blacke and cursed Chus came all these blacke Moores which are in Africa."[24] At a particular historical moment, emerging racism adopted patriarchy for its own ends.

Jews, the primary Other in Europe for much of the Middle Ages, were also receptacles of European Christian men's projections, and also received punishment. The Christian Crusades of the eleventh century intensified religious anti-Semitism in Europe, as did the role that Jews were forced to play in the money economy that emerged in part from the Crusades. Usury, like sexuality, was considered a sin, so Jews were forced as moneylenders into the marginal economy until that cash economy became profitable, then forced out in country after country, until capitalism replaced feudalism in Europe, with Christians in firm control of financial resources and with Jews as a convenient buffer class to obscure the real source of class oppression and to hedge Christians against their own guilt over a burgeoning materialism.

When the British turned to the West in search of profits for the private London Company, the history of European anti-Semitism, racism, and sexual repression shaped the laws and attitudes of their first permanent settlement at Jamestown, the entry point of the Cobbses into the history of North America.

Ambrose Cobbs died in 1656. His son Robert Cobbs had been born in 1620, the year the Pilgrims landed at Plymouth Rock. Robert Cobbs lived his sixty-two years in York County, Virginia, eventually holding the authority of justice of the peace and high sheriff. His life spanned the period when the practice of African chattel slavery developed in Virginia, a shift that also brought the emergence of white identity.

The British in America followed Spanish and Portuguese patterns of genocide of indigenous people and enslavement of Africans. Some historians feel, however, that British racism was even harsher than the Spanish variety, partly because the British did not have to reckon with the competing interests of the Catholic Church and partly because British capitalism was more ruthless as Britain gained control of the slave trade.[25] The British policy regarding the racial identity of the offspring of interracial unions was also much more rigid than that of the Spanish. British colonies used what Marvin Harris calls the "rule of hypo-descent," which categorized anyone with any African parentage as belonging to the subordinate race. This practice allowed plantation masters to have sexual access to Black women without jeopardizing the inheritance of white children; it also ensured that "whites" would remain relatively "pure," while "Blacks" became increasingly hybrid.[26]

The British employed slavery first on their sugar plantations in the Caribbean. As with Spanish silver, profits from the slave trade fueled European industrial development. The Royal Africa Company had been chartered in the 1670s, and between 1680 and 1688 it paid 300 percent in dividends, although 35 percent of its (human) African cargo did not survive the Middle Passage. Slave traffic made Bristol, its shipping center, Britain's second-largest city and Liverpool the world's largest port. Liverpool slave merchants made more than 1.1 million pounds a year from the Caribbean trade (at a time when an Englishman could live on six pounds a year). Banks grew, and Lloyds made money by insuring each step of the process. These slave profits financed Britain's Great Western Railway and its industries, and subsidized the invention of the steam engine.[27]

The slave trade profited New England as well. In the mid-1700s, northern slave ships left Boston for Africa with rum to trade for slaves, then sailed to the Caribbean and traded slaves for molasses, bringing that back to Massachusetts to distill into rum, with big profits made from each transaction. This slave trade helped develop the northern naval industry and distilleries and created a market for agricultural and manufacturing exports.[28]

This history of European-U.S. economic development provides the context we need to understand programs such as affirmative action, which seem a puny enough redress to centuries of rape of resources and labor and women. According to the 1990 U.S. census figures, African Americans still made only half the wages of whites but had one-tenth the wealth, because many whites still inherited the cumulative effect of centuries of appropriation.[29]

Sugar made slavery profitable in the Caribbean. Tobacco was the cash crop on the Atlantic seaboard, and in the tobacco colonies of Virginia and Maryland African slavery developed in three phases.

Between 1619, the year before Robert Cobbs was born, and 1640, the year after his family received a land grant, the British imported Africans gradually, with no set policies. But by 1640 evidence mounts that Africans were being subjected to the twin characteristics of slavery—lifetime servitude and inherited slave status. Both of these were very different from the indentured servitude of Europeans and the "tendency toward liberty" of English common law. Along with this emerging practice came the debasement of Africans through discriminatory laws and practices, such as the barring of interracial sexual unions and not allowing Africans to purchase arms.[30] British jurisprudence—the American version of which various Cobbses would help to implant—codified an emerging American racism. Little wonder that when I sat in North Carolina courts monitoring trials of racist attackers I despaired of justice from a legal system that itself helped to invent the racist distinctions between "slave" and "free."

The Cobbses probably used their 350 acres to grow tobacco, the main cash crop of Virginia. That acreage hardly made them part of the planter aristocracy, but it was probably a large enough tract to "require" a small number of slaves. The Cobbses were probably also affected in the 1660s when the price of tobacco dropped in Virginia, and with this economic pressure "unmitigated capitalism" (in Stanley Elkins's terms) became "unmitigated slavery," as colonists realized the extra dividend of inherited slave labor.[31] As a justice of the peace, Robert Cobbs doubtless reacted to Bacon's Rebellion in 1676, an uprising of African slaves and white indentured and unemployed workers against the planter aristocracy.

To forestall such revolutionary alliances across race lines, colonial rulers had already begun extending to all European settlers the rights initially given to Englishmen. By 1671, the British began encouraging the naturalization of Scots, Welsh, and Irish to enjoy "all such liberties, priviledges, immunities whatsoever, as a naturall borne Englishman."[32] In the same decade, the Virginia Assembly passed a law that "the conferring of baptism doth not alter the condition of the person as to his bondage or freedome": Africans could be converted to Christianity but still remain slaves.[33] (I wonder whether Robert Cobbs in his role as first vestryman of Bruton Parish Church in

Williamsburg agonized at all over the contradiction between "saved" soul and enslaved soul.) Historian Winthrop Jordan comments, "From the initially most common term *Christian*, at mid-century there was a marked drift toward *English* and *free*. After about 1680, taking the colonies as a whole, a new term appeared—*white*."[34]

Robert Cobbs's life spanned the period in U.S. history when white people were "invented" to give Europeans a common identity against Africans. His son Robert Cobbs Jr. was born in 1660 and lived until 1725, serving as constable and vestryman. It was during Robert junior's lifetime that slavery was finally consolidated into a police state in the mid-Atlantic colonies. By 1705 Virginia consolidated a generation of random statutes into a "slave code." With police power and the legal equation between Africans and slavery in place, African slaves were brought to the colonies in unprecedented numbers in a period that Jordan calls the "unthinking acquiescence" to slavery and its presuppositions.[35]

This creation of white identity in late seventeenth-century Virginia is what James Baldwin recognized. The implications are profound: if we white folks were constructed by history, we can, over time and as a people, unconstruct ourselves. The Klan knows this possibility and recognizes those whites who disavow this history as "white niggers," "race traitors," and "nigger lovers." How, then, to move masses of white people to become traitors to the concept of race?[36]

2

Industrial Capitalism

"Slavery Is Nothing Compared to It . . ."

My great-great-great-great-grandfather James Cobbs was a captain of the militia in the American Revolution—he is my claim to membership in the Daughters of the American Revolution. He was born in 1735. After the war, he was granted large tracts of land in Kentucky and South Carolina, which he willed to his sons at his death on or before 1800. During James Cobbs's lifetime, Europe entered a new phase of capitalism, its industrial phase, made possible by technology that adopted new energy sources and machines for manufacturing and by the development of the factory system. Profit-making from manufacturing was at the heart of industrial capitalism, as money became concentrated in the hands of the middle class. Both the American Revolution and the Civil War would be fought over who would reap the profits of industrialism on the vast continent. In the British colonies, commerce capitalism had demarcated whiteness against and above both Africans and Indians; in the new nation, industrial capitalism would add Mexicans and Asians to a racially demarcated underclass.

As the market revolution expanded, African, Indian, Mexican, and Asian peoples were written into sectors of the economy differently.

African Americans were tied to the southern agrarian/slave economy, Mexicans to the "free" and soon-to-be-freed territory of the Southwest appropriated after an official war, and Asians to the "free" agricultural and industrial labor system of California and Hawaii. Indians resisted incorporation into any labor system and thus were the objects of open warfare, land appropriation, and the reservation system.

The American Revolution was fought on the cusp of the Industrial Revolution in America. It was precipitated by England's victory over France in a struggle for control of increasingly profitable colonies in North America, the West Indies, and India. After four global wars fought in the first half of the 1700s, England emerged in 1763 as the leading colonial power in the world, a position the British would hold until the mid-twentieth century, when the United States assumed hegemony. England's victory over France, however, eventually led to the loss of England's richest claim, the thirteen colonies in North America, because England began to tighten the bonds of empire that previously had been laxly enforced in America, in order to pass on the costs of the war. British taxation, through such acts as the Stamp Act and the Tea Act, led to the colonials' cry of "no taxation without representation" and to the Continental Congresses and the Declaration of Independence.

The "self-evident truths" that Jefferson used to explain the colonists' revolt were not merely the more cold-blooded "right" to profit but also the "inalienable rights" of "life, liberty, and the pursuit of happiness"—hardly consistent with the practices of genocide or chattel slavery that had helped create the profits the colonists were so loath to have taxed. In fact, the new Constitution, created in 1787, wrote racial inequity into the new nation's founding document in the Three-Fifths Compromise, in which slaves were counted as three-fifths human for the purpose of determining the population base for propertied white male representation. Abolition of the slave trade ("the Migration or Importation of such Persons as any of the States now existing shall think proper to admit") was forbidden for twenty years.[1]

If the white framers of the Constitution did not apply natural rights to Blacks and Indians, the people of Haiti did, as Haiti became the next country in the Americas to follow the revolutionary example, overthrowing French domination in a bloody revolt. The aftershocks of Haiti's uprising persuaded Napoleon to sell off the Louisiana territory to the United States in 1803, ironically opening up more territory for slavery and for relocation of Indians. The Haitian Revolution also terrified the white authors of American liberty, inspired North American slaves, and sent tremors through southern households, including, perhaps, the Cobbses'.

One of the first concerns of the new nation was economic independence from Britain. The large-scale agriculture of the plantation system in the South was the southern face of the Industrial Revolution. Textile manufacturing in the North using the new technology ushered in the beginning of the factory system in the United States, which was based in New England but used southern cotton. Thus when the Industrial Revolution reached American shores, it set up interdependent but competing economic systems, one dependent on "free" white labor, the other on the slave labor of Africans.

James Cobbs's son Thomas Cobb (born in 1764, the year after the Treaty of Paris) sold off part of the land he inherited from James and moved to Georgia.[2] He was a lawyer and became a judge. He died in 1816, willing his farm to his son. Perhaps he moved south in the years after the Revolution because of depleted soil and a glutted tobacco market, which brought a severe depression in the tobacco colonies. The price of slaves declined, and there was reason to believe that slavery as a practice might pass. But here the momentum of racism overrode short-term economic motives, and the planters sustained losses. The invention of the cotton gin in 1792 broke the bottleneck in textile production and ushered in "a period of economic change . . . that, in degree, compared favorably with any changes in the history of agriculture."[3] Cotton became the new cash crop on which slavery could thrive. The United States produced 6,000 bales of cotton in 1792; by 1810 it was producing 178,000 bales, and by 1860 over 5 million.[4]

About the time Thomas Cobb left Virginia and headed with his family to Georgia, the economic center of the slave colonies shifted from the mid-Atlantic to the "Cotton Kingdom" of the Deep South, where soil had not been depleted by tobacco production. The new states of Louisiana (admitted to the Union in 1812), Mississippi (1817), and Alabama (1819) were swelled by slaves and by immigrants like Thomas Cobb. The population of the Cotton Kingdom rose from forty thousand in 1810 to one million thirty years later.[5] The abolition movement won the end of the international slave trade in 1808, but a white supremacist economy adjusted, as the Atlantic states substituted breeding slaves as the "cash crop" to replace tobacco—what historian John Hope Franklin calls "one of the most fantastic manipulations of human development in the history of mankind."[6] In 1790 there were fewer than seven hundred thousand slaves in the United States. By 1830 there were two million. By 1860 there were almost four million slaves.[7] Boston judge Samuel Sewall at the turn of the eighteenth century had declared, "[Africans can] never embody with us and grow up into orderly Families, to the Peopling of the land."[8] Clearly, the American "family" was being ideologically constructed as white. The bonds of biological and emotional families outside of whiteness had no protection, an inhumanity that, I suspect, has considerably eroded emotional bonds within white families as well.

Southern and westward expansion created the need for a new Indian policy. From the first colonial settlements in the early 1600s, North American Indians (in less hierarchical, more egalitarian tribal arrangements than the Aztecs or Incas) had resisted assimilation into the labor system.[9] At first, settlers in clearly vulnerable positions on the edge of the continent had been friendly to the Indians who helped them survive. Then, when the English settlements became permanent and stockpiled arms, their attitudes shifted. The Massachusetts colonists massacred the Pequots only sixteen years after the first settlements in New England, at about the same time slavery was consolidating in Virginia. As one colonist described the attack: "[Many Indians] were burnt in the fort, both men, women, and children; others [who were] forced out . . . our soldiers received and entertained with the point of the sword. Down fell men, women, and children."[10] The Pequots were the first New England tribe to feel the genocidal effect of the English and the implications of their style of battle, which was intended, in the words of one officer, to "conquer and subdue." By the French and Indian War (1754–63), every colony but Georgia and

Pennsylvania had engaged in a bloody war with the tribes in its region, as native resistance to the colonial presence intensified.[11]

After the Revolution, the "white lie" of the new nation showed in an Indian policy that developed in the highest councils of state into a cold-blooded rationale for "extinction." In 1783, Congress forbade white settlement on Indian lands, the first of many such statements to be ignored by settlers and land speculators. In 1786, Secretary of State Henry Knox shifted Indian policy from "right of conquest" to "right of purchase" unless in a "just war"—a shift that led mainly to manipulative purchases and an increase in legalistic explanations for war.[12]

President Thomas Jefferson, "author of American liberty," began a two-faced Indian policy of urging assimilation but planning for Indian removal. He viewed the hunting, nomadic life of most tribes as lazy because it did not fit into the mostly agrarian U.S. economy. He urged "his children" to give up hunting and learn to farm—to "persuade our red brethren then to be sober, and to cultivate their lands; and their women to spin and weave for their families."[13] On the other hand, he waged a secret campaign for Indian land, regarding the territories newly acquired by the Louisiana Purchase as a good place to relocate Indian tribes. One deliberate intent of encouraging Indians to abandon hunting was to turn them into debt-ridden consumers at government trading posts: "To promote this disposition to exchange lands, which they have to spare and we want, for necessaries, which we have to spare and they want, we shall push our trading uses, and be glad to see the good and influential individuals among them run in debt," Jefferson wrote to Governor William Henry Harrison, who was legally responsible for keeping white settlers away from Indians in his territory. If any tribe fought back, the government would "[seize] the whole country of that tribe and [drive] them across the Mississippi."[14]

By the 1820s, the western territories opened by the War of 1812 were viewed by settlers as good places to relocate native peoples, since the West with its treeless plains was considered unsuitable for white people.[15] Between 1816 and 1848, twelve new states joined the union, carved out of Indian country. John Adams wrote to a friend in 1818, "Shall we say that a few handfuls of scattering tribes of savages have a right of dominion and property over a quarter of this globe capable of nourishing hundreds of millions of happy human beings?"[16] According to President John Quincy Adams's memoirs, Secretary of State Henry Clay explained in an 1825 cabinet meeting how it was "impossible to civilize Indians," so they were "destined to extinction," and

> although he would never use or countenance inhumanity towards them, he did not think them, as a race, worth preserving. He considered them as essentially inferior to the Anglo-saxon race, which were now taking their place on this continent. They were an improbable breed, and their disappearance from the human family will be no great loss to the world.[17]

In 1828, Georgians such as Thomas Cobb's son William, itching for land of the "Five Civilized Tribes," passed laws extending the state's control over Indian lands, in clear violation of the Constitution. When the Cherokees refused to emigrate after the Indian Relocation Act of 1830, Supreme Court Chief Justice John Marshall upheld their position, but President Jackson refused to enforce it, forcing relocation instead, explaining that contact with whites would "degrade and destroy Indians." In 1812, Jackson had led forces that killed 850 Creeks at the Battle of Horseshoe Bend, "those deluded victims doomed to destruction by their own restless and savage conduct."[18] On the Cherokees' "Trail of Tears," a forced march to Oklahoma begun in 1836, one-quarter to one-third of the sixteen thousand Cherokees died. President Jackson's blatantly unconstitutional action was a disregard for the facade of "justice" that Jefferson could not have mustered.

Several thousand Seminoles in Florida refused to relocate, many of them escapees from Georgia and South Carolina. They were joined by several hundred African Americans, escaped slaves or the descendants of slaves, who could slip on and off plantations, bringing information gathered by slaves. Under the leadership of Chief Osceola, they waged a guerrilla campaign (the Second Seminole War) against the U.S. troops Jackson sent with instructions to find their villages and to capture or destroy the village women.[19] "If strong measures are not taken to restrain our slaves, there is but little doubt that we should soon be assailed with a servile as well as Indian war," reported Major Benjamin Putnam to the secretary of war.[20] William Cobb of Columbia County, Georgia, was thirty-eight when he served under Jackson against the Seminoles and escaped slaves.

The Seminole Wars were only one of many acts of resistance by people of color to the racist practices of Europeans. From the beginning of the slave trade, as Vincent Harding chronicles, Africans had seized control of slave ships or jumped overboard, preferring drowning to slavery; once in the Americas, many Africans ran off to join bands of Maroons in the Caribbean or the Seminoles in Florida, or to initiate slave rebellions on plantations. In 1831, several years before the Second Seminole War, Nat Turner led a slave uprising in Virginia that killed sixty whites in twenty-four hours, explaining to his followers that theirs was not a war "for robbery, nor to satisfy our passions; . . . [but a] struggle for freedom."[21] From the beginning, Indian tribes had engaged in prolonged warfare against white encroachment.

While William Cobb was soldiering for Jackson, the movement to abolish slavery became the first strong interracial anti-racist movement in the United States. The egalitarian strain in Christianity, combined with a rise in humanitarianism, produced the white abolition movement, which for the first time among whites challenged slavery in an organized way. Of the fifteen known white condemnations of slavery before 1750, all were by Quakers, who themselves had undergone years of persecution for doctrinal heresy.[22] White abolitionism coincided with a growing number of free Blacks in northern states. The doctrine of natural rights that justified the American Revolution, if it did not in fact protect African Americans or Indians, did give ideological impetus to both white and Black abolitionists. In 1794, delegates from nine anti-slavery societies met in Philadelphia. Northern states abolished slavery in the two decades after the Revolution, and many southern states allowed manumission, or voluntary freeing of slaves. By 1808, the first year after the constitutional protection of the slave trade expired, abolition sentiment and fear of Black uprisings were enough to abolish the international slave trade—the high-water mark of early abolitionist struggle.

The 1830s brought a new upsurge in abolitionist organizing, as sharpening economic differences between the slave states of the Cotton Kingdom and the wage labor of the Northeast caused increasing sectional conflict. White abolitionists led by William Lloyd Garrison took on a more militant stance, abandoning gradualism to argue for immediate abolition. In 1831 the New England Anti-Slavery Society was founded, followed in 1833 by the American Anti-Slavery Society.

It was from this interracial abolition movement that the first feminist organizing emerged. Black women such as Maria Steward, Harriet Tubman, Sojourner Truth, and Sarah Redmond and the white Grimké sisters (who had been run out of South Carolina for their opposition to slavery) joined the question of racial slavery with that of women's rights. They had the cooperation of male supporters of women's rights such as Frederick Douglass. This radical analysis emerged as a contradiction to the moment when growing industrialism encouraged the "cult of true womanhood," confining pious, domestic, submissive, and pure—therefore middle class—"true" women to the home at a time when more and more poor women were entering the factory workforce.[23] Disagreements over the role of women in the abolition movement eventually helped to split the American Anti-Slavery Society. White racism also split the abolition movement.

Martin Delany observed that African Americans within the abolition movement occupied a similar "underling position" to whites as in the general culture, racist practices that contributed to increasing autonomy in Black organizing. By 1830, there were 319,000 free Blacks in the United States, many of whom were subject to the northern racism of white mob violence and denial of education and jobs and land that would become the model for Jim Crow. A radical Black analysis began to emerge from such people as David Walker and Martin Delany, who began to target not just slavery but the federal government for its anti-Black policies, combining an analysis of racism for the first time with an analysis of economic exploitation. Delany began to advocate for more separatist and nationalist Black strategy, while Frederick Douglass continued to argue for integration into the U.S. political system.[24] Historian Vincent Harding points to a similar emergence in the 1960s of Black nationalist strategies from a disillusionment with interracial activism.

Indian fighter William Cobb's life spanned the advent of the market economy in the United States. In the early years of the nineteenth century, the "Market Revolution" marked the takeoff of the U.S. economy in a period of entrepreneurial ferment. In 1800, the cost of transporting a ton of goods thirty miles overland was as much as shipping it three thousand miles to Europe. Advances in transportation and increasing urbanization (the U.S. urban population increased from 5 percent to 20 percent of the country's total from 1800 to 1860) broke down barriers and created the space in which a sectored market emerged as a central force in U.S. society, with the East providing manufactured goods and commerce, the West foodstuffs, and the South cotton, both for eastern textile mills and for Europe. Because cotton was the commodity that sold on an international market and thus brought in extra capital, the entire economy depended for its growth on the cotton trade, which depended on stolen Indian land and unpaid African labor.[25]

The Jackson administration (1829–37) had been a period of increased democratization for white U.S. citizens as frontiersmen challenged the patrician rule of the previous forty years. Constitutional changes in a number of states widened suffrage, in some cases giving the vote to all adult white males. These votes brought Jackson to the White House. In the late 1600s, white rights had expanded at a period of intense contraction of rights for Africans (the consolidation of chattel slavery). In the 1820s, expanding white political freedom across class lines came at the same historical moment as Indian removal and Sam Houston's appropriation of Mexican land and a viewing of African Americans as "anti-citizens."[26] White democracy, it seems, gets built on the backs of people of color, a fact that gives white people a very different subjective experience of U.S. democracy than many people of color have. Congressman Alexander Duncan observed without conscious irony in 1845: "There seems to be something in our laws and institutions peculiarly adapted to the Anglo-Saxon American race, under which they will thrive and prosper but under which all others wilt and die. . . . There is something mysterious about it."[27]

The Market Revolution reshaped U.S. citizens not only as consumers, but also as workers subject to the labor discipline required by industrial capitalism. A white working class emerged, defining itself in Republican terms as "free laborers" in contradistinction to the despised and forced-labor roles of African slaves. Labor historians George Rawick and David Roediger have suggested that Blacks came to symbolize their pre-industrial way of life for whites: "Increasingly adopting an ethos that attacked holidays, spurned contact with nature, saved time, bridled sexuality, separated work from the rest of life and postponed gratification, profit-minded Englishmen and Americans cast Blacks as their former selves."[28]

William Cobb's son James was born in 1835, the year before his father went off to fight in the Second Seminole War. James would himself fight in the Civil War to defend the agrarian slave economy against the wage labor system of the North as the culmination of the competition over which form of economy would prevail in the expanding U.S. territories. If Robert was the first "white" Cobb, James was the first "southern" one, since defense of the increasingly profitable slave system rose to fever pitch and consolidated the identity of the slave states as "southern" in the three decades before the Civil War broke out. Like Thomas Cobb's migration to Georgia, his grandson James's migration to Texas in 1857, where he went to practice law, was made possible by appropriation of land—this time, the land of Mexico. After the Louisiana Purchase, the next major block of territory to the west belonged to Spain. Jefferson had commented in 1809, "[The Spanish borderlands] are ours the first moment war is forced upon us."[29] It was the kind of "just war" that the U.S. government had become expert in rationalizing against Indians.

"New Spain" reached from what is now Utah to Central America in 1810, when the native or mestizo inhabitants of Mexico began their revolution against Spanish colonial control. The country of Mexico that they won in 1821 was already sapped of many of its resources because of three hundred years of colonial rule. Mexico was bankrupt and needed time to build a unifying infrastructure. The United States, on the other hand, was an expanding white settler state, its southern economy underwritten by slave labor and its profits firmly in the hands of its industrial class. The U.S. population encompassed seventeen million people of European descent, three million slaves, and fewer than a million Indians; Mexico's population was four million Indians and three million mestizos and Europeans.[30] Anglo Americans began to covet Mexican territory more aggressively after Mexican independence. Sam Houston's and Stephen Austin's men took over a million square miles and established the Republic of Texas by defeating the army of Santa Anna in 1836. Then in 1845, the United States annexed Texas and provoked a war with Mexico by claiming territory to the Rio Grande. U.S. victory resulted in Mexico's ceding what is now California, New Mexico, Nevada, parts of Colorado, Arizona, and Utah for only $15 million. The statement of rights for former Mexican citizens that Mexican negotiators fought to include in the Treaty of Guadalupe Hidalgo was uniformly violated, and Mexican Americans quickly became an underclass in the rapidly expanding Anglo American political and economic system.[31]

With California part of U.S. territory, the country had reached the Pacific Ocean; the invention of steam transportation, both trains and boats, opened up Asia as a source of markets and labor. European imperialism in Asia was likewise creating conditions that propelled its workforce toward the United States. Most of the Chinese immigrants came from Guangdong, driven to the United States by peasant rebellions and the British opium wars of 1839–42 and 1856–60. Many Chinese immigrated to avoid starvation.[32]

Asians were the only non-European peoples during the nineteenth century who immigrated to the United States for economic opportunity. (Mexicans were incorporated by land appropriation, as were Indians. Africans were imported for slave labor.) They were treated very differently than European immigrants, however. Immigration policy, repression, and racist violence were used to keep Asians as a "reserve labor force." Like Africans in the Caribbean, the pattern of Asian labor was established on island sugarcane plantations in Hawaii. William Hooper, a Boston visitor to a sugar mill on the island of Kauai in 1835, noticed a small group of Chinese workers and wrote home to the New England businessmen who had sent him there: "They have to work all the time—and no regard is paid to their complaints for food, etc., etc. Slavery is nothing compared to it."[33]

At about the same time the Royal Hawaiian Agricultural Society was importing Chinese to Hawaii, Chinese also began immigrating to the West Coast of the United States. The year after the Treaty of Guadalupe Hidalgo ceded California to the United States, gold was discovered there, bringing a wave of new settlers to the great Gold Rush of '49. There were 325 Chinese among the prospectors in 1849. Three years later, 20,000 Chinese had immigrated, and by 1870 there were 63,000 Chinese in the United States, 77 percent in California, where they constituted one-quarter of the entire workforce. In the first year or two, they were welcomed, but the nativism of white miners rapidly contracted the space in which they were allowed to operate.[34]

James Cobb lost his law library in a fire in 1860. Penniless, he taught school in Liberty, Texas, until Texas seceded from the union. James joined Company F of the Fifth Texas Regiment as a private, and he was soon promoted to second lieutenant, then first lieutenant. He was captured at the Battle of Gettysburg and spent the rest of the war in a series of northern prisons. Soon after the war, he settled in Alabama. According to family records, there he "made a name and fame as a jurist and statesmen of which Alabama may well be proud . . . succeeding in every thing that he undertook and with energy and foresight made his impress in politics, in the church, and in his daily intercourse with his fellow man." Other records show that he was one of many white men instrumental in reasserting white supremacy, both regionally and nationally, in the decades following the South's defeat in the Civil War.

3

Finance Capitalism

"Nothing We Could Do but Take Them All . . ."

James Cobb returned to Alabama part of an army whose defeat had settled the issue over whether slave or wage labor would prevail and opened up all the mainland territory to the expanding industrial economy. In Europe and the United States the years between 1870 and 1914 brought a new surge of industrial and technological progress. The invention of electricity, wireless telegraphy, refrigeration, the dynamo, and the gas engine helped create the "New Industrial Revolution." It was fueled by industrial research that systematized inventions, mass production techniques, and the assembly line, and breakthroughs in chemistry that created new synthetic materials, such as early plastics. Business consolidated into huge new structures such as trusts and cartels to control markets and sources of raw material necessary for the new products. Increasingly, the chief source of profits would come from the process of finance itself. The northern United States, Germany, and Japan emerged to rival Britain as industrial powers.

Within the United States, burgeoning industry brought suddenly skewed distribution of wealth. In 1889, total manufacturing capital in the United States was $5,697 trillion; in 1900 it was $8,663 trillion. In 1890, the wealthiest 1 percent of families owned 51 percent of real and personal property, while the 44 percent of families at the bottom owned only 1.2 percent. The 88 percent of families in the poor and middle classes combined owned only 14 percent of the wealth.[1] These inequities, periodic depressions, and the expanding power of business brought intense labor agitation in the late nineteenth century, as new waves of immigrants from eastern Europe entered the industrial work-force. These eastern European workers were often viewed as being of different "races" than northern Europeans.[2] However, much like in the 1600s when other northern Europeans were given the privileges of Englishmen, after Reconstruction the category of "whiteness" was expanded to take in all Europeans (even Jews). Eastern Europeans battled their way into the white working class, while non-Europeans were often excluded from the unions and the economic progress that resulted from labor struggles.[3] Like the "cult of true womanhood" that worked to draw the line around who was a "real woman," race ide-ology created a highly elastic "cult of true whiteness"; both of these seemingly biological categories drew their power in part from their volatility and their power to exclude.

This expanding economy, whose benefits within the United States flowed differentially according to race, led the United States for the first time to carry out imperial conquests beyond the limits of North America and eventually to overtake Britain as the world's foremost imperialist power. The imperialism that accompanied finance capital-ism linked people of color in the United States even more closely to their continents and nations of origin. As in industrial capitalism, in finance capitalism the roles of various nationalities and communities of color within the United States depended in part on that group's role in a sectored economy.

When James Cobb returned from Yankee prison camps, eman-cipated slaves in the South were experiencing a brief period of in-creased freedom and economic promise during Reconstruction. The Thirteenth, Fourteenth, and Fifteenth Amendments helped to rectify the injustice built into the original Constitution, not only for Afri-can Americans but for other people of color as well. But after four decades of intense sectional conflict, northern and southern whites closed ranks, to the detriment of all people of color both in the United States and globally.

In 1874, James Cobb was elected judge in Macon County on the Democratic ticket, and he did his part to restore white rule to his county, sentencing two Black legislators to the chain gang for larceny and adultery and persuading a white Republican to leave town by indicting him for perjury. Judge Cobb opposed the white businessmen in Tuskegee who supported Booker T. Washington's plans to build a school for African Americans. Cobb was elected to Congress in 1884.[4] James Cobb's training as a lawyer and his role as a judge was in keeping with his Cobb forebears, who were consistently part of the judiciary and police in the emerging racist disciplinary structures. He was not, nor were they, part of the capitalist class who owned the plantations or, after the war, profited hugely from the development of an industrial economy. During his lifetime, New South industrialists would link up for the first time with northern capitalists. Sharecropping and debt peonage replaced slavery for Black workers who were shut out of most union organizing during this period as white workers joined the mill villages in the textile industry of the newly industrializing South.

As the South shifted back toward white control, marking James Cobb's passage from defeated soldier to Democratic judge, northern opinion also began to shift. Former abolitionists, like "neoconservatives" a century later, moved to the right, speaking for the prosperous, educated classes. In publications such as *The Nation* and the *Atlantic Monthly*, these men "mouth[ed] the shibboleths of white supremacy regarding the Negro's innate inferiority, shiftlessness, and hopeless unfitness for full participation in the white man's civilization."[5] A succession of Supreme Court decisions between 1873 and 1898 closed the political space opened by the post–Civil War amendments, leading to "separate but equal" segregation in *Plessy v. Ferguson* in 1896.[6]

As racist propaganda and state-instituted repression surged, racist violence escalated, fueled by a racist mythology. Philip Bruce explained in *The Plantation Negro as a Freeman* (1889) that Black males, cut off from the civilizing influence of whites, had regressed to African type and were raping white women.[7] Whites rioted and murdered all over the South, lynching 2,060 Blacks between 1882 and 1930, some of the victims children and pregnant women. It was not the African who had regressed: some of the Black victims were castrated, burned at the stake, decapitated, or blinded with hot pokers.[8]

In the 1880s and 1890s, a severe economic depression fueled an insurgent interracial populism that offered a radical challenge to the southern elite. Tom Watson, foremost leader of southern populism, declared that the Populist Party would settle the race question "by presenting a platform immensely beneficial to both races and injurious to neither." Watson explained that race hatred rested on "the keystone arch of financial despotism which enslaves you both . . . [and] a money system which beggars you both." In Georgia in 1892, two thousand armed white farmers came to the defense of a Black populist threatened with lynching, and in 1896 Georgia populists denounced the lynch law. Blacks were admitted to the inner circles of the party, serving with whites as party delegates and officials and speaking from the same platform to interracial audiences.[9]

This class alliance alarmed southern conservatives, who had made their alliances with northeastern financial interests, and they mounted a campaign of repression, using fraud, terror, and race-baiting. Conservatives stole Black votes, and Populist Party candidates were defeated by these forged ballots. The resulting frustration and bitterness dissolved the Black-white coalition, leading the way for intensified racial repression and violence. Tom Watson turned racist and campaigned in 1906 on what Woodward calls a platform of "Negrophobia and progressivism."[10]

In the 1890s, James Cobb seems to have stolen at least one, if not two, elections from Populist candidates. Voter fraud was so obvious in 1894 that Congress threw out his election and seated his Populist opponent. By the turn of the century, the South was in the throes of a resurgent white supremacy. All over the South, legislatures enacted segregation laws and disenfranchised Black as well as poor white voters, inaugurating the rule of Jim Crow. One of James Cobb's last official acts in 1901, at the age of sixty-six, was to participate in the Alabama constitutional convention that brought segregation and disenfranchisement to Alabama before he went to New Mexico for his final years.

African Americans, numbering about eight million, were the largest non-white population in the United States at the turn of the century. But the rising racism fueled by expanding capitalism devastated other communities of color as well. The Chinese had migrated to the West Coast in large numbers in the 1840s, 1850s, and 1860s. Capitalists in California looked to the Chinese to do the hard labor that white workers refused to do: the building of the western section of the transcontinental railroads, service work in mining camps, backbreaking agricultural production, and manufacturing in western cities. "The introduction of machinery was rendering Black labor obsolete, it was claimed, for what was required in an industrial mode of production was a 'much higher standard of intelligence.'" Chinese became both servants and factory proletariat.[11] In 1882, organized labor turned against "coolie" workers, and Congress passed the Chinese Exclusion Act, barring the entry of Chinese laborers into the country and denying them the vote and citizenship. Chinese were also the targets of white mobs, with eighteen Chinese lynched in Los Angeles in a single incident in 1871 and twenty-eight Chinese murdered in Rock Springs, Wyoming, in 1885.[12] Like the African presence during slavery, the Chinese presence on the West Coast helped to consolidate the white working class. Many white workers got a start toward economic self-sufficiency, as one railroad builder explained, "by controlling Chinese labor on our railroad."[13] The Chinese functioned as a kind of internal colony of "nonwhites allowed to enter as 'cheap' migratory laborers and members of a racially subordinated group, not future citizens of American society."[14]

Indians, who were not willing to be assimilated into the U.S. workforce, fought a new set of wars for western territory. The federal government's genocidal policy toward Indians, established in the early years of the century, played itself out. After the Civil War western expansion into "treeless" territory once thought unfit for white habitation led to demands for a new wave of military conquest of Indian tribes. There were bloody battles in the 1870s and 1880s, with surviving members of tribes put in reservations, land that government policy then set out to steal. The Dawes Severalty Act of 1887 intended to break up communally owned reservation land and allow for purchase of "surplus" by white settlers, leading to a decline in reservation land from 138 million acres in 1887 to 78 million in 1900. In 1890 at Wounded Knee, the U.S. Army attacked warriors of the Ghost Dance, the last burst of Indian resistance in the nineteenth century, killing 146 men, women, and children. By 1910, the policies of Jefferson and Jackson had borne their deadly fruit: there were only 222,000 Indians in the United States, a population reduced by two-thirds in only a hundred years.[15]

In the Southwest, the years of rapid industrialization after the Civil War brought the appropriation of Mexican American land and the forcing of Mexicans into a dual-wage labor system in mining and agriculture. New Mexico and Arizona remained territories until the twentieth century because their populations were not white majorities. In New Mexico, where land was the major resource, the Anglo American colonizers destroyed communal land holdings through use of private land grants. Anglos also took control of the open range, where cattle raisers established monopolies on grazing and pushed out Mexican subsistence farmers, who began to accumulate in urban barrios.[16]

The completion of the railroad opened the Southwest to an intensified exploitation of its mineral and agricultural resources in which Mexican American workers became the lowest level of labor in the mines, on the railroads, and on communal farms. Often Anglo workers insisted on twice the wages of Mexican workers.[17] Throughout the Southwest, Mexican Americans fought back against white violence, and armed rebellion was common. When even the most radical unions excluded Mexican American workers, they organized in *mutualistas*. In the Clifton-Morenci strike of 1903, upward of fifteen hundred miners—80 percent to 90 percent Mexican or Mexican American—armed themselves and occupied the mines. Strikes in 1906, 1915, and 1917 convinced mine owners that Mexicans were hardly "docile" laborers, and farmers began to import Filipino workers to replace them.[18]

The treatment of the four major non-European populations by whites in the United States over the course of the nineteenth century shows the way in which an expanding white supremacy scripted people of color into specific economic and psychological roles. "Next to the case of the black race within our bosom, that of the red on our borders is the problem baffling to the policy of the country," former president James Madison explained in 1826.[19] Slavery in the nation's "bosom" made anti-Black racism inescapably intimate and domestic; the relative independence of indigenous peoples on the "frontiers" caused open warfare that led to the decimation of Indian peoples and the reservation policy. These racist practices and ideas were then extended to other non-European people. Sam Houston explained glibly when he took over Texas that the United States had always cheated Indians, and Mexicans were no better than Indians.[20] Planters in Hawaii expected to find "coolie" labor "far more certain, systematic, and economic than that of the native," as one explained.[21] There, planters systematically diversified immigrant populations, paying Portuguese, Japanese, Chinese, and Koreans different wages for the same work to prevent class solidarity. "By employing different nationalities, there is less danger of collusion among laborers and the employers [are able to] secure better discipline," a planter explained.[22] On the U.S. mainland, the Chinese were identified with the already developed stereotypes used on African Americans and were called "nagurs."[23] The Chinese were also viewed as quieter and more intelligent and generally more fitted for an industrial labor force. By playing off national and racial groups, capitalism created not one but a series of racisms that buttressed each other and a series of working classes that allowed people of color to be played off against one another. It was a potent strategy.

It was not just white men who shifted sharply to the right in the last half of the nineteenth century. White women leaders of the women's rights movement accompanied them, breaking with the interracial, anti-racist origins of U.S. women's organizing in the abolition movement. The split came with the debate on the Fifteenth Amendment. By 1867, it became clear that Republicans would allow female suffrage or Black suffrage, but not both (and excluding, in both cases, Black women). White feminist leaders Susan B. Anthony and Elizabeth Cady Stanton teamed up with millionaire Democrat George Train, who financed *The Revolution*, their women's rights newspaper, and implemented an increasingly racist suffrage strategy. "While the dominant party have with one hand lifted up TWO MILLION BLACK MEN and crowned them with the honor and dignity of citizenship," it read, "with the other they have dethroned FIFTEEN MILLION WHITE WOMEN— their own mothers and sisters, their own wives and daughters—and cast them under the heel of the lowest orders of manhood." Stanton, writing of a lynching in Tennessee, said, "The Republican cry of 'Manhood Suffrage' creates an antagonism between black men and all women that will culminate in fearful outrages on womanhood, especially in the southern states."[24]

The American Equal Rights Association, founded by Susan B. Anthony, Elizabeth Cady Stanton, and Frederick Douglass, split into two suffrage organizations after its 1869 meeting because of increasing racism within the movement.[25] After 1870, when the Fifteenth Amendment was passed, both Black men and women agitated for the female vote, including Black elected officials in Reconstruction governments. Black women's rights activists again came in conflict with white women leaders during the anti-lynching campaign spearheaded by Ida B. Wells-Barnett. "The colored race multiplies like the locusts of Egypt," Frances Willard of the Women's Christian Temperance Union had written, "and the grogshop is its center of power."[26] In white feminist circles, there were no anti-racist leaders in the tradition of the Grimké sisters. The complicity of white women in the mythology of rape doubtless contributed to the escalation of racist violence, as right-wing feminism emerged. By the 1910s, Black women had organized independently in the club movement and were fighting not only for women's votes but also for the votes of Black men lost to post-Reconstruction disenfranchisement in the southern states. In 1918, after the Nineteenth Amendment passed the House, white feminist organizers again capitulated to racism to get the support of southern senators. "Negro men cannot vote in South Carolina and therefore negro women could not if women were to vote in the nation," Alice Paul of the Women's Party told the New York *World*.[27] After the eventual passage of the Nineteenth Amendment, Black women continued to press white feminist organizations to work against their disenfranchisement in the Jim Crow South, with little success. In the South, however, Jesse Daniel Ames and the Society of Southern Women for the Prevention of Lynching took on the white power structure in the name of "white womanhood," and an interracial YWCA movement brought women together to work against racism.

Like the suffrage movement, the birth control movement took a decidedly racist and elitist turn, as leaders like Margaret Sanger capitulated to the eugenics movement. "More children from the fit, less from the unfit—that is the chief issue of birth control," she explained in 1919, and by the 1930s her rhetoric was virulently racist and she began to advocate sterilization of the "whole dysgenic population."[28]

One major factor in the national move to the right was a new wave of U.S. imperialism toward peoples of color globally. In 1898 the United States went to war with Spain over Cuba and the Philippines, and U.S. victory brought eight million people of color under U.S. control. To many whites, the new colonial possessions symbolized national greatness, a coming of age on the world stage and expanded access to new markets, especially in Asia.[29] The "English virtue" of empire sparked a new sense of brotherhood among English-speaking peoples and a sense of Anglo-Saxon superiority. In the United States, these concepts echoed the race theories being propagated in Europe in the late nineteenth century, where "scientific racism" gave ideological justification for European imperialism. From the beginnings of colonialism, the intellectual machinery of Europe had been busy explaining what "race" meant in a context that justified European dominance, shifting from a religious to a scientific explanation as Europe emerged from the Middle Ages. Early race theories that supplanted the interpretation of the story of Ham in Genesis were concerned with whether humans developed from a single stock in a short period of time or whether many races evolved differently in different places.

Opposition to the slave trade at the end of the seventeenth century prompted European scientists to consolidate the theory of race, drawing on both anthropology and evolution to justify racist practices. In 1843, the English Ethnological Society grew out of the activities of the Aborigines' Protection Society. British scientists felt a need to understand "the whole mental condition of the savage . . . so different from ours." These "savages" were subjects of the empire that represented

"almost every known modification of the human species whose varied and often conflicting interests have to be regulated and provided
for."[30] Although Charles Darwin did not himself assign superiority to
particular traits or place races in position on the evolutionary scale,
his followers did. They used the doctrine of natural selection, or "survival of the fittest," to explain the superiority of conquering European
culture: "As the Indian is killed by the approach of civilization, to
which he resists in vain, so the black man perishes by that culture to
which he serves as a humble instrument."[31] Cultural traits such as
language and physical traits such as facial features were dangerously
confused into a biological determinism designed to show European
superiority.

Within this biased framework, various tests were used to classify
humanity into racial groupings: the test of language arrived at groupings of three or seven main races. Physical characteristics such as
skull size were used to clarify the Frontal (European), Parietal (Mon-
gol), and Occipital (Negro). Facial angle was used to conclude that
the "receding forehead and projecting jaws of the Negro" represented
"ignorance and brutality," in contrast with the "harmonious" Saxon/
Celt/Scandinavian "broad forehead . . . a special fullness in the intellectual and moral regions." Often the reason scientists would challenge a particular system would be that it lumped in Europeans with
less "evolved" races. While all non-European "races" were inferior, in
British thought the Negro came in for special fear and hatred: "His energy is considerable: Aided by the sun, he repels the white invader."[32]

Darwin himself underlined the subjectivity—thus the irrationality—
of racial classifications:

Man has been studied more thoroughly than any other organic
being, and yet there is the greatest possible diversity amongst
capable judges whether he should be classed as a single species
or race, or as two (Virey), as three (Jacquinot), as four (Kant),
five (Blumenbach), six (Buffon), seven (Hunter), eight (Agas-
siz), eleven (Pickering), fifteen (Bory St. Vincent), sixteen (Des-
moulins), twenty-two (Morton), sixty (Crawfurd), or sixty-three
(Burke).[33]

Anti-Semitism evolved within this race-conscious European climate from eighteen hundred years of Christians persecuting Jews as a religious group ("Christ killers" or "poisoners of wells") to the persecution of Jews as a race. Not unlike his British counterparts, French writer Arthur de Gobineau was convinced that "the racial question overshadows all other problems of history, that it holds the key to them all, and that the inequality of the races from whose fusion a people is formed is enough to explain the whole course of its destiny."[34] In Germany, nationalism fed by Germany's defeats fueled a sense of Teutonic destiny. Race was seen to determine the fate of civilizations. German philosophers fused the ideas of the German people, or *Volk*, with the idea of the state as a transcendental essence to which the Jew was the primary outsider. The term "anti-Semitism" itself was coined during this period by a German racist, Wilhelm Marr, to promote hatred of Jews.

Hitler and his party of National Socialists would take these racist anti-Semitic ideas to their genocidal conclusions. In *Mein Kampf*, he wrote, "The racial question gives the key not only to world history, but to all human culture," for "in the blood alone resides the strength as well as the weakness of man." The Aryan race is the "bearer of human cultural development" and was therefore chosen to rule the world. The state must "set race in the center of all life . . . not only of assembling and preserving the most valuable stocks of basic racial elements in this people, but slowly and surely of raising them to a dominant position."[35] "The mightiest counterpart of the Aryan is represented by the Jew," Hitler explained. "Jewry is without question a race and not a religious fellowship" because "if worst came to the worst, a splash of baptismal water could always save the business and the Jew at the same time."[36] At the end of the nineteenth century, Jews were being allowed into the white working class in the United States, at the same time that they were being cast as the most reviled racial Other in Europe (an indication, among other things, of the extreme malleability of the concept of race).

The climate that fostered scientific racism also began to evolve medical distinctions between homosexuals and heterosexuals. Doctors such as England's Havelock Ellis who were investigating questions of sexuality in the late 1800s reported an outpouring of stories from the newly labeled homosexual population. Many indigenous cultures in North America had allowed cross-gender identification for community members such as the *berdache*, practices severely discouraged by Christian missionaries. With urbanization, white medical writers came to see homosexuality not as sodomy, a punishable but discrete offense, but as a kind of gender identity, a personality type with specific behaviors that they usually assumed to be pathological. Between the 1880s and World War I, homosexuals emerged as a "sexual minority of sorts."[37] Scientific racism as well as psychiatry contributed to early homophobic discourse. In an atmosphere where the propagation of the white race was the key to a nation's destiny and the fittest were assumed to be white, the newly discovered white homosexual's alleged inability to have children was seen as "degenerate."[38]

In the United States by the beginning of the twentieth century, Anglo-Saxons, not "Aryans," were the superior racial group. The virtues of these Anglo-Saxons, according to *Our Country*, an influential report on missions published in 1887 and paraphrased by historian Nell Painter, were "a sense of fair play, the ability to gain wealth honestly, the enjoyment of broad civil liberties in democracies in which every man had an equal vote, the genius for self-government and for governing others fairly and the evolution of the highest civilization the world had ever known."[39] Theodore Roosevelt, imbued with a sense of Anglo-Saxon manhood, declared in 1895 that "this country needs a war."[40] President McKinley explained his decision to keep the Philippines after the Spanish-American War, which came three years after Roosevelt's declaration: "We could not leave them to themselves—they were unfit for self-government—and they would soon have anarchy and misrule over there worse than Spain's was . . . there was nothing left for us to do but to take them all."[41] The white lie refined its concept of democracy as an exclusively Anglo-Saxon preserve at a time when the United States was extending increasingly anti-democratic control over huge numbers of people of color.

My grandfather Ben Cobb, one of Judge James Cobb's seven children, lied about his age and, perhaps harking to Roosevelt's call to Anglo-Saxon manhood, went off at sixteen to enlist in the

Spanish-American War. He didn't get to fight in 1898, but spent his time camped in Florida, where he did get malaria. He later became an engineer and spent a good bit of time in Central America working on the Panama Canal. But his health had been weakened by disease, and he died in the influenza epidemic of 1918, when my mother was three. It is with James and Ben Cobb that I begin to pick up the trail, the emotional scent, of family history. "Men and wars! Men and wars!" Mama would sometimes exclaim bitterly; but she too was an Anglophile, reading my brother and me to sleep at night with tales of English adventure, from *Robin Hood* and *King Arthur* to *When Knighthood Was in Flower* and *Under Drake's Flag.* She loved her daddy the way women love men they never knew except through other people's stories. Mother said that my grandmother hated Judge Cobb because he beat his children. Ben was a wanderer, an adventurer, maybe trying to escape his power-hungry father; I don't think it was coincidental that many of the places to which my mother liked to travel—often needing to get sick to get to do it—were places he had been. In my forties I have begun to deal with the effects of my sense of abandonment from her absences, my panic from her sickness: issues usually privatized in therapy discussions of "dysfunctional families," but in fact with historical causes and dimensions, racism not the least of them.

The Spanish-American War that eventually killed Ben Cobb marked the beginning of the United States' rise to global economic supremacy in a century when intense rivalries among industrial powers would contribute to two world wars. World War I brought the beginning of the watershed shift from Britain to the United States as premier imperial power. The Allies turned to New York to borrow money to finance the war. The dollar joined the pound as a major reserve currency—a national currency (and/or gold) that can be used to pay off the balance of payments of nations that import more than they export. These reserve dollars act as IOUs that can only be used to purchase U.S. goods at U.S. prices, making the role of the dollar an instrument of massive economic control.[42] The increased trade that resulted helped the United States to shift to a creditor nation and begin international lending on a large scale, bringing profits from the interest. In 1913, the Federal Reserve Act made international branch banks legal, the beginning of a web of U.S. financial networks that would increasingly span the globe. When World War II devastated Europe for a second time, the dollar finally beat out the pound as primary reserve currency, requiring that the leading trading nations keep their reserves in U.S. banks.

As the United States gained its status as the premier capitalist country, for the first time in four centuries serious challenges emerged to the capitalist/imperialist system. The threat of international socialism manifest in the Bolshevik Revolution in 1917 presented an alternative to imperialism.[43] Within the United States, the Great Depression, brought on by excesses of capitalism such as stock speculation, high tariffs, and skewed distribution of income, brought riots and strikes from both white workers and people of color: armed white farmers in Arkansas seized food supplies, five hundred unemployed people rioted in Detroit, Boston children raided a luncheon for Spanish-American War vets, three hundred thousand southern textile workers went on strike, and Black Alabama sharecroppers fought off sheriff's deputies when they came to confiscate their land.[44]

This last uprising occurred near my home county. The fact that Black sharecroppers fired on white law enforcement officers to defend their property brought immediate reprisal. Vigilante violence by white groups followed the incident, and two of the Black farmers died in jail of untended wounds. Survivors received prison sentences of up to twelve years.[45] My paternal grandfather was sent by local law enforcement out to the hospital to question one of the surviving members of the Sharecroppers' Union shootout about possible communist influence. These and other insurgencies necessitated a "New Deal" between workers, owners, and government—a reorganization of U.S. capitalism through increased federal regulation, deficit spending, and a co-opting of socialist policies in a range of welfare-state reforms. Both world wars also weakened Europe's hold on its colonial empires, which became too expensive to maintain. After World War I, strong national movements across the globe won political independence from former European colonizers, a process accelerated by World War II and extending into the 1960s.

Fascist movements emerged in the 1920s in Germany, Italy, and Japan and were propelled into power by the Great Depression. They offered a challenge both to communism and to the leading industrial countries, but not to capitalism itself. As Hitler explained, "Let these 'well-bred' gentry [capitalist leaders] learn that we do with a clear conscience what they secretly do with a guilty one."[46] Bertram Gross explains that the fascists were "heretics seeking to revive the old [capitalist] faith by concentrating on the fundamentals of imperial expansion, militarism, repression, and racism." They mobilized the discontented and alienated in order to "channel the violence-prone," and they manipulated and tolerated anti-capitalist currents to ultimately build a firmer base for capitalism. "Above all," Gross explains, "the fascists wanted 'in.'"[47]

Albert Speer explained Nazism as "the first dictatorship of an industrial state in this age of technology, a dictatorship which employed to perfection the instruments of technology to dominate its own people."[48] The Germans employed unprecedented repression on their own people, focusing, as Hitler explained, on "the annihilation of the Jewish race throughout Europe."[49] Concentration camps built and supplied by German firms became the focus of wholesale gassing and cremating of twelve million people (six million Jews, as well as communists, Gypsies, homosexuals, and the sick or insane), slave labor (7.5 million civilian foreigners working for the Reich), medical experiments, and "recycling" of human remains. Beyond the concentration camps, fascists in all three countries "destroyed the very liberties which industrialization had brought."[50] The needs of the master race justified imperialism and the militarism required for it and for domestic repression. These racist theories were used not only against Jews but also against Africans (by Italians), Slavs (by Germans), and Chinese and other Asians (by the Japanese).[51]

My two uncles, Ben Cobb's sons, fought in World War II, as did my own father, who was in the Air Force. He was shot down over Germany, and he spent two years in a German POW camp before being liberated by Allied armies in 1945. The defeat of fascism made World War II a "good war," although the internment of Japanese Americans, the decision to drop the atomic bomb on Hiroshima and Nagasaki, and the experience of Black soldiers on their return home showed that there was a need to defend democracy beyond its white preserves at home as well as abroad. Like many men and women of their generation, my parents turned from the defeat of German Nazism to a fervent Cold War confrontation with communism. They also began to anticipate the postwar uprising of African American southerners that announced itself most publicly with *Brown v. Board of Education* in 1954.

As bankers and industrialists in the United States had anticipated, the victory of the Allies over the Axis brought the United States to an unprecedented role of global leadership in what *Time/Life* magnate Henry Luce dubbed "the American century." World War II had brought unprecedented cooperation among political and military leaders, businessmen, and scientists. At the close of the war they worked to consolidate a world capitalist bloc under the leadership of the United States with myriad channels of influence, "a loose network of constitutional democracies, authoritarian regimes, and military dictatorships described as the 'Free World,'" Gross explains. The net result was "a remarkably flexible control system in which competing views on strategy and tactics make themselves felt and are resolved through mutual adjustment," allowing business to operate both through and beyond the state.[52] As colony after colony won independence, they were brought into the burgeoning capitalist financial networks as the price of their independence, a process known as neocolonialism.

Within these networks, the poorer, "underdeveloped" countries were at a permanent disadvantage. When they ran up deficits that their stores of reserve currency could not cover and were refused credit by banks, they were forced to undertake severe internal adjustments, austerity measures that raised prices, lowered wages, and shifted spending from social services toward the military. The United States, on the other hand, could for decades maintain yearly deficits without having to implement the kind of austerity measures that would have had severe political repercussions, both in terms of encouraging domestic revolutionary movements and in terms of increasing governmental repression. The United States used the money from its deficit to finance its military machine, to lend military and economic aid to its allies (including forgiving debts for its client states who behave and for foreign investments that brought countries more tightly into its economic sphere). The United States maintained a deficit because of its flexibility of resources, because it generated much of its income from its financial services, and because it could extend itself credit, since other countries wanted dollars in a way that they did not want Third World national currencies. "If we had not been world banker . . . we would have been in the same situation as other countries face," explained treasury secretary C. Douglas Dillon in 1963; "as soon as we got into deficit we would have had to balance our accounts one way or another."[53] Once again, political openness in the United States was built on the backs of people of color.

World War II also brought a shift within the United States away from self-sufficiency in raw materials, one of the "striking economic changes of our time," according to the Commission on Foreign Economic Policy.[54] And the intensified need for overseas raw materials coincided with the growth of the "Second World" of the communist empire. Three-fourths of the imported materials in a Department of Defense list of necessary stockpiles came from underdeveloped areas, a "Third World" beyond Europe, North America, Japan, and the Soviet Union.[55] Explained W.W. Rostow, President Johnson's adviser on national security affairs, to a joint congressional committee: "The location, natural resources, and populations of the underdeveloped areas are such that, should they become effectively attached to the Communist bloc, the United States would become the second power in the world. . . . In short, our military security and our way of life as well as the fate of Western Europe and Japan are at stake in the evolution of the underdeveloping areas."[56]

These far-reaching shifts in world finances helped to shape racial policies and practices within the United States. Intensified racism at the end of the nineteenth century had brought an upsurge in Black anti-racist organizing, marked by the beginning of the NAACP and the Urban League. World War I brought increased economic opportunities to as many as one million African Americans who left the South looking for industrial employment formerly denied by industries and by white unions but now available because of war-induced labor shortages. Black soldiers came home from fighting a war to make the world "safe for democracy" to race riots, lynching, and a resurgence in the Klan. With a powerful and growing urban base in the North, the 1920s saw increasing Black militancy with an international focus: W.E.B. Du Bois called a Pan-African Congress to meet in Paris during the Versailles conference, Marcus Garvey promoted Pan-Africanism with his Universal Negro Improvement Association, and the Harlem Renaissance brought an unprecedented cultural resurgence.

Immigration policy shifted under the new global pressures of the American century, affecting especially Asian immigration, which had been severely limited since the Chinese Exclusion Act in 1882. World War II had also brought the internment of 110,000 Japanese Americans here while German Americans went on with their daily lives. But after the war, the quotas limiting non-European immigration, in place from the beginning of the century, finally gave way under pressure from Cold War competition for Third World resources. In 1952, the Immigration and Nationality Act (also called the McCarran-Walter Act) finally made legal the naturalization of any person regardless of race, for the first time making immigrants from Japan, Korea, and other parts of Asia eligible for citizenship.[57] In 1956, the Republican Party came out in favor of easing immigration restrictions—the same year its platform called for "the establishment of American naval and air bases all around the world."[58] Political refugees from Cuba and Indochina were admitted in large numbers after the United States failed to dislodge communist governments. In 1965, the McCarran-Walter Act was amended to abolish the national-origins system and substitute seven preferential categories, including refugees "fleeing a Communist or Communist-dominated country." Asians began to immigrate to the United States in record numbers—one and a half million people between 1966 and 1983, creating a brain drain and siphoning off wealth from the Asian continent.[59] Capitalism's economic competition with communism helped to shift immigration policy and thus the racial demographics of U.S. society.

The deficit in U.S. mineral resources contributed to a shift in policy toward American Indians as well, as mineral resources on reservation lands became more coveted. Indian policy after the Dawes Severalty

Act had followed a colonial pattern, destroying collective structures and fostering dependence on an emerging welfare apparatus. From 1880 to 1930, fifty thousand Indian children were sent, by force or otherwise, to Indian boarding schools to encourage assimilation. Between 1881 and 1934, Indian land declined from 155 million acres to 70 million acres.[60] In 1924, Congress granted full citizenship, finally, to Indians. In 1928, the Meriam Survey described unrelieved poverty on reservations as a result of land policies. Because corporations wanted access to mineral leasing, the Indian Reorganization Act of 1934 gave power for economic planning to a "tribal council" system, setting up Indian leadership that would collaborate with corporate pillaging and further usurp traditional structures.

Roosevelt's New Deal and World War II helped to dislodge the biological approach of "scientific" racism, whose genocidal ends Hitler made clear. From the 1930s to 1965, the "ethnicity theory" of race operated as the progressive/liberal consensus. First articulated by sociologists at the University of Chicago in the 1920s, it theorized a "race cycle" of contact, conflict, accommodation, and assimilation based largely on the experience of European immigrants, an approach that has been increasingly challenged by class-based (mostly Marxist) and nation-based (anti-colonial) theories of race.[61] Jim Crow still gripped the South, but the integrationists won the confrontation within the Democratic Party in 1948.

As the United States competed with the Soviet Union for Third World resources, domestic racism became an international issue. "We cannot escape the fact that our civil rights record has been an issue in world politics," Truman admitted in 1946. "Those with competing philosophies have stressed—and are shamelessly distorting—our shortcomings."[62] Third World revolutionary movements were growing in Indochina, the Philippines, Indonesia, and Africa. Truman appointed a Committee on Civil Rights in 1946 and in 1948 issued an order barring racial segregation in the armed forces. In 1954, after decades of work by the NAACP to shift court findings, in *Brown v. Board of Education* the Supreme Court reversed the 1896 *Plessy v. Ferguson* ruling that had made "separate but equal" school facilities legal at the end of Reconstruction. Challenging the southern apartheid put in place as Jim Crow, the Black freedom movement erupted in the South, targeting school desegregation and voting rights.

In early January 1965, Sammy Younge, one of the young Black men and women across the South who responded to this movement, was shot and killed by a man named Marvin Segrest, a cousin of my father's, when Younge had insisted on using the "white" bathroom in the gas station where Marvin Segrest worked. Segrest claimed he had shot in self-defense and was acquitted by an all-white jury. Activist James Forman called Younge "the first Black college student in the movement to have been killed," a murder that "marked the end of tactical nonviolence."[63] That year, I was sixteen and deeply disturbed by the eruptions of racist violence around me.

School desegregation and voting rights arrived in the South with federal enforcement much reviled by white southerners. The need for the United States to consolidate its relationships with newly independent Third World countries probably helped motivate the Kennedy administration to overturn the Jim Crow structures put in place in the South after Reconstruction. As Black freedom struggles moved north and became less assimilationist and more militantly nationalist, the federal "support" of the civil rights movement turned to opposition, as George Wallace had predicted. Martin Luther King Jr. was assassinated after he linked Black civil rights struggles in the United States with the issue of domestic poverty and with anti-imperialist struggles in Vietnam. Numerous Black Panthers and other Black leaders were murdered by federal and state law enforcement officers.

This militant Black organizing triggered renewed militancy in other Third World communities within the United States, as well as student rebellions and the anti-imperialist opposition to the war in Vietnam. Vietnam became the first U.S. military defeat in history, and the militant anti-war movement at home helped to put some brakes on U.S. military power. This revolutionary upsurge also triggered a "second wave" of feminism, in a way similar to the emergence of early women's rights out of the abolition struggles. Gay and lesbian liberation movements also erupted from the homosexual subcultures that had been developing since the late 1800s, inspired by and using political models of both feminism (itself highly influenced by anti-racist struggles) and Black freedom struggles. It was this lesbian-feminist politics into which the great-great-great-great-great-great-great-great-granddaughter of Ambrose Cobbs of Yorktown came out in the mid-1970s.

In this essay, I have tracked ten Cobbs, from the sweating pews of Virginia churches to Florida swamps, dodging gators and searching for human prey, and to the Alabama bench, gaveling Reconstruction officials off to the chain gang. I have traced my white history through a particular set of white men because they are the ones who constructed white history and because my mother's papers did not include the genealogy of daughters and mothers. I suspect from my knowledge of my own mother's and grandmother's experiences that this matrilineal history is fraught with much more ambivalence and opposition. My father's side of the family would bring a more working-class worldview. Likewise, if I have tracked ten of these ancestors back to English origins, I find it hopeful that I am left 1,014 more possibilities of something other than "pure" European blood.

"It is the Black condition, and only that, which informs the consciousness of white people," wrote James Baldwin. And on another occasion: "As long as you think you're white, there's no hope for you."[64] I have worked in this essay to both think myself, and unthink myself, white (the related project, in which I engaged in the memoir, to feel myself both white and not-white), in order to regain the power, in Baldwin's terms, to "control and define" myself by excavating the Black (and "red" and "brown" and "yellow") condition within my own white history. For it is only through acquiring a consciousness of racist consciousness (a necessary corollary to anti-racist practice) that we white people will ever have any other community than the community of the lie.

Part Three

A BRIDGE, NOT A WEDGE

For Leah Wise

A Bridge, Not a Wedge

This essay was originally delivered as a keynote at the National Gay and Lesbian Task Force's "Creating Change" conference in Durham, North Carolina, in November 1993. I have elaborated the remarks to conclude this [first edition of this] book. The reflections on the economy in the 1980s and 1990s complete the assessment of capitalism undertaken in "On Being White and Other Lies" and show the emergence of what I believe is a fourth stage, beyond commerce, industrial, and finance capitalism, driven by the technological advances of the information age. The remarks on racism, while targeted to white gay and lesbian organizers, are relevant to other predominantly white movements within the United States. I have also expanded my reflections on the ways that homophobia hurts heterosexuals, especially the way that the Right is attempting to seed homophobia in communities of color. I certainly hope that homophobia will not prevent heterosexuals reading this piece from seeing its relevance to their lives.

Good morning, and welcome to Durham. Those of you making your first trip South may already be disoriented by our peculiar blend of hospitality and repression, which comes from having spent 246 of the last 374 years as a slave culture. But it's important for all of us to understand the history of racism in the United States—in which the South has played a particularly visible but by no means singular role. If coming South reminds us of this, so much the better. If the South is the cradle of the Confederacy and of many subsequent right-wing movements, it is also the mother of all resistance, the heir to generations of Africans' determination to be free, from the moment they set foot on the slave ships, all across the Middle Passage, to the long, cold, white nightmare on this continent. The South is the heir to their creativity. For however destructively white supremacist culture has defined them, African Americans have continually re-created themselves, have known in their songs and in their hearts *before I'll be a slave, I'll be buried in my grave.* I call some of their names, a verbal libation: Harriet Tubman, Frederick Douglass, Ida B. Wells-Barnett, Ella Baker, Martin Luther King Jr., Rosa Parks, Fannie Lou Hamer. We meet on their ground, and on the ground of Tuscaroras, Algonquians, Cherokees, Lumbees, Sioux, who fought their own wars with the U.S. Army, the long and brutal history of which should remind our movement what it means to take on the U.S. military, arguably the most repressive force in the world.

I feel honored to address you this morning, but I also feel urgent. I am afraid that I will not explain clearly enough my conviction that the gay and lesbian liberation movement must understand racism more fully if we are to survive, and that we cannot understand racism if we do not understand the anti-human virulence of capitalism. If we did understand these two great barriers to human liberation, we would behave differently—position our movement differently, structure our organizations differently, develop and respect our leaders differently. In this regard, I think we are similar to many progressive movements in the United States. But we gay people are at a critical juncture. In November 1992, Amendment 2 was passed in Colorado, prohibiting the passage of gay rights laws and repealing existing anti-discrimination ordinances in three cities. In November 1993, just last week, we lost three similar homophobic ballot initiatives—in Maine, Cincinnati, and Portsmouth, New Hampshire. New Right groups in at least twelve other states plan Amendment 2–type initiatives in 1994. The demise of the Rainbow Curriculum in New York City was another frightening victory for the Right and a model of how effectively it can use homophobia and racism as a wedge between communities of color and gay and lesbian communities, limiting the aspirations of both as a result. The Right is building its base on a homophobia as volatile as the fires that recently swept through the canyons of southern California.

Yes, the gay movement has more visibility, more access to corridors of power, than we have ever had. But, unfortunately, our biggest ally, the president, is a weak man in a weak position. We have only to look at the degeneration of Clinton's honorable intent to lift the ban on gay men and lesbians in the military to the capitulation policy of "don't ask, don't tell" that still leaves lesbian and gay servicepeople at the mercy of military intelligence. Bill Clinton will not save us. We have to "save" ourselves by organizing our own people and bringing them into coalitions on a range of justice issues. To meet the emergencies the Right presents us will require a conceptual shift, a new paradigm to take us into a new century.

Our failure to understand racism is killing us. Maybe twenty years ago, our movement and institutions had the luxury of stupidity. Maybe twenty years ago, white queers could approach issues of racism out of guilt, or a desire to be liked, or to be "good." Maybe then we could offer token jobs and token recognition to people of color, saving the decision making, the real power, for the folks who looked like the president, or the chief justice, or the CEO of Exxon. But the Right has called our diversity bluff. Their most recent and effective propaganda, such as the video *Gay Rights, Civil Rights*, uses African American spokespeople to proclaim that we are not a "genuine" minority in the tradition of Martin Luther King Jr. but a privileged group after "special rights." Many Black people have no illusions that the producers of this propaganda have their best interests at heart. However, these divisive strategies become most apparent as the lies they are where our movement has relationships with people of color (including those in our own midst). In all those towns and cities where there are few links between visible gay organizations and people of color, such strategies are dangerously effective among both people of color and straight whites. The wildfire of the Right's insurgent fascism is sweeping down the canyons that divide us, and we must respond to racism now for our own survival—to save our little white asses. And we should be thankful for the opportunity.

When we don't get race, it kills us. When we don't understand capitalism, not only are we more confused about race, not only do we confuse power with money, not only do we deny our clearest voices—we also fail to understand the forces driving the history of our times. We won't have successful strategies if we don't understand our times. If we don't understand why things are happening to us now, we will never have the vision and the strategy to seize the future and shape it.

Last year, as part of my new job for the Urban-Rural Mission of the World Council of Churches, I traveled to Juarez, Mexico, to visit the *maquiladoras*. Fortune 500 companies built these "twin plant" factories along the U.S.-Mexico border in the 1970s when the Mexican president, faced with mounting pressure from his country's international debt, developed "free trade zones." (Many other Third World countries were saddled with similar huge debts when the International Monetary Fund and the World Bank encouraged them to borrow too much money. The consequence has been to keep those poor countries' people and resources at the disposal of richer countries and under the control of domestic authoritarian regimes, since democracies are less inclined to starve their people.)

In Juarez, first we toured the industrial districts, driving past rows of seemingly innocuous factories. Then we went behind one of the *maquilas*. On the other side of a drainage ditch, Mexican families lived in houses made from cardboard and scrap lumber. There was an acrid smell rising from ditch water the bright green color of Astroturf. A pipe from the plant fed unprocessed waste the color and consistency of breast milk into the water. Families washed and dried their laundry in the polluted water. Our guide later showed us pictures of babies born to women *maquila* workers in Brownsville, Texas—babies who had no brains. The workers in these factories are 70 percent women.

Then we went to visit a *colonia*, a poor neighborhood that feeds workers into the *maquilas*. As we rounded the hill, I looked out to the horizon, and all I could see were scores of the same cardboard houses. They stretched from mesa to mesa for acres, the pattern broken only by an occasional power line or by water brought in in old chemical barrels.

There on the hill outside of Juarez, the taste of its dust in my mouth,

I found myself face-to-face with the latest manifestation of a virulent capitalism in which masses of humanity become pawns for massive profits for a few.

What does this mean, I thought, to gay people?

While the New Right's "family values" campaigns of the 1970s and 1980s pumped up hostility against gay men and lesbians, the forces that eventually brought Reagan and Bush to the White House stole this country. Corporate profits from the postwar boom peaked in the mid-1960s, then began to decline, squeezed by increasing foreign competition from both established and newly industrializing countries. In the 1960s and 1970s, the men who run the multinationals responded with mergers and hostile takeovers to try for fast profits, rather than using the money to retool basic industries and maintain our infrastructure. They did not improve our products—how many of you began driving Volkswagens or Hondas rather than American cars in the 1970s and 1980s? Rather, they cut labor costs—by attacking unions and by sending our basic industries to Third World countries, where people work for one-tenth the wages (*maquila* workers make $4 a day).[1]

New computer technologies have allowed this rearrangement of the global assembly line because now production and assembly of particular products can be dispersed to countries with the "comparative advantage" of cheap labor costs and lax labor and environmental standards. "Money" is reduced to electronic impulses, both highly concentrated and rapidly deployed.

Between 1970 and 1990 conservative administrations and Congress restructured our federal tax policy to provide incentives for corporations to invest overseas, decreasing the percentage of corporate taxes that constitute the total federal budget from 23.4 percent to 9.7 percent. Reagan gave so many corporations "tax expenditures"—deductions and credits—that many Fortune 500 companies stopped paying taxes altogether and even got money back from previous years. IBM paid virtually no U.S. taxes between 1986 and 1988 on U.S. assets of $39 billion and a worldwide profit of $26 billion.[2]

The people in control of our economy "deindustrialized" the United

States, leaving us a service economy with lower-paying jobs. These corporate and governmental decision makers "feminized" the workforce, because the way they could save the most money was by eliminating the unionized, higher salaried, white men's jobs. By 1973, the standard of living from the postwar expansion had peaked, and wages began to fall. In the 1970s for the first time since World War II, the standard of living for white workers began to decline.

The New Right, which would mobilize a racist, sexist, and homophobic backlash to the justice movements of the 1960s, was born just at this moment of declining white living standards. In 1973, Kevin Phillips had articulated in *The Emerging Republican Majority* the formula for forging a right-wing populism based on racist backlash to issues such as busing and affirmative action. The "New Right" movement had been brewing since Barry Goldwater's 1964 presidential campaign brought conservatives together and generated a mailing list. It was fed by the success of George Wallace's populist racist presidential campaigns, which garnered ten million votes in 1968 and showed the "Old Right" a way to break up the Democratic coalition that had dominated U.S. politics since the Depression. At the same time, ultraconservative strategists Howard Phillips and Paul Weyrich recruited televangelists Jerry Falwell and Pat Robertson to shape the national organizations that formed the basis for a religious right politicized by issues of prayer in schools, feminism, and the new gay liberation movement. These two thrusts—one racist, the other based on gender and sexuality—took separate courses but sprang from the same impulse and the same ultraconservative strategy.[3]

While the ideologues blamed feminists, people of color, poor people, and gay people for the national decline, the stage was set for business moguls to siphon off billions. In 1980, Barry Goldwater's disciple Ronald Reagan was elected president on a platform of deficit reduction. Then his administration pumped up the deficit from $79 billion to $155 billion and the national debt from $1 trillion to $2.6 trillion with inflated military spending. In 1986, 63 percent of the tax dollar (not counting trust funds such as Social Security) went to pay for past, present, or future wars.[4]

While Reaganites inflated the war budget, they slashed the "safety net" that was put in place in the 1930s and 1960s to protect us from the ravages of unrestrained capitalism. The federal government cut federal social spending and passed on insufficient block grants to the states. Cities cut taxes to draw investments and concentrated on service, not manufacturing jobs, then, many went bankrupt in the 1980s under the double pressure of increased responsibility for social services and a reduced tax base. States became the managers of social spending and in the 1990s will increasingly face bankruptcy under this pressure. In 1991, New York carried a $6 billion deficit, California $10 billion. Then there is the savings-and-loan scam, which is costing us $100 billion a year. The United States in the 1990s is facing the kind of "structural adjustment" economic policies that we have long foisted on Third World countries, likely with the attendant volatile social movements and beefed up police state to repress them.[5]

The collapse of the Soviet bloc in the late 1980s (due in part to its own massive military spending) has left capitalism without the counterforce that the USSR offered for the past seventy years, speeding up the process of economic integration of global markets as three huge trading blocs have emerged: in the Pacific Rim (dominated by Japan), in Europe (dominated by Germany), and in the Americas (dominated by the United States). The situation in the *maquilas* is one result of the policy of deindustrialization and hemispheric economic integration that U.S. economic elites helped to put in place with the political support of the same white workers they have begun to dislocate; and with the passage of the North American Free Trade Act (NAFTA), the *maquila* economy will spread to all of Mexico, and eventually all of Latin America and back north.

With the communist threat suddenly diminished, the G.H.W. Bush administration dropped a lot of its military hardware on the unfortunate people of Iraq in half-million-dollar smart bombs over Baghdad— with every bomb, *bam!* another school, *bam!* another AIDS research project, *bam! bam!* bridges and sewer systems, *bam!* low-income housing complexes. We also killed two hundred thousand people.

In the 1990s, expect many more politicians to blame crises in the economy on our most vulnerable people, such as "welfare mothers," "illegal immigrants," and "homosexuals wanting special rights." Suddenly, there is not enough money for baby formula, supposedly because welfare mothers are having too many children. States are making massive, homicidal cuts in public assistance: currently in Pennsylvania the proposed cut is a quarter of a million people, mostly women and children. White workers are facing hard times, and many people repeat the lie planted by ultraconservative strategists: that affirmative action is giving people of color all the good jobs—when actually the "good jobs" are disappearing altogether. The United States has lost 2.6 million manufacturing jobs since 1978.[6] In 1986, the median income of a white family was almost double that of a Black family.[7]

How does this economic stuff affect us as gay people? Pitiful funding for AIDS and breast cancer is an obvious answer, but let's look deeper. Since we are meeting in Durham, let's consider where homophobia fits into the social and economic fabric of this city and state. You are meeting in Buck Duke's town—James B. Duke, nineteenth-century tobacco baron, built his fortune by teaching the world to smoke his cigarettes. If you walk a block east up Chapel Hill Street, you come to the post office. In the tobacco heyday of Durham it sold $1 million a day in revenue stamps for the ninety million packs of cigarettes shipped out each day from Durham's tobacco factories.

If you go in the other direction past Brightleaf Square (tobacco warehouses converted to shops and restaurants) you come to Ninth Street—bookstores, lesbian ice cream, a great bakery, and, across the street, expensive condos. They used to be Erwin Mills, one of the many textile mills built at the turn of the century in the rapidly industrializing South. These factories had prospered by drawing poor whites off depressed farms for low wages and white privilege. Many jobs came to these southern textile mills from the Northeast because the South had cheaper wages than unionized northern shops. In the 1930s, strikes all across the Southeast were brutally repressed by companies, governors, and the National Guard. In the past fifteen years, we have lost many of these jobs to automation or to even cheaper labor in Third World countries, where the World Bank, the International Monetary Fund, and the U.S. military have maintained poverty conditions and a ready workforce—as similar forces did in North Carolina.

Lesbian and gay male professionals working in the universities and medical and research facilities of the Triangle have benefited from this new wave of development. At the same time, a cadre of some-times marginally employed gay and lesbian activists such as myself have shaped a largely middle-class movement that does not include many of the "queers" working in the mills and factories and convenience stores, people whose low wages make North Carolina a state of the "working poor."

In 1990, North Carolina ranked forty-sixth among the fifty states in overall labor climate from the workers' perspective—and number one in labor market opportunities from the perspective of the employer, according to the Southern Labor Institute. This month, *Fortune* named Durham/Chapel Hill/Raleigh as the best place to do business in the United States.[8] Yet one-third of Durham's families live in poverty, and these are mostly Black, mostly female-headed households.

Walking southeast several blocks from the Omni where we meet today, you come upon the massive construction for Durham's new jail. Governor Jim Hunt has called a special session of the legislature in 1994, which is considering a $200 million bond initiative for building new prisons that will cost $100 million a year to maintain.

Now some of you may be thinking, *Why is she going on so about Durham and North Carolina? What is all this economics? I'm just here for the weekend.* So let me approach it another way. If you have concerns about Jesse Helms and the havoc he wreaks for lesbians and gay men—his attack on the National Endowment for the Arts for its support of "homoerotic art," his demonization of us, his attacks on AIDS funding, or just for aesthetic reasons—then you care about these conditions in North Carolina. North Carolina created Helms because hard times create demagogues everywhere. Helms came to his homophobia relatively late (the 1978 Senate race). He cut his political teeth on the anti-communism of the 1950s working in Willis Smith's no-holds-barred Senate race against Chapel Hill liberal Frank Porter Graham. He gained a following in the 1960s as a television commentator defending segregation. Every six years, he wins his Senate seat again by a 2 to 3 percent swing vote, drawn from his base of free-enterprise Republicans (owners of factories and mills), middle-class religious conservatives, and the working-class whites whose economic interests he seldom serves. Economic conditions like we have had for much of this century in North Carolina are creating others like Helms all across the country.

Similar circumstances in Virginia have bred Pat Robertson of the Christian Coalition, Jerry Falwell's Moral Majority, and a Religious Right that draws on deep regional roots. You are meeting in the Bible Belt, but originally it was those folks in Massachusetts who were the theocrats, who were burning women as witches and merging government with their Führer's version of God. Thomas Jefferson, the slave-master from Virginia, insisted on the separation of church and state. But in the three decades before the Civil War, the South called on all its institutions to defend slavery against growing opposition. Under this pressure, government merged with reactionary religion in this repressive way as slavemasters quoted the Bible to maintain their way of life. Now the Virginia-based Christian Coalition's 386 radio stations reach all over the globe.[9]

As the South goes, so goes the nation. As North Carolina (the most industrialized state in the country, losing jobs to automation and "economic integration") goes, so goes your state. And the real problem, with this region and this country, is that slavery was never really abolished. It just got reinstituted in other forms: Jim Crow, sharecropping, subsistence "wage labor" jobs for people of color that often amount to involuntary servitude. Today's proposals for "free enterprise zones" in blighted and abandoned cities and even "don't ask, don't tell" are descended from the heinous logic of biological and social superiority and an economic system that requires a dehumanized category of workers to reap its profits. We gay men and lesbians should not be surprised when this country does not treat us well.

We can meet till the cows come home and discuss how to "Fight the Right" without recognizing that in some cases we *are* the Right. Lance Hill, who directed the Louisiana campaigns against neo-Nazi David Duke's candidacies, told me that Duke's campaign for governor in 1990 was active in the gay bars of the French Quarter in New Orleans. Neo-Nazis could have access there because those bars are largely segregated.[10] I offer this example not to say that Louisiana is an anomaly but to say that the Duke campaign brought out a weakness of gay movements in most cities. We gay people look with justified concern at the way the religious right uses homophobia to divide, for example, the African American community, to persuade some of its church people to organize against us, to their own detriment and destruction. We need to look with equal concern at the practices of our movement, our community, which are also the dry wood on which fascism burns. For many gay and lesbian people of color, it is every bit as much an expense of spirit to be in a room with us radical queer white activists as with the most hair-raising fundamentalist minister—just as exhausting and insulting. We can no longer take for granted the presence of our brothers and sisters of color among us, their talents and their resources. The arsonists of the Christian Coalition have lit their fires, and the hot winds are rising.

As we go on the defensive, state by state, fighting the religious bigots, we should seriously consider the possibility that it's not the men (or women) who can write checks for $100,000, $500,000, or $1 million who know most strategically how to spend that money. Maybe acquiring that much money has buffered these people from the need to come together with the broadest range of people. Yes, we need "powerful allies." But we must always ask ourselves how this power is constituted. A congressperson may have debts to liberal donors, but popular conservatism can cancel that debt at any moment.

The demographics of the United States will shift radically over the next half century, fed by Latino immigrants from war-torn and economically ravaged Central American countries; Asians, who began to immigrate in greater numbers when Congress repealed racist immigration quotas during the Vietnam War; and declining white birth rates. By the middle of the next century, there will be as many people of color in this country as white people. We lesbians and gay men will have a chance to build a potentially new kind of power base at the local, state, and national levels with progressive people of color, marginalized workers both within and outside of unions, and progressive feminists. Will our racism allow us to make that choice? (Feminists will face similar decisions, and we are already seeing the emergence of a right-wing feminism as well as the cultivation of right-wing Black leadership such as Clarence Thomas and General Colin Powell.) As we walk the corridors of power, it may be not our lobbyists, our congresspeople, the queer members of a Democratic administration who carry our hopes of success. It may be the unseen lesbian secretaries and gay janitors, the Black Congressional Caucus, and the National Conference of Mayors who are as much the source of our power.

Many of these people know that no movement or person in this country can escape the repression and dehumanization that was required for the genocide of Native peoples and the enslavement of Africans. That's what we fight when we "Fight the Right." Let our presence in the South this weekend remind us of that. The only "special right" that the United States gives to minorities is the right to be the target of genocidal policies. We have only to look at AIDS policy to confirm this truth. Just as we do not want people of color buying the Right's homophobic argument that we are after "special rights," not civil rights, it is also vital that our movement does not buy the racist backlash to affirmative action propagated over the last two decades by the same Republican forces. When we put both parts of their strategy together, it's clear that, to them, *all* civil rights are "special rights" that victimize privileged white men.[11] When any "minority," whether racial, ethnic, gendered, or sexual, buys into these wedge strategies, we play ourselves for fools and disrupt the possibility of a transformative political majority in the next century.

It's my belief that racism shapes all political movements in the United States, for better and for worse, but because white people so seldom talk about how we are affected by racism, we don't understand how to counter it. We just act it out. In the lesbian and gay movement, much of our analysis has flowed from an understanding of gender, leaving race and class at two removes from our analysis. But approaches to racism have shaped the debates within our own community on issues such as passing and assimilation, radical transformation versus reform, and legal strategies versus empowerment of the grassroots. One of the dominant paradigms for dealing with race in the twentieth century emerged from the University of Chicago in the 1920s. It was called the ethnicity model, and it theorized that immigrants to the

United States go through cycles of contact and conflict, then assimilation.[12] Now, on the one hand, this theory was an improvement over the dominant paradigm it replaced, which was the biological approach to race, that saw racial differences as inherited and that justified slavery and colonialism. (This context should make us beware of the biological theories of homosexuality now being advanced.)

But the ethnicity paradigm was based on European experience, not the experiences of people of color. At the same time that European immigrants were being assimilated—if painfully—into our economy, Jim Crow reigned in the South for African Americans, Asians were kept out of the country altogether by immigration quotas, Native Americans were suffering record rates of poverty on a land base once again decimated by white theft, and Chicanas were forming their own *mutualistas* in the Southwest in the face of racist white unions. So this business of assimilation operates differently above and below the color lines, as do most manifestations of American "democracy." If we generic gay and lesbian white folks set as our movement's goal being assimilated into American culture, getting "our piece of the pie," we ignore or deny the reality that gay and lesbian people of color will never be assimilated in the same way within this system because it was constituted to exclude them. And, as Derrick Bell has argued in reference to African American liberation, and as Colorado proved in regard to gay civil rights, wherever assimilation goals may become enshrined in law, they can just as easily be overturned.[13]

If we follow the ethnicity theory, we perpetuate the belief that the issue of "homophobia" is mainly a matter of personal prejudice, which contact with us will diffuse. We ignore the extent to which the most powerful political and economic forces in this country have an investment in our degradation. Literally, right-wing groups invest millions in slandering us, knowing that these efforts will build up their grassroots base and their funding chests. In the Oregon Citizens Alliance campaign, they put back into their vicious homophobic ballot initiative campaign only one dollar out of every three raised. The rest of the money, according to the Task Force's "Fight the Right" organizer Scot Nakagawa, went into a range of regressive causes. Such campaigns also distract people from the corporate theft that may beggar us all.

The assimilation model leads us to try to smooth the rough edges of our community, putting limits on visible leadership by people of color, working-class white gay men and lesbians, and anyone else who doesn't look and act like most lobbyists. It leads to "outing" powerful, rich people to show that they, too, are gay. It leads to surveys that tout the marketing power of the gay dollar and position us as a movement of the middle to upper class, with higher-than-average spending power. This dynamic sets us up to be a "buffer class," in a way similar to how Jews were portrayed in Europe, to draw off class anger from the economic elite who are really making the decisions and reaping the rewards in a period of national economic crisis and decline. It makes us appear narrow and selfish (which I do not think we are) and cuts us off from allies, increasing our vulnerability to insurgent right-wing populist movements agitated by economic unrest. This is classic fascism, and its foundation has already been laid in our time and our nation.[14]

The two models of race thinking that emerged to counter the ethnicity model were nationalism and socialism. I would argue that we have opted for the wrong model. We don't need a queer nationalism— as powerful as the militancy and anti-assimilationist stances of Queer Nation have been. We need a queer socialism that is by necessity anti-racist, feminist, and democratic; a politic that does not cut us off from other people, but that unites us with them in the broadest possible movement. Now, I live in a state where folks shoot both "commies" and "queers," so I had better explain first what I do *not* mean by socialism: I don't mean the KGB, or the Berlin Wall, or Stalin's gulags, or the repression of spirituality or creativity or initiative. What I really mean is a more genuine *democracy*, where the citizens of our country have more direct access to *all* the decisions that affect us, not only in the political but also in the economic arena. (The NAFTA vote was important because it offered a rare occasion where the U.S. Congress got to vote on what multinational corporations do.) What I mean is a less *lonely* society, where we think collectively about resources for the common good, rather than struggling individually against each other for material and psychic survival. What I mean is a more humane society, where our driving motive is abundant life for all rather than increasing extravagance for a few and suffering for many more. Nor do I think there is presently any complete blueprint for how this political and economic democracy would occur in the United States. We are called on to invent it, as the "New Left" set out to do thirty years ago.

With the collapse of socialist governments around the world, we are called on to reinvent the movements for a society where, in Margaret Randall's words, "everyone contributes and everyone is cared for." Randall feels that many of these socialist movements failed because they would not develop a feminist agenda. Queer socialism would occur within a profoundly feminist revolutionary context, defined by Randall as "a feminist discourse based on an ideology embracing democratic relations of power, a redefinition of history and of memory, and a world view that favors life over the signs of imminent death that we experience on so many fronts."[15]

This queer socialism of a "Newer Left" would recognize the damage done by five hundred years of colonial rule. People of color have suffered for five hundred years from the European/Christian war between mind and body, soul and body, projected onto all women and onto cultures that often had more holistic worldviews and darker skins. The mind/body split allows the one hundred white men owning poultry plants in Mississippi to tell the Black women workers, "We only want your bodies, not your minds," as those men lock the women into plants where twenty-seven out of thirty in one factory acquired carpal tunnel syndrome.[16] It generates rape and devastating physical and psychological violence against women. It also defines gay men and lesbians in this period as only perverse bodies engaged in sinful/sick/illegal physical acts, as "abominations." And it discards the old and the disabled. When we lesbians and gay men see that Black women in Mississippi poultry plants and Mexican women in *maquilas* are also defined as only bodies, to be used and discarded, machines without feelings and souls, we can understand more fully how our fates are implicated in theirs. When we don't respond to others being hurt by similar forces, how can we expect them to respond to our crises and pains? As Rabbi Hillel taught two thousand years ago, "If we are not for ourselves, who will be for us? [But] if we are not for others, who are we?"

As queer socialists, we would bring our insights and strengths to a range of progressive struggles. A queer socialism would be inevitably inflected for gender, would have our anger and our militancy, our humor and our flair, and would shape a movement that includes gay and lesbian homeless people, many of them cross-dressers, and many, people of color. We know that in some cultures that do not hate the body, the male and female principles are not so much at war as they are in this culture, and that gender-transgressive people like the *berdache* in American Indian societies are considered holy people— as we are holy people. A queer socialism would clarify our roles as workers, as "means of production." But we gay people also bring the knowledge that humans are not only "means of production," however much capitalism seeks to define us that way. We know and insist that our needs include not only the survival needs of food, shelter, health care, and clothing but also dignity, pleasure, intimacy, and love.

In adding our lavender stripe to the rainbow, we bring our grief and our creativity in the too-familiar face of death. I have watched my gay brothers care for one another to the grave, joined in their care, of course, by lesbians and heterosexuals. I've been around a good bit, and I have not witnessed this particular tender brotherhood in the face of disease and death in other places in the same way. Many of these are white men, middle-class men, who have taught me about courage and compassion. None of what I urge here is about categories we cannot escape. It is about who we choose to be.

Gay men and lesbians also bring the ability to create familial love that does not depend on biology, on the worship of our own gene pools. Those non-biological parents among us know that we can love and parent any child—it mainly requires our rapt attention to an unfolding wonder—and that the children in the inner cities, the babies born in the *maquilas*, are also our children. As an African proverb teaches, "It takes a whole village to raise a child." These days, it must take a whole country unwilling to write off any of its young.

A queer socialism would not be provincially urban. It would

recognize that the most crucial battles for gay/lesbian politics in the next decade will not be in the cities where we have our power base, where most of our people are concentrated. The Right has finally figured out to take us on their turf, not ours. These battles will be in areas that are more rural and historically more conservative. In those areas, we will develop new models not dependent on a critical gay mass and gay infrastructure. We will create broad-based movements against homophobia and all forms of social injustice rather than movements only for gay and lesbian rights. These movements will hold heterosexuals accountable for heterosexism, generating heterosexual allies and then trusting them to do their jobs. The trust we will gain through this process is one of the opportunities within the crisis. Heterosexuals will increasingly learn how their fates are implicated in ours, how homophobia erodes their most intimate relationships and corrupts their institutions, building repression into our military, fear into our schools' quest for understanding and knowledge, and meanspiritedness into proclamations of love from churches, mosques, and synagogues. If the Religious Right has its way, they will use homophobia as an ax against the very taproot of this country's democratic potential, the revolutionary concept of human dignity and equality.

In my vision of a reinvigorated movement, the National Gay and Lesbian Task Force would take a stand on major issues of our time, such as the North American Free Trade Act: against NAFTA and in solidarity with working people, who are most of our people; in recognition that unemployed people (whose numbers NAFTA will increase) are six times more likely to commit acts of violence than people who are employed, and some of that will be hate violence; and in recognition that NAFTA will override our national and local laws on labor and environmental standards (as "unfair labor practices"), constricting once again this country's democratic possibilities.

In my movement, the Task Force would call up Ben Chavis, the new NAACP director, and say, "Rev. Chavis, thank you for your support of the March on Washington"—for which he came under serious attack from within his own organization—"and we'd like to return the favor." We'd say, "The next time a big vote on racism comes up in Congress, we'll be there with you, with our hundred thousand members and $4 million budget, because we appreciate your help and because that's about our people, too." My movement would not avoid these stands for fear it would divide our constituency—which is already divided; it would take leadership stands to unite us around broader principles.

In *our* movement, we see the opportunity in the crisis to do what we should have done twenty-five years ago: increase our determination to keep faith with one another by not tolerating racism, sexism, anti-Semitism, ageism, the fear and neglect of the disabled, or class divisions in ourselves or in our organizations.

In our movement we don't panic or blame ourselves; we stay accountable and take the long view. The quincentenary of Columbus's arrival in the Americas gave us the opportunity to reflect on five hundred years of resistance. The people of color among us let us know that this is not a decade's or even a lifetime's struggle. If we sacrifice our relationships to immediate victories, we will lose in the long haul. How we treat one another matters more than any particular "win" because our goal is a transformed culture, which also requires transformed human relationships.

In our movement, we seize the opportunity to face our own self-destructive fears and isolations in the messages of the Right, and to stare them down. As Creek poet Joy Harjo wrote:

Oh, you have choked me, but I gave you the leash,
You have gutted me, but I gave you the knife,
You have devoured me, but I gave you the heated thing.
I take myself back, fear.[17]

In our movement, we claim no more or less than our human place among the creatures on the planet. Queer socialism moves us to the post-queer.

This reenergized movement will be, in Suzanne Pharr's eloquent terms, "not a wedge, but a bridge"; not a point of division, but of expansion and connection. To those who insist on denying us our full humanity, we will insist on the sacred humanity of all people. *A bridge, not a wedge. A bridge, not a wedge.* It has a nice ring to it. We can say it like a mantra when we feel the Right getting too hot. Folks from San Francisco can help us in this imaging—all those bays, all that steel hanging up in the air, and people got the nerve to drive across it. How does it stay up there, anyway, across the blue expanse?

Yes, the fires are burning. But think of all that water.

And, even in a hot wind, bridges will sing.

Afterword

I wrote this section for the new edition to catch readers up on at least a slice of events that have transpired since Race Traitor's *publication in 1994. The major updates are on "cold cases" from the earlier era, in Robeson County and for White Patriot leader Glenn Miller. I'll also provide brief updates on key individuals who chose to share them with me. There are other huge resonances with contemporary events that the original book will provoke.*

In the fall of 2014 two villainous characters from this book reemerged: Joe Freeman Britt, the infamous "Death Penalty DA" from Robeson County, and Glenn Miller, former head of the White Patriot Party.

I opened the *New York Times* one day in September 2014 and saw the story of Britt's role in the false convictions of Henry McCollum and Leon Brown.[1] It resulted in over a quarter of a century of unjustified incarceration of two mentally impaired African American men on charges of rape and murder, even as the prosecution ignored the probable culprit, who lived adjacent to where the body was found and who would kill again in a similar manner less than two months after the first killing. As Miller's White Patriot Party rampaged out of his farm near Angier and from Fort Bragg, a separate but equal set of events in North Carolina unfolded around a succession of murders of Indian and black men allegedly connected to Robeson County's active drug trade and the alleged complicity of local law enforcement and DA Britt. (We used "alleged" a lot in those days.)

The most infamous was the murder of Julian Pierce, a Lumbee attorney who headed up Lumber River Legal Services and was running against Britt for North Carolina Superior Court judge. After getting his law degree from the North Carolina Central University School of Law, Pierce worked for the U.S. Securities and Exchange Commission, earned a master's degree in tax law from Georgetown, and accepted an invitation to direct Lumber River Legal Services.[2] Pierce realized that if they could pull together a coalition of Black, Indian, and white voters, they could defeat Britt and substantially shift the balance of power in the county. But as chapter 8 explains, he was murdered in his home the Saturday before the election, and the Sheriff's Department (also implicated with Britt in the drug trade) soon turned up a suspect, who allegedly committed suicide as law enforcement was closing in on him; the Sheriff's Department closed the case. In the election the Tuesday after his murder, Julian Pierce received 10,787 votes and Britt received 8,231. But Pierce was dead, so Britt became Superior Court judge. The interracial coalition against the drug trade went on to win elections and make substantial changes in the county.

Julian Pierce's children never accepted the sheriff's version of the story. For years they have worked to get the investigation reopened. His daughter Julia, a University of Virginia graduate, is a senior lawyer for the Indian Health Service, a department within the U.S. Department of Health and Human Services, and she serves as its highest-level Indian attorney. In their search for justice for her father, Julia and her family were assisted by Attorney General Roy Cooper (who is now governor). A family delegation got an appointment with the North Carolina State Bureau of Investigation (SBI) to raise a series of questions about the investigation. They were particularly concerned about discrepancies between law enforcement descriptions of the suicide of Pierce's alleged murderer and the autopsy reports. In February 2017, Julia finally got an audience for herself, her mother, the Lumbee tribal chief, and her lawyer to see SBI representatives, who refused to reopen the case.[3]

Ian Mance, an attorney for the Southern Coalition for Social Justice who works with the Pierce family, summarized for me where the case stands. An article written by Joseph Neff for the *News and Observer* article correctly reported: "Two people interviewed by Pierce's lawyer pointed to law enforcement relatives as being involved in the murder. The son of a local drug dealer said that his father was allied with Sheriff Stone and that his father was involved in the murder. The dealer was never investigated." Mance gave these names and the substance of these interviews to the SBI and Attorney General Cooper in 2015. Despite these efforts, the SBI has refused to interview these individuals.

Last year, Mance received a letter from the state informing him that the SBI had done a second review of the case file in response to his continued letters and calls. The letter did not provide any details about the nature of this review, but it seemed to be simply a review of existing materials and did not include any new interviews. Mance and Julia Pierce continue to push the state to send investigators to talk to these individuals.

There is a new district attorney in Robeson County, Matt Scott, who is the first Lumbee DA in county history. He knows the Pierce family. His office ceded jurisdiction of the case to the attorney general's office in 1988, but it's possible his election may provide new opportunities for an investigation that would finally resolve who killed Julian Pierce and why.

Malinda Maynor Lowery, an associate professor of history and director of the Center for the Study of the American South at the University of North Carolina at Chapel Hill, recently published a powerful history, *The Lumbee Indians: An American Struggle*. Chapter 6 of that book, "They Can Kill Me, but They Can't Eat Me: The Drug War," puts the struggles of the 1980s in Robeson County into the encompassing narrative of the Lumbee people.[4] There is also a new podcast, *The Murder of James Jordan*, about the father of basketball superstar Michael Jordan (James was killed in Robeson County); early episodes talk about Julian's murder.

Julia Pierce and I spoke on March 27, 2019, thirty-one years to the day since her father was murdered. She shared that the current target in her unending quest for justice is Governor Roy Cooper, since he has the authority to order the reopening of the investigation into her father's murder; she and others she is working with have repeatedly requested a meeting. I shared my own memories of the devastating week her father died and what a brave man he was—a hero. Julia appreciated my words and agreed that he had been doing his best to address the inequities and injustices facing minority communities in the whole state. She noted that the Robeson County community that is the home base for the Lumbee tribe still recognizes her father's contributions and goals in many ways to try to keep his vision alive.

On April 13, 2014, Frazier Glenn Miller turned up again like a very bad penny, or one of those recurring nightmares from which it is difficult to awaken. That week a reporter from the Durham-based *Indy Weekly* called me in Brooklyn for a comment, and I learned that the neo-Nazi leader whose increasingly wild activities were the focus of my North Carolina life in the late 1980s had that Sunday shot dead a fourteen-year-old and his grandfather outside the Overland Park Jewish Community Center near Kansas City, then proceeded to Village Shalom, a Jewish retirement community a mile away, to kill a woman on her way to visit her mother.[5]

My God, I wondered from Brooklyn at reading about Britt's role in the McCollum/Brown convictions and now Miller's triple murder in Kansas City. *Is this some Carolina night of the un-living undead?*

The trajectory of the first two-thirds of this book rises and falls on the career of Miller, who during the 1980s in North Carolina organized the most effective neo-Nazi organization in the United States. Today Glenn Miller sits on death row in Kansas City, Missouri. Miller had dropped off of my radar screen about the time that he entered federal prison in 1990. In this new edition, it is worth picking up the rest of his story for several reasons. First, today we know more about past events, both from Miller's self-published 1999 autobiography and from subsequent reporting on his case. However miserable a failure he was, the vision he embraced plays out today on a much broader stage. Also, Glenn Miller's neo-Nazi organizing left his white family shattered, with two sons' graves as markers of the filial tragedy. These sons of Glenn provide a cautionary tale of one white supremacist who was so intent on saving the white race that he destroyed his

white family—his own contribution to "white genocide" on an intimate scale. It suggests, as I argue in this book, that white supremacy
is white genocide.

Race Traitor records how Miller participated in the November 3,
1979, Klan and Nazi caravan whose members killed five anti-Klan
demonstrators in Greensboro. Remarkably, none of the assailants
were ever convicted of any crime, although their rampage was caught
on film by cameras from two TV stations. In the next decade Miller
went on to organize the Carolina Knights, then the White Patriot
Party (WPP), and to assemble up to five hundred foot soldiers to
march through North Carolina towns. He ran for office frequently,
garnering additional publicity, and boasted that he was organizing "a
white Christian army to take back the South," which would happen
once a thousand followers mobilized in one of his marches. Through
the intervention of the Southern Poverty Law Center (SPLC) rather
than actual work by NC lawmen, Miller was put under a consent
order not to do paramilitary organizing. In January 2017 the Justice
Department issued a twelve-page indictment of several of the WPP
leadership. When the SPLC brought Miller back into court for violating the consent decree, he faced a year in prison, and his cadres were
facing a trial for conspiracy to obtain weapons and explosives from the
U.S. armed forces to "maintain, train and equip a paramilitary armed
force . . . to further the goals of the White Supremacist Movement."[6]

When *Race Traitor* went to print, I did not use rumors circulating
in the summer of 1987 that Miller had been arrested on a charge of
soliciting prostitution around the time of his turning state's evidence,
after a Raleigh police officer saw a car parked on a deserted street at
night and found Miller in the backseat with a black transsexual. One
rumor implied that he was not prosecuted on that charge because
he had already turned state's evidence. Another was that the arrest
helped law enforcement turn Miller into an informant. Back then, I
could not confirm any of these rumors. But Miller himself explained
years later, in a rambling interview on the SPLC website, that the account of his arrest was true—though he explained that he was really
just "carrying [the person he was found in the backseat with] out to
whip his ass," one episode in his practice of "going around picking up

niggers and beating the hell out of them, particular nigger faggots."[7]
But it seems Miller was "whipping his ass" *after* sex, not before. The
other party's name was Peaches.[8]

Then as now, I wonder: how much of this history of beating up
black queers and trans folk did the North Carolina police know or
care about? As the editor of the *Aurora Advertiser* said of the always
media-obsessed Miller after his 2014 rampage in Kansas City, "Everyone thought he was harmless."[9] But we at NCARRV never did. As
NCARRV often argued in the 1980s, much of Miller's constitution-
ally protected speech was in fact admission of crimes. What really
made law enforcement go after these white supremacists was their
targeting of police and federal officials.

If in years past the Order targeted law enforcement and the president, now the president, former attorney general Jeff Sessions, and
many far-right groups line up with the Blue Lives Matter movement.
In the 1990s, NCARRV pressured law enforcement to prosecute law-
breaking white supremacists. Today prison abolitionists encourage
communities to solve conflicts within their communities when they
can, and restorative justice practices give communities tools to practice doing so.

Miller turned out to be a lousy witness in trials that mostly
brought acquittals of his trailer-park friends and other white supremacists. He testified in exchange for plea bargains on charges
that could have kept him in prison for a hundred years. In 1989,
Douglas Sheets was acquitted of the Shelby killings, having claimed
that Miller was the culprit. The case was never solved. In 1990,
Miller went to jail for three years and then into the federal witness
protection program.

In April 2014 when Miller set out for the Overland Park Jewish
Community Center, he left his wife, Marge, back in the Aryan home,
apparently ignorant of what he intended to do. With this second wife,
he had three boys and two girls. In 2008, their son Jesse died on the
side of a Missouri road after he inexplicably shot to death a man who
stopped to help him after a traffic accident. Then Jesse also shot a
police officer who arrived on the scene; the officer returned the fire
and killed Jesse on the spot. Marge was in the vehicle with him that

day—they were on the way to put flowers on the grave of her son Mike, his brother.

Mike had died in a car wreck at age nineteen in 1998, not long after being released from jail for tossing a Molotov cocktail in 1995 into a crowded trailer that housed an interracial couple. Mike's ex-partner Connie explained that Mike had been saved during his 120-day incarceration (presumably by Jesus, not by Odin) and rejected his father's teachings. But he had gotten caught up in drugs, "meth, Valium, whatever he could get," Connie explained. "Mike was encouraged to be violent and fight his whole life, so I think that was Mike's escape route, the drugs." Connie said that Miller's third son, Frazier III, "never bought his father's crap" and left home as soon as he could.[10]

Michael and Jesse Miller lie side by side, on their gravestones matching declarations: "Our Young Rebel—Saxon Braveheart. Ride now forever, my son, with Valkyrie angels in the heavens. Dad."

Recent reports show that of all racial-ethnic groups, whites are the only group with rising mortality rates. The additional deaths are largely due to "unprecedented levels of suicide, alcohol-related liver disease and overdoses of heroin and prescription opioids" among white Americans between forty-five and fifty-four with a high school education or less.[11] These Americans are facing a "sea of despair" from the collapse of "the high school educated working class after its heyday in the early 1970s," according to research by Ann Case and Angus Deaton.[12] White nationalists argue that this decline in the "white race" was caused by affirmative action for people of color. In fact, the roots of this despair are the decision by white elites to abandon their contract with white workers during the structural shift in the economy that started in 1969, as the global economy began its realignment to an information and service mode. In the 1970s, capital flight, corporate consolidation, attacks on unions, and a shift to a contingent workforce destabilized white families and decimated people of color. For a fuller explanation of this shift, see "A Bridge, Not a Wedge," the final section of Race Traitor.

In April 2014, when I saw images of Miller on TV, he was hardly the dapper, clean-shaven ex–Green Beret in camo gear that I had tracked, or the Saxon Braveheart he projected onto his dead sons. He was a ramshackle old man, unkempt, wheeled into court looking very naked under the peculiar black sleeveless garment that more or less covered his thighs but threatened to reveal what was left of the Aryan Nations' family jewels. (This vest is designed as suicide protection, I later read.) He cleared a mental competency test, defended himself, and was convicted of murder. On November 10, 2015, Miller was sentenced to death by lethal injection. Given the state of his health, he is more likely to die while waiting on death row than on the gurney.

White supremacist Don Black's assessment of Miller at the time of Miller's deeds shed light on Miller and on the nicer distinctions of the media-conscious Klan's aspirations to respectability. Black knew Miller in the 1980s, when he was "something of an alcohol-driven blowhard," and more recently Black denied him access to his online hate forum Stormfront.org. Black observed, "We have enough of a problem with how we are portrayed without some homicidal whack job coming along and reinforcing that." (Black himself spent time in prison for attempting in the 1980s to overthrow the government of the Caribbean island of Dominica to establish a white state, which apparently is more Nazi-normal.) Black also pointed out the "weird and suspicious" fact that none of the Kansas victims were Jewish.[13] A less critical online response from one cyber-Nazi read, "Miller's motives were pure, but his execution was disastrous."[14]

Donald Trump has changed the algebra on such sensitivity about media portrayals for Klansmen and neo-Nazis—they are all now "good folk." Trump has so lowered the bar on speech and behavior that the far-right "politics of respectability" (such as it was) are no longer needed. The gloves are off, if they ever were on.

Given his many disasters, the goals Miller set for himself back then are instructive. In the 1980s, our job in North Carolina was to see that Nazi and Klan forces did not strengthen and to stop their racist, homophobic, and anti-Semitic violence. With a strong coalition that today would be described as intersectional, we set out to strip away Klan and Nazi leaders' pretense of being merely the "white person's NAACP." Glenn Miller never achieved his goals, but he had a vision of what white supremacist organizing might achieve. In 1984 white "revolutionist" Robert Mathews met Miller outside Benson to drop off

$200,000 from the group's cache of stolen money. Miller mused about this meeting in *A White Man Speaks Out*: "I often since then fantasized a scenario wherein he and I were leaders in a great above-ground organization, with hundreds of thousands of members, and with millions of dollars with which to build the Cause of racial unity, strength and survival. . . . We would have the best young minds leading the growing formations of awakened White people in every community, town and city throughout the South, and their fanaticism would create inspiration and social upheavals so that the White masses would overcome their fears and brainwashing and would love and support them."[15]

At about 9:00 on the night of the 2016 elections it began to sink in with a pit-of-the-stomach ferocity that Donald Trump would win the U.S. presidency. I attended an election-watching party at my friend Laura Flanders's flat on Canal and Broadway in Lower Manhattan with a phalanx of other longtime freedom workers. We experienced the collective shudder when the networks declared Trump's victory because we knew viscerally the multitude of terrible historical forces his election would unleash. It was a huge white supremacist tipping point, marked by a white supremacist meeting located only blocks from the White House in which participants celebrated Trump's election by shouting "Heil!" and giving a Nazi salute.

In terms of the reach of current white supremacists and white nationalists, a contrast with the 1980s is instructive. As he explained in 1999, Glenn Miller "unloaded the 20,000 *White Carolinians* [his newspaper] and stacked them neatly in a corner of [his] living room," then he "rolled the rest in rubber bands for distribution to the public." Meanwhile his wife, Marge, "was busy sticking address labels onto envelopes, and sorting them by zip codes." Then Glenn drove to the post office with envelopes in "neat stacks" loaded into "postal shipping bags." (Any organizer from that era sympathizes.) All of this, he calculated, required "30 to 40 man-hours, or in our case, woman hours, because Marge did most of it by herself." But when Glenn "pondered the financial and mathematical results," he concluded that "it took distribution of a thousand papers for one new member, supporter or subscriber. And a meeting or rally brought only $1 per attendee in donations."[16] As much as Marge worked, it was hard to reach a tipping point with these odds. Miller used phone lines with answering machines dedicated to WPP propaganda; by July 1986 he was operating a total of twenty-eight machines. In 2019, a marauding killer in a New Zealand mosque wearing a live-streaming camera on his head got 1.5 million hits on the Internet as he killed peaceful Muslim worshippers.

Also different from the 1980s is the degree to which the far right is armed, in public and in private. In 2017 Virginia governor Terry McAuliffe claimed in Charlottesville that if "you saw the militia walking down the street, you would have thought they were an army."[17]

Miller's ragtag band is hardly the model or the greatest danger for this new era, in which a lone white man with enough guns is his own army, especially when he takes on children, worshippers peacefully assembled in prayer, or people at a concert. Far-right organizers no longer need cell structures like the Order when they can get susceptible young white men to upload their ideology and tactics right into their heads from the World Wide Web. "Surplus" arms and tanks from Iraq and Afghanistan show up in local policing in places like Ferguson, where tightening grids of racist coercion reach flash points, as they did in the police killing of Michael Brown.

Erik Prince, another former soldier operating out of North Carolina, made a lot more than Glenn Miller did out of paramilitary organizing. In 1997, Prince used his $1.35 billion inheritance from his father, also a right-wing Christian bent on global conquests, to open Blackwater USA on seven thousand acres near North Carolina's Great Dismal Swamp. Blackwater would become "the world's largest private military facility," and Prince's enterprise would draw millions of dollars in contracts from the U.S. government.

So when Glenn Miller dreamed of having access to "millions of dollars" to run his own personal army, it was a pipe dream. He did not have Erik Prince's daddy's $1.35 billion at his disposal.

Where Are They Now?

John Fletcher Segrest Jr. My father died in 2005 in a nursing home in Columbia, South Carolina, where he lived after suffering a stroke in 2000. My sister Dallas cared for him carefully, as did her children, many of whom now live with their partners and children in and near Columbia. My father was accompanied in assisted living by his stuffed squirrel but not his shotgun; his stoicism served him well, as he withstood the flirtations of the many women who sought his attention on the walk to dinner. Because of the work we did together on *Race Traitor*, he remained my good friend to the end, and I thanked him and we bid each other goodbye shortly before his death.

John Fletcher Segrest III. My brother John died of complications from colon cancer in 1998 in Alabama. For my story of his death, see "Requim for My Brother" in *Born to Belonging: Essays on Spirit and Justice* (New Brunswick, NJ: Rutgers University Press, 2001).

Barbara Culbertson. Barbara writes, "From my sweet adobe home in Santa Fe I offer traditional Ka Ta See healing, teaching and counseling. The Ka Ta See people have been around for at least 30,000 years and live a deep respect and for self, others, Earth and all her inhabitants. To them fun is important. They have much wisdom for us. Here in Santa Fe, the sun is intense, the stars close by, and the mountains big and nourishing."

Leonard Zeskind. His book *Blood and Politics: The History of the White Nationalist Movement from the Margins to the Mainstream* was published by Farrar, Straus and Giroux in 2009. He is working at the Institute for Research and Education on Human Rights to fight the white-ists and the far right.

Mac Legerton. Mac continues to direct the Center for Community Change in Lumberton, and is involved in environmental struggles such as the challenge to the Atlantic Coast Pipeline, which runs through Robeson County.

Marty Nathan. She will be in North Carolina in 2019 for the fortieth anniversary of the Greensboro Massacre. She writes: "I live in Northampton, Massachusetts, with my husband of thirty-three years, Elliot Fratkin. Our daughter Leah is married and has two kids, and we adopted two children, Mulugetta and Masaye Fratkin. They are twenty-seven and twenty-six and live in New Mexico and Brooklyn, respectively. Eli is a retired Smith College anthropologist, and I am almost retired from family practice at an urban Latino clinic in North Springfield, Massachusetts. I head a project there, the Cliniquita, that provides health care to undocumented workers, and also direct the Markham-Nathan Fund for Social Justice, which raises and distributes grants to small grassroots groups in western Massachusetts. I also work with local climate justice organizations and write a column for our newspaper about climate change."

Eddie Hatcher. The man who masterminded the hostage takeover of the *Robesonian* died in a North Carolina prison in 2009 of complications from AIDS. In 2001 he was convicted of murder in a drive-by shooting, which Hatcher denied, saying it was harassment.[18] In the 1990s and 2000s in prison Eddie lived openly as a gay man, advocating from his cell for gay people and for human rights.

Christina Davis-McCoy. Christina sent this assessment: "In many ways the current resurgence certainly confirms how deeply white supremacy and racial superiority are embedded/entrenched in the American psyche. It only takes 'one voice with authority' to sanction and ignite hatred smoldering underneath. Now it is ablaze! Anyway . . . we did great work together during the eighties and into the early nineties. Tracking activity, reporting, organizing communities, and making the breadth of the problem clearly evident were vital to arresting that resurgence then. The lessons we learned could/should continue to serve as touchstones needed for retooling today's ongoing struggle toward Racial Justice. For sure, those lessons have served me well in this my rural roots place of Raeford, Hoke County, North Carolina, where I returned and have remained for the past twenty-five years doing community development work. The 'unabashed courage to confront injustice' we supported in each other has been key to enduring here. That audacity was vitally instrumental during the local sheriff's campaign of 1998, when my brother Jim became the county's first Black elected sheriff. The struggle here continues."

Notes

Introduction to the New Edition

1. Combahee River Collective, "The Combahee River Collective Statement," in *Home Girls: A Black Feminist Anthology* (New York: Kitchen Table: Women of Color Press, 1983), 272.

2. *This Bridge Called My Back: Radical Writings by Women of Color*, ed. Cherríe Moraga and Gloria Anzuldúa (New York: Kitchen Table: Women of Color Press, 1983; 4th ed., Albany: State University of New York Press, 2015). There are many other brilliant women, books, and sectors of movements involved in these years of struggles, particularly the rich and complex contributions by feminists of color. This is my attempt in broad strokes to identify the ones that most influenced me and this book.

3. Patrick Kingsley, "New Zealand Massacre Highlights Global Reach of White Extremism," *New York Times*, March 15, 2019.

4. Nicolas Vinocur, "How European Ideas Motivated Christchurch Killer," *Politico,* March 16, 2019. Much of the manifesto was drawn from Renaud Camus, a French right-wing extremist and openly gay academic; its central idea echoed white supremacist fears of "white genocide" from the nineteenth century, most recently targeting Muslim immigrants fleeing the civil war in Syria and other "wars on terror" to arrive en masse in Europe, in particular France.

5. Tina Vasquez, "Samuel Oliver-Bruno, Deported After Immigration Appointment, in His Own Words," *Rewire News*, December 14, 2018.

6. Meagan Flynn, "Feds Deport Undocumented Immigrant Whose Church Supporters Went to Jail to Protect Him," *Washington Post*, November 30, 2018.

7. Felony charges of incitement to riot were dismissed against all twelve defendants. Misdemeanor charges of injury to property, defacing public buildings or monuments, and conspiracy to deface were either dismissed for

lack of admissible evidence or, in one case, tried and found not guilty. See Sarah Willets, "Judge Tells Durham GOP Why He Didn't Convict Protestors Charged with Toppling a Confederate Monument," *Indy Week*, March 9, 2018. See Southern Vision Alliance, "Our History," southernvision.org/about /letter-from-the-southern-vision-alliance-our-history, and Workers World, "Defend Durham Anti-Racists," February 12, 2018, www.workers.org/2018/02/12 /defend-durham-anti-racists.

8. The SONG website is http://southernersonnewground.org.

1. Osceola's Head

1. See Adrienne Rich, "What Would We Create?," *What Is Found There: Notebooks on Poetry and Politics* (New York: W.W. Norton, 1993), 21.

2. James Forman, *Sammy Younge, Jr.* (New York: Grove Press, 1968), 25.

3. This story is also recounted in Patricia R. Wickman's *Osceola's Legacy* (Tuscaloosa: University of Alabama Press, 1991), 144–45.

2. The Typical American Democracy

1. Thomas Dixon Jr., *The Leopard's Spots: A Romance of the White Man's Burden—1865–1900* (New York: A. Wessels Company, 1906), 385–86. "Can the Ethiopian change his skin or the leopard his spots?" asks the title page.

2. W.J. Cash, *The Mind of the South* (New York: Alfred A. Knopf, 1941; reprint, Garden City, NY: Doubleday Anchor, 1954), 51–52.

3. Workers' Viewpoint Organization news release, "WVO Calls for Demonstration and Conference Against the Klan," October 11, 1979, in Elizabeth Wheaton, *Codename Greenkil: The 1979 Greensboro Killings* (Athens: University of Georgia Press, 1987), 104. I rely on Wheaton's book for many of the details about the events on and around November 3, but I disagree with her thesis that "there were no heroes in this story; there are only many, many fools" (4). I cannot accept "fool" as the final assessment of the five people killed in Greensboro on November 3. They were isolated by their ideology both before and after the attack on November 3. They were also heroic in their commitments to each other and to a vision of a more just society. I find that Wheaton makes much more severe judgments about the people whose politics and philosophies are closer to hers and, in a strange way, lets the Klan and Nazi killers morally off the hook. For example, she recounts the outbreak of violence at the anti-Klan rally in the third person and often accepts as fact the Klansmen's versions as to their motives; e.g., "To [David] Matthews, Mike Nathan and his 'Death to the Klan' sign were just another 'nigger with a shotgun.' He pulled the trigger" (147).

4. The footage by cameramen Ed Boyd of WTVD in Durham and Jim Waters of WXII-TV in Greensboro was used as evidence in all three trials.

5. As news accounts and court documents demonstrated, Ed Dawson was the Greensboro Police Department informant and Bernard Butkovich was the Bureau of Alcohol, Tobacco, and Firearms agent.

6. The men initially charged with murder and conspiracy to commit murder were Roland Wayne Wood, Coleman Blair "Johnny" Pridmore, Terry Wayne Hartsoe, Lisford Carl Nappier, Billy Joe Franklin, Jerry Paul Smith, Michael Eugene Clinton, Lee Joseph McLain, Roy Clinton Toney, David Wayne Matthews, Lawrence Gene Morgan, and Harold Dean Flowers (Wheaton, 157). Later, the conspiracy charges were dropped and first-degree murder and felony riot indictments were issued for David Matthews, Jerry Smith, Jack Fowler, Wayne Wood, Johnny Pridmore, Lawrence Morgan, Roy Toney, Junior McBride, Harold Flowers, Billy Joe Franklin, and Terry Hartsoe. Carl Nappier, Lee McLain, and Michael Clinton were indicted only on riot charges (Wheaton, 203). Six defendants went to trial together: Fowler, Smith, Pridmore, Morgan, Wood, and Matthews. When they were acquitted, the state dropped the charges against the other men.

7. Rand Manzella was indicted for going "armed to the terror of the public"; Nelson Johnson, Allen Blitz, Dori Blitz, Lacy Russell, and Percy Sims were charged with misdemeanor riot, and Willena Cannon for interfering with an arrest. Later, the district attorney's office asked the grand jury for felony indictments against all of them, but dropped all the charges after the acquittals in the state murder trial (Wheaton, 182, 204).

8. Wheaton, 152.

9. CWP press statement, released November 5, 1979; quoted in Wheaton, 170.

10. The prosecution had expert Bruce Koenig analyze the audio portion of the videotapes to determine the source of shots; in his testimony in the murder trial, he was 90 percent certain that shots three, four, and five came from an indeterminate place that could have been near the demonstrators and could have been near the Klan caravan. When pressed in court, Koenig identified a spot where defendants said they had seen demonstrators with guns. In the later federal trial, Koenig changed his testimony, saying that the three shots could have come from another area where Klan were—an area, he testified, he was not asked by the prosecution to consider in the state trial. State prosecutors angrily denied the truth of Koenig's statement (Wheaton, 218, 259).

11. *McCullum v. Smith* was bounced out of district court on the grounds that it had no standing. While the Center for Constitutional Rights was appealing, the Justice Department changed its position, deciding that it did have jurisdiction to prosecute racially motivated violence under the Thirteenth Amendment.

12. No one was ever arrested in this incident.

13. The people were Leah Wise, the Martins, Reverend Lee, Mardie McCreary (a lawyer who had recently moved to Durham and soon began working

part-time for Southerners for Economic Justice, taking on the staffing tasks for the emerging anti-Klan effort), Kira Dirlik (a friend of Leah's), Taylor Scott (an Episcopalian minister), Bob Hall (from the Institute for Southern Studies), C.P. Ellis (a white union organizer who had been a Klan leader until he underwent a change of heart), and Chip Hughes (active in farmworker and Brown Lung Association organizing). Later Carol Kirschenbaum of the Progressive Jewish Network joined, about the same time that I did. Marty Nathan, widow of Mike Nathan, had begun to organize the Greensboro Civil Rights Fund in response to the Greensboro slayings. She also attended early meetings, in spite of remaining tensions that existed between the Communist Workers Party and some of the members of the working group.

14. Court Order, *Bobby Person v. Carolina Knights of the Ku Klux Klan*, 84-534-Civ-5, U.S. Dist. Court, Eastern District of N.C., January 18, 1985.

15. The station was WTVD; the program was *Reflections*. It eventually aired in February 1984.

16. The defendants in *U.S. v. Griffin* (835301-G, U.S. Dist. Court, Middle District of N.C.) were Virgil Griffin, Ed Dawson, David Matthews, Wayne Wood, Jerry Paul Smith, Jack Fowler, Roy Toney, John Pridmore, and Milano Caudle. They were charged with violating Section 371, Title 18, U.S. Code; and subsections 245 (b)(2)(B) and (b)(4)(A) (Wheaton, 253).

3. Statesville

1. This incident occurred on January 29, 1983, and was later cited by the FBI as the beginning of their investigation, which eventually brought to justice the Klan men and women involved in attacks in Iredell and Alexander counties. "Man Faces Trial, Another Pleads Guilty in Cross-Burnings," *Charlotte Observer*, July 24, 1985.

2. Dee Reid, "Rev. Wilson Lee," *The Independent*, December 20, 1985.

3. Unpublished paper by Mary Beatty, "Wilson W. Lee and the Struggle for Civil Rights in Statesville, North Carolina."

4. "Federal Unit Is Probing Racial Threats at MCC," *Statesville Record and Landmark*, March 25, 1985.

5. Letter received by Bernard Robertson, March 15, 1985.

6. "Judge Orders Trial in Shooting Incident," *Charlotte Observer*, April 10, 1985. John McCann, Donald Ray McCann, and James Wesley Meyers were each charged with one count of felonious discharge of a weapon into an oc-cupied dwelling and two counts of assault with a deadly weapon, charges that could have brought a maximum of fifty years. Statesville police said that no facts indicated racial motivations for the gunfire, in spite of the fact that one witness testified that one of the men ran into the middle of the street and said, "We're going to get us some niggers now."

7. "Economy" information sheet, Statesville Chamber of Commerce, 1984.

8. "Civic Section . . . for Statesville, North Carolina," compiled by the Statesville Chamber of Commerce, 1985, for the Iredell County phone book.

9. Dee Reid, "A Window on Racism: Is Statesville Peculiar, or Typical?," *The Independent*, September 13–26, 1985, 5–6.

10. Jubilee House, where we stayed when we were in Statesville, was an intentional Christian community, at the core of which were Michael and Sarah Woodard, Kathleen Murdock, Mike and Sarah's children Tiff and Jessica, and Margaret Carpenter and her daughter Beth. They ran a battered women's shelter, a homeless shelter, and a winter emergency shelter, as well as participating in a range of progressive activism, especially Central American solidarity work. I met Kathleen on a Witness for Peace trip to Nicaragua in winter 1985. Reverend Lee had told me to be sure to meet Kathleen on our trip, that she and the other folks at Jubilee House were "wonderful people," which proved to be true. Many an evening, Chris and I returned exhausted to their home to their fellowship, home cooking and laughter.

11. *Gomillion v. Lightfoot*, 167 F. Supp. 405 (M.D. Ala., 1958); 365 U.S. 399 (1960).

12. See Robert J. Norrell, *Reaping the Whirlwind: The Civil Rights Movement in Tuskegee* (New York: Random House, 1986), chapters 9 and 10, for an account of the desegregation of Tuskegee High. Norrell's account reminds me that, even though a sense of isolation in a chaotic world is what I took from those events, there was in fact a faction of white liberals who had hoped to lead a peaceful school integration that would provide a model for other Alabama communities to follow. I am especially moved to reread Norrell's account of Alice Wadsworth, a white woman who attempted with her children to run the line of troopers the first day of school. Upset by events, she went to the Presbyterian church to cry and pray. The division over integration split every institution in town and dissolved lifelong friendships. Our family became rapidly and permanently estranged from families with whom we had celebrated our joys and shared our sorrows, and many of my friends left town. The aftermath of September 1963 made my adolescence lonelier than it would have been had I had my old girlfriends to share it with. I write about this period in *Born to Belonging*.

13. I gave my father a version of this manuscript to read in spring 1993. He remembers this incident differently. "I was not in church that Sunday," he wrote. "Three other men and I were on our way to Farmville, Virginia [to visit private schools]. When we heard the news, the feeling was it was an awful thing to happen and did no one any good." His version has as much authenticity as mine in its detail—the snapshot memory of where I was when I heard certain news. It also fits Norrell's account of Daddy, McDonald Gallion, Howard Rutherford, and Andrew Cooper traveling up to Prince Edward County, Virginia, to visit segregated private schools there. I have my own clear memories of his presence at our dinner table that Sunday. Perhaps he made the comment later, perhaps I

heard it from other church folks, or perhaps my memory is the correct one. At any rate, that story became for me a hook, a place to hang my sadness and my anger, a growing fear of my own kind.

14. Bitty Martin shared this perception with me during a conversation when I visited Ithaca in 1990. The insight about boundaries came from a Black woman who participated in an anti-racism workshop I conducted in Atlanta in 1991 in preparation for the National Lesbian Agenda Conference.

15. Forman, 154. This tactic was not lost on white church people, who justified refusing the Black demonstrators with the rationale that they didn't really want to come to church, they just wanted to make trouble.

16. See Norrell, 174–76; Forman, 157–59.

17. Forman, 166–69.

18. Forman, 173.

19. Forman.

20. Forman, 192.

21. Norrell, 180.

22. Letters to the Editor, *Statesville Record and Landmark*, May 7, 1985.

23. "Violence Cited by Klan Leader," *Statesville Record and Landmark*, March 12, 1985.

24. "Anger, Demands for Action Ignited by Saturday Ku Klux Klan Gathering," *Mooresville Tribune*, June 5, 1985; "Klan Planning Recruitment Rally in Western Rowan," *Salisbury Post*, July 17, 1985.

25. Monitors' reports.

26. Jeff Byrd, "Feeding on Fear, a Sore Festers in Iredell County," *Iredell Neighbors*, July 7, 1985.

27. "Group Seeks Opposition to Klan Statewide," *Charlotte Observer*, October 27, 1985.

28. "Cross-Burning Guilty Plea Is Entered," *Charlotte Observer*, August 20, 1985. Childress was actually Mary Suits's son and Jerry Suits's stepson. The charges for Eidson, Rector, and Childress were civil rights violations of interfering with their victims' right to "hold and occupy a dwelling without injury, intimidation or interference because of their cohabitation and association therein with persons of another race." Rector pled guilty on similar charges. *U.S. v. Grady Herman Rector, Jr.*, ST-CR-85-29, U.S. Dist. Court, Western District of N.C.; *U.S. v. Alvin Wayne Childress*, ST-CR-85-29, U.S. Dist. Court, Western District of N.C.

29. "Son of Ku Klux Klansman Convicted of Cross Burnings in Iredell County," *Winston-Salem Journal*, August 22, 1985.

30. See "Two Cross-Burning Incidents Reported," *Statesville Record and Landmark*, September 4, 1985.

31. *U.S. v. Jerry Douglas Suits, Mary Vestal Suits, Jerry Albert Henderson, Michael Thomas Chambers, Rodney Eugene Pope, Tony Douglas Earp, Alfred S.*

Childers, Dan Pritchard and Kenneth Ray Blankenship, CR-ST-85, U.S. Dist. Court, Western District of N.C. They were charged in a conspiracy to violate the civil rights of seven people, shooting firearms and igniting crosses in front of their residences in order to interfere with their rights to hold and occupy a dwelling because of association with persons of another race. Two counts violated Title 18, United States Code, Sections 241 and 2; and Title 42, U.S. Code, Section 3631(b)(1).

32. The McCanns and Meyers were given six months' active time for assault with a deadly weapon with intent to kill.

33. Rodney Pope pled guilty to aiding and abetting and Michael Chambers pled guilty to one count of conspiracy; Jerry Suits, Mary Suits, Jerry Henderson, and Kenneth Blankenship pled guilty to conspiracy; Jerry Suits to one additional cross burning and Henderson to four. "Four More Cross-Burning Suspects Plead Guilty During Statesville Trial," *Kingston Daily Free Press,* December 18, 1985. Indictments against Tony Earp, Dan Prichard, and Alfred Childers were dropped because they had been linked to the wrong crimes. The men were reindicted in January 1986, along with others.

34. "Klan Activity Outlined by Suits in Testimony," *Statesville Record and Landmark,* April 23, 1986.

35. Bruce Prichard and Dan Prichard were acquitted. Tony Douglas Earp was convicted on one count of conspiracy and two counts of perjury before a grand jury, and he was given seven years; Alfred Steven Childers was convicted of one conspiracy and one perjury count, and he was given six years. Billy Carrigan, Dennis White, and Clyde and Ethel Hodge were convicted on one conspiracy count, and they were given suspended sentences. Michael Treadway pled guilty to misdemeanor cross burning and received a suspended sentence. Judge Woodrow Jones sentenced Jerry Suits to five years, Jerry Henderson to four years, and Michael Chambers to two years. Kenneth Blankenship, Kenneth Clay Baldwin, Thomas Ray Moore, and Junior Lee Vestal were given suspended sentences for their guilty pleas. Bruce Henderson, "Jury Convicts 6 Former Klan Members in Cross-Burning," *Charlotte Observer,* April 26, 1986.

36. See NCARRV Newsletter 3, "Operation Crossfire," Spring 1986.

37. "The Klan's Haunting Violence: 2 Years of Terrorism Forced Iredell County to Examine Black-White Relations," *Charlotte Observer,* April 20, 1986.

4. Coming Out

1. "The Woman Identified Woman," by Radicalesbians, was first distributed as a leaflet at a New York City conference in 1970.

2. These women included Susan Ballinger, Sherry Kinlaw, Helen Doerpinhaus, Aida Wakil, Sharon Funderburke, and Raymina Mays.

5. Bad Blood

1. Randy Shilts, *And the Band Played On: Politics, People and the AIDS Epidemic* (New York: St. Martin's Press, 1987), 55.

2. Shilts, 186.

3. Shilts, 580.

4. Kirkpatrick Sale, *SDS* (New York: Random House, 1974), 8.

5. Carl Wittman, letter to Elizabeth Freeman, July 30, 1962; Wittman, "Students and Economic Action," originally published in 1963 as an SDS working paper; reprinted in *The New Student Left: An Anthology*, ed. Mitchell Cohen and Dennis Hale (Boston: Beacon Press, 1966), 171.

6. Carl Wittman, letter to *Swarthmore Student Newsletter*, vol. II, no. 1, July 1, 1963.

7. Sale, 104.

8. Carl Wittman and Tom Hayden, "An Interracial Movement of the Poor?," in *The New Student Left*, 208, 215.

9. Wittman and Hayden, 191.

10. Carl Wittman, letter to "Bob and William SDS People," Hoboken, New Jersey, January 5, 1966.

11. Carl Wittman, mimeographed letter to friends from Jersey City, New Jersey, November 20, 1966.

12. Sale, 149.

13. Sara Evans, *Personal Politics: The Roots of Women's Liberation in the Civil Rights Movement and the New Left* (New York: Vintage, 1980), 146, 182.

14. Carl Wittman, letter to Elizabeth Freeman from Wolf Creek, Oregon, March 25, 1969.

15. Carl Wittman, "A Gay Manifesto," in *Out of the Closets: Voices of Gay Liberation*, ed. Karla Jay and Allen Young (New York: World Publishing, 1972), 330–41.

16. Author's interview with Michael Bronski, October 1993.

17. Lucy Dawidowicz, *The War Against the Jews, 1933–1945* (Toronto: Bantam Books, 1975), 85.

18. J. Wellington Byers, "Diseases of the Southern Negro," *Medical and Surgical Reporter* 43 (1888), 735, in James H. Jones, *Bad Blood: The Tuskegee Syphilis Experiment* (New York: Free Press, 1981), 21.

19. Jones, 1.

20. Shilts, 532–33.

21. Shilts, 531–32.

22. "Judge Orders U.S. to Release HIV-Positive Haitian Refugees," *Raleigh News and Observer*, June 9, 1993.

6. The White Patriot Party

1. Interview with Joe Fahy, "Militant Groups Growing: Neo-Nazi Links on Rise in N.C.," *Virginia Pilot and the Ledger-Star*, February 16, 1986.

2. Shep Moyle, "Grand Dragon Vows All-White Nation," *Aelous Magazine* (Duke University), April 15, 1981. Duke students Moyle and Robert Satloff drove down to Angier to interview Miller. Satloff, a Jew, had taken precautions to hide his identity. But Miller decided he was Jewish and made him sit in his car, under armed guard, while Moyle conducted the interview.

3. Transcript of Carolina Knights' message on Angier phone line, November 14, 1983.

4. For more complete information on these groups and tendencies, see the opening section of *When Hate Groups Come to Town* (2nd ed., 1992), published by the Center for Democratic Renewal, Atlanta, Georgia.

5. NCARRV published annual reports on hate violence and far right activity each year beginning in 1985; they contain an extensive chronology of incidents, analysis of trends, and recommendations.

6. See *Quarantines and Death* (Atlanta: Center for Democratic Renewal, 1989), 23.

7. Leah suggested that I include this struggle between Lenny and me. "You make these alliances sound too easy," she said, "as if they just fall out of the sky."

8. *The Protocols of the Elders of Zion* was a forgery that originated in czarist Russia in the early part of the twentieth century delineating a "Jewish conspiracy" to control the world. *Instauration* is a racist high- to middle-brow publication written anonymously but published by Howard Allen Enterprises in Cape Canaveral, Florida. The title means "rising from the ashes."

9. Twenty-three members of the Order were indicted for these and other crimes in Seattle on April 12, 1985, on federal racketeering charges in a ninety-three-page indictment that accused them of robbing banks and armored cars, counterfeiting, murdering Berg and white supremacist Walter West, and stockpiling illegal explosives and weapons. Indicted were Bruce Carroll Pierce, Gary Lee Yarbrough, Randolph George Duey, Andrew Virgil Barnhill, Denver Daw Parmenter II, Richard Harold Kemp, Richard E. Scutari, David Eden Lane, Randall Paul Evans, Robert E. Merki, James Sherman Dye, Sharon K. Merki, Frank Lee Silva, Jean Margaret Craig, Randall Eugene Rader, Kenneth Joseph Loff, Ronald Allen King, David Charles Tate, Thomas Bentley, Ardie McBrearty, Jackie Lee Norton, George Franklin Zaengle, and William Anthony Nash. The Merkis, Dye, Parmenter, Norton, Rader, Zaengle, and Bentley pled guilty. During the trial, Parmenter testified that they discussed assassinating Henry Kissinger, Norman Lear, the heads of the three TV networks, Morris Dees, and a federal judge in Texas, among others. On December 30, a jury convicted the defendants on all major counts. See the following *Klanwatch Intelligence Report* articles: "23 Nazis Indicted in Seattle," July–August 1985; "Rico Trial Begins in

Seattle for Members of the 'Order,'" October 1985; "The End of the Order: The Klan-Nazi World in Upheaval," February–March 1986. On November 17, 1987, David Lane and Bruce Pierce were found guilty in federal court of conspiring to deprive Berg of his civil rights. Craig and Scutari were found innocent. Denver's district attorney had decided not to bring state murder charges, so federal prosecutors sought convictions on charges of violating civil rights. It marked one of the first government attempts to use federal civil rights laws to prosecute defendants for killing a Jew. See "Lane, Pierce Found Guilty in Berg Murder," *Klanwatch Intelligence Report*, December 1987.

10. Raymond Godfrey, "Klan Rally Draws Cool Reception in St. Pauls Saturday Evening," *St. Pauls Review*, November 21, 1984.

11. "Aryan Warrior Falls," *Confederate Leader*, February 1985.

12. "Second Raleigh Klan Rally Shows Alarming Links," NCARRV press release, February 1985.

13. "White Patriot Party News Statement," March 19, 1985.

14. Jon Healey and John Downey, "Items Taken from Neo-Nazi Could Implicate Him in Crimes," *Winston-Salem Journal*, April 4, 1985.

15. Wheaton, 283.

16. Testimony from Order members soon bore out my predictions. Denver Parmenter testified during the Seattle trial of Order members on racketeering charges that Glenn Miller had received $200,000 in stolen Order money in fall 1985. See "Rico Trial Begins in Seattle for Members of the 'Order,'" *Klanwatch Intelligence Report*, October 1985.

17. *James Waller et al. v. Bernard Butkovich et al.* (U.S. Dist. Court, Middle District of N.C., May 9–10, 1985), a $48 million civil suit, made claims under federal civil rights laws and state wrongful death and assault and battery statutes. After a three-month trial, the jury voted in June 1985 to hold white supremacists David Matthews, Jerry Smith, Wayne Wood, Ed Dawson, and Jack Fowler and police officers Paul Spoon and Jerry Cooper liable in the wrongful death of Mike Nathan and in the assault on Nathan, Paul Bermanzohn, and Tom Clark. They awarded damages of $394,959.55; the City of Greensboro opted to pay $351,000 to Nathan's estate rather than appeal. Wheaton, 281.

18. "Two Bodies Found During Raid on Farm," *Kansas City Times*, August 19, 1985; "One of 2 Rulo Bodies Believed to Be Child," *Kansas City Star*, August 19, 1985; "Raid Confirmed Her Worst Fear: Grandson's Dead," *Kansas City Times*, August 20, 1985. Mike Ryan was later convicted of first-degree murder and sentenced to death in the Stice killing. Dennis Ryan was convicted of second-degree murder in the Thimm killing and given life in prison.

19. David L. Rice was convicted of first-degree murder for killing the Goldmarks and was sentenced to death.

20. "Specialist Jim Bailey," letter to the *Shelby Star*: "When the W.P.P. marches and exercises the sacred constitutional right to peaceful assembly,

this is labeled 'bigotry' and 'racism' by Mab Segrest and her lackeys. In turn I will label Mab Segrest, the North Carolinians Against Racist and Religious Violence and anyone who agrees with her as cowards, communists, traitors and agitators."

21. Fahy, "Militant Groups Growing," February 16, 1986.

22. Nadine Gordimer, "Living in the Interregnum," *The Essential Gesture: Writing, Politics and Places* (New York: Alfred Knopf, 1988), 270.

23. Lillian Smith, "Dialogue Between King and Corpse," in *The Winner Names the Age: A Collection of Writings by Lillian Smith*, ed. Michelle Cliff (New York: W.W. Norton, 1978), 191.

24. My father responded to this passage: "I do not believe that any person manipulated Marvin Segrest. He was well informed about current events. He hitchhiked over the western states as a young man. He was very much concerned about the way the Indians had been and were treated."

25. Trial transcript, 409–11.

26. Testimony of Simeon Davis and Wendell Lee Lane in *U.S. v. Stephen Samuel Miller, Robert Eugene Jackson, Anthony Todd Wydra, Wendell Lee Lane and Simeon Davis*, 87-2-01-CR3, U.S. Dist. Court, Eastern District of N.C. Davis and Lane pled guilty in early 1987 as part of a plea bargain in which they agreed to cooperate with the government. Davis received a sentence of four years and nine months; Lane's sentence was thirty months. Pat Reese, "Supremacists Get Prison Terms in Murder, Theft Plot," *Fayetteville Observer*, May 17, 1987. Miller, Jackson, and Wydra went to trial in April 1987; Miller was convicted of conspiracy, illegal possession of a machine gun, and making a silencer. He received a twenty-five-year sentence, which a judge later reduced to ten years, saying that Stephen Miller was not a violent person. Adam Seessel, "Judge Reduces Term for Avowed Racist in Robbery Scheme," *Raleigh News and Observer*, December 2, 1987. Jackson was convicted of conspiring to acquire stolen government property and received a six-month sentence with five years probation and a $50 fine. Sheets was fined $4,000, sentenced to six months, and ordered to disassociate himself from the white supremacist movement. Wydra was acquitted. "Ex-Fayetteville Man Sent to Jail in Explosives Case," *Fayetteville Observer*, July 14, 1987.

27. "State Pursues Racist Groups Diligently, SBI Agent Says," *Raleigh News and Observer*, January 23, 1987.

7. Mama

1. Joel W. Martin, *Sacred Revolt: The Muskogees' Struggle for a New World* (Boston: Beacon, 1991), for Muskogee cosmology, especially 24–27. Martin, like myself, is a white Alabamian trying to "imagine [the South] differently and inclusively." I gave his book to my father in 1992 and later retrieved it when I began to focus on Osceola in this narrative.

8. Robeson, Bloody Robeson

1. See W. McKee Evans, *To Die Game: The Story of the Lowry Band, Indian Guerrillas of Reconstruction* (Baton Rouge: Louisiana State University Press, 1971).

2. See Evans, especially chapter 2, for the early history of Robeson County; see also Martin, 49.

3. Myles Horton, *The Long Haul: An Autobiography* (New York: Doubleday, 1990), 125.

4. Evans, 19.

5. "The Appearance of a Whitewash Given," *The Robesonian*, November 16, 1986. The verdict actually read "accident or in self-defense."

6. Lee Freeland Hancock, "Slaying of Lumbee Rocks Robeson," *Raleigh News and Observer*, December 21, 1986.

7. *Coroner's Inquest in the Matter of Jimmy Earl Cummings*, November 13, 1986, 19.

8. Stan Swofford, "Blacks, Lumbees Want Answers," *Greensboro News and Record*, December 14, 1986. Hunt made similar statements to Ellen Scarborough, "Fairmont Slaying Testimony Questioned," *Fayetteville Observer*, November 28, 1986.

9. *Coroner's Inquest*, 40.

10. Hancock.

11. *Coroner's Inquest*, 42.

12. Hancock; Swofford.

13. *The Robesonian*, November 16, 1986.

14. *Coroner's Inquest*, 61.

15. R.L. Godfrey, "Cummings' Death to Be Investigated," *The Robesonian*, November 23, 1986. The ACLU officially agreed to represent the Cummings family in early January 1987. R.L. Godfrey, "ACLU Agrees to Represent Cummings," *The Robesonian*, January 7, 1987.

16. Pat Jordan, "The Passions of Joe Freeman Britt," *Southern Magazine*, March 1987, 97, 99.

17. Testimony of Maurice Geiger in *U.S. v. John Edward Clark A/K/A Eddie Hatcher and Timothy Bryan Jacobs*, 88-7-01-CR3, U.S. Dist. Court, Eastern District of N.C., October 12, 1988, 19.

18. Fund for Rural Justice, Memoranda to Chief Justice Branch, North Carolina Supreme Court, December 1983 and January 1985. Geiger's summary is from a January 5, 1989, letter and affidavit to Governor Mario Cuomo requesting that the State of New York not extradite Timothy Jacobs to North Carolina for trial on state kidnapping charges.

19. North Carolina Commission on Indian Affairs, *Report on the Treatment of Indians by the Criminal Justice System*, September 1987, 25, 38–40. See also Greg Hitt, "Reports Allege Racism," *Winston-Salem Journal*, February 14, 1988.

20. Lee Freeland Hancock, "Cocaine Trade Rich in Robeson, Officials Say," *Raleigh News and Observer*, February 9, 1986.

21. R.L. Godfrey and Larry Blue, "Robeson Is Focus of Drug Probe," *The Robesonian*, December 21, 1986.

22. Between 1975 and February 1984, there were fourteen unsolved murders in Robeson County, according to *The Robesonian*. In the fall of 1985, when Joyce Sinclair was murdered, three Indians were found dead in a locked car in a gangland-style shooting. However, *Charlotte Observer* reporter Elizabeth Leland found in 1988 that Robeson County often did as well if not better than other counties in solving murders. "Robeson Sorts Out Murders," *Charlotte Observer*, April 18, 1988.

23. Ellen Scarborough, "Robeson DA Accused of Rushing Inquest," *Fayetteville Observer*, November 15, 1986; Malissa Talbert, "Residents Discuss Shooting," *The Robesonian*, November 14, 1986.

24. SBI agent Timothy Batchelor testified at Stevens's trial that he had received information from another law enforcement officer that confessed drug dealer Johnny Lee Jones had paid either Burnis Wilkins or Kevin Stone to set up the theft. Lee Freeland Hancock, "SBI Agent Says Deputy May Have Had Help," *Raleigh News and Observer*, March 18, 1987.

25. "Slain Lumbee, Stolen Drugs Linked," *Greensboro News and Record*, January 5, 1986.

26. Ellen Scarborough and Tim Bass, "Cummings Left Out of Cocaine Probe, U.S. Attorney Says," *Fayetteville Observer*, January 8, 1987.

27. Lee Hancock, "Incidents Past the County Line Hint at Robeson Cocaine Trade," *Raleigh News and Observer*, February 9, 1987.

28. Dennis Garcia, "Sinclair Murder Investigation Centers on 1 Man," *The Robesonian*, November 14, 1985.

29. *State of North Carolina v. John Quincy Parker*, 85 CrS 23109-10, Sup. Ct., August 14–15, 1986, 39–40. Testimony describes Parker's criminal record, including three counts of breaking, entering, and larceny; assault on a female; assault and burglary; common law robbery; two counts of larceny; and twice escaping from prison.

30. *North Carolina v. John Quincy Parker*, 26–27.

31. R.L. Godfrey and Jeralene Gibbs, "Parker Sentenced to 30 Years," *The Robesonian*, February 26, 1988.

32. Johnny Parker, "I Did Not Kill Sinclair," *St. Pauls Review*, December 17, 1987.

33. Testimony of Mitchell Stevens, *U.S. v. Mitchell Stevens*, 86-91-01-CR3, U.S. Dist. Court, Eastern District of N.C., 96.

34. Testimony of Arthur Robertson, *U.S. v. Mitchell Stevens*, 189.

35. Lee Freeland Hancock, "Trial of Former Deputy Goes to Jury," *Raleigh News and Observer*, March 20, 1987.

36. Brian Innes, *The Tarot: How to Use and Interpret the Cards* (New York: Crescent Books, 1976), 44.

37. *Hold On! The Fight for Justice in Robeson County*, video produced by NCARRV, 1988.

38. Memorandum from North Carolina Secretary of Human Resources David T. Flaherty to the Robeson County Task Force on the Subject of Billy McKellar's Death, March 25, 1988. See also Greg Hitt, "Robeson Jail Employees Partly to Blame for Death, Report Says," *Winston-Salem Journal*, April 22, 1988.

39. Innes, 44.

40. Roy Pattishall, "Political Prisoner?," *The Independent*, November 23, 1989.

41. Roy Pattishall, "Justice in Robeson County," *The Leader*, April 12, 1989.

42. Wheaton, 183.

43. Pattishall, "Justice in Robeson County."

44. Hatcher's source later changed his story about what the maps represented, saying they showed people he would watch for the SBI.

45. Interview in *Hold On! The Fight for Justice in Robeson County*.

46. John Day, "Indian Activist Slain in Robeson," *Raleigh News and Observer*, March 27, 1988.

47. John Day, "Investigators Follow Leads in Robeson Killing," *Raleigh News and Observer*, March 28, 1988.

48. John Moser, "Robeson Leaders Fend Off Violence," *Greensboro News and Record*, March 29, 1988.

49. Joe Dew, "Key Suspect in Robeson Kills Himself," *Raleigh News and Observer*, March 30, 1988; Greg Hitt and Terry Martin, "Young Lumbee Killed Pierce, Then Himself, Authorities Say," *Winston-Salem Journal*, March 30, 1988.

50. Sharon Grove, "Britt Seeks Special Prosecutor in Slaying of Judicial Opponent," *Raleigh News and Observer*, March 31, 1988.

51. *Hold On! The Fight for Justice in Robeson County*.

52. Dee Reid and Julia Harper Day, "The Assassination of Hope," *The Independent*, April 7–20, 1988.

53. Adam Seessel, "Indians Promise Witnesses for Immunity," *Raleigh News and Observer*, June 18, 1988.

54. Nicki Weisensee, "Defense Lawyers Say They Have Evidence of Robeson Corruption," *Durham Herald*, June 15, 1988.

55. Eddie Hatcher received eighteen years and Tim Jacobs six years for fourteen counts of kidnapping.

56. Chavis plea-bargained from first-degree murder to accessory and got time served.

57. Roy Pattishall, "The Trials of Eddie Hatcher's Attorneys," *The Independent*, November 23, 1989.

58. "Media Coverage of Robeson County Is Source of 'Problems,'" *Fayette-ville Observer*, October 21, 1988.

59. The legislature agreed, in a compromise worked out between Representative Sidney Locks and white Robeson legislators, to appoint a second Superior Court judgeship for the district, which would go to an Indian. Senator David Parnell, one of the white representatives from the county, blocked financing the second judgeship until Britt's seniority was ensured. Britt would be the senior judge, but without the power to appoint the public prosecutor, whom the junior judge would appoint. The senior judge's powers include appointing magistrates, setting and enforcing court calendaring, and setting bond policy. A white man replaced Britt and a Black man was appointed public prosecutor. Tim Funk, "Robeson Reveals Judgeship Compromise," *Charlotte Observer*, June 25, 1988.

9. Take What You Need

1. Alice Walker, "Beyond the Peacock: The Reconstruction of Flannery O'Connor," *In Search of Our Mother's Gardens: Womanist Prose by Alice Walker* (San Diego: Harcourt Brace Jovanovich, 1983), 58–59.

10. The Bookstore Murders

1. Indictment, *U.S. v. Stephen Samuel Miller, Robert Eugene Jackson, Anthony Todd Wydra, Wendell Lee Lane and Simeon Davis*, 87-2-01-CR-3, U.S. Dist. Court, Eastern District of N.C.

2. Michael Goforth, "3 Killed in Adult Book Store; Officers: Shootings Planned"; and Joe DePriest, "Officers Believe Store Linked to Organized Crime," *Shelby Star*, January 19, 1987.

3. Robert Field, "Victims' Lives Varied," *Shelby Star*, January 29, 1987.

4. June 6, 1985, correspondence.

5. *U.S. v. Miller.* See 87 and 251 n. 27 for this text.

6. "Mud people" is one of the neo-Nazi epithets for people of color.

7. Bill Haynes, "Federal Agents Seek Miller, Official Says," *Raleigh News and Observer*, April 19, 1987; "Miller Promises Race War Unless Demands Met," *Raleigh News and Observer*, April 26, 1987.

8. Adam Seessel, "Officials Agree to Meeting with Miller," *Raleigh News and Observer*, April 28, 1987.

9. This felony charge is punishable by up to five years in prison and a $1,000 fine. It was later included in a plea bargain for lesser charges. Karla Jennings, "Miller Charged with Using Mail to Threaten U.S. Government," *Raleigh News and Observer*, May 7, 1987.

10. Pat Reese, "White Supremacists Suspects in Killings," *Fayetteville Observer*, September 4, 1987.

11. Pat Reese, "Reporter Intermediary for Informant's Clues," *Fayetteville Observer*, September 4, 1987; Pat Reese, "White Patriots Had Arsenal, Agent

Testifies," *Fayetteville Observer*, September 5, 1987. Stoner later testified in Wilmington and Shelby.

12. Pat Reese, "Miller Agrees to Plea Bargain," *Fayetteville Observer*, September 15, 1987.

13. Ken Soo, "Extremists Indicted in Attack," *Charlotte Observer*, November 17, 1987.

14. It was the second trial, the first (held in New Bern in October 1987) having ended in a hung jury.

15. Testimony of Robert Eugene Jackson in *U.S. v. Jackson*, 87-12-01-CR-2, U.S. Dist. Court, Eastern District of N.C., Vol. 1, 60–62. Jackson denied having been on salary for Glenn Miller.

16. Testimony of Douglas Sheets, *U.S. v. Jackson*, Vol. 1, 128–33.

17. Sentencing memo filed in U.S. District Court in Raleigh.

18. "Ex-Fayetteville Man Sent to Jail in Explosives Case," *Fayetteville Observer*, July 14, 1987.

19. Robert Field, "White Supremacists' Convictions Pave Way for Extradition Here," *Shelby Star*, April 14, 1988.

20. Faye and Bobby were later interviewed by a gay journalist. Darell Yates Rist, *Heartlands: A Gay Man's Odyssey Across America* (New York: Dutton, 1992), 381, 385–86.

21. *Shelby . . . It's Home*, 21.

22. Dixon, 385–86.

23. Shelby Chamber of Commerce, "Demographic and Income Forecast Report," December 3, 1985.

24. Cash, 52.

25. Lillian Smith, letter to Marvin Rich, December 11, 1964, in *How Am I Heard? Letters of Lillian Smith*, ed. Margaret Rose Gladney (Chapel Hill: University of North Carolina Press, 1993), 316–17.

26. "White Supremacist Is Killed When Gun Discharges," *Greensboro News and Record*, January 8, 1989.

27. Bruce Henderson, "Activists Say Violence Aimed at Gays Goes Unchallenged," *Charlotte Observer*, May 4, 1989.

28. Michelle Morris, "Shelby III—Testing Parameters of Society's Conscious [*sic*]," *Gastonia Gazette*, May 11, 1989.

29. Susan McBrayer, "DA Says Trial Is Like a Puzzle," *Shelby Star*, May 5, 1989.

30. McBrayer.

31. Susan McBrayer and Joe DePriest, "Shelby III Survivor: They Continued to Shoot All of Us," *Shelby Star*, May 6, 1989.

32. Chip Wilson, "Survivor Can't Identify Gunmen," *Charlotte Observer*, May 6, 1989.

33. McBrayer and DePriest.

34. "Inmate Testified 2 Men Discussed Bookstore Killings," *Charlotte Observer*, May 17, 1989, and my notes.

35. Susan McBrayer, "Witness Says Sheets Linked with Murders," *Shelby Star*, May 11, 1989.

36. Susan McBrayer and Elisa Hoagland, "Threats Made at Shelby III Before Murders," *Shelby Star*, May 13, 1989.

37. Bruce Henderson, "Trial Engrosses Shelby Shooting Victims' Families," *Charlotte Observer*, May 9, 1989.

38. Susan McBrayer, "Sheets: He Will Help Jury 'Find the Truth,'" *Shelby Star*, May 18, 1989.

39. Susan McBrayer, "Sheets Denies Being in State During Killings," *Shelby Star*, May 19, 1989.

40. Susan McBrayer and Elisa Hoagland, "Sheets Knew About Shelby III Before It Happened," *Shelby Star*, May 20, 1989.

41. Susan McBrayer and Joe DePriest, "Defense: Don't Judge His Beliefs," *Shelby Star*, May 25, 1989, and my notes. The judge dismissed five counts of kidnapping; earlier he had dismissed assault charges based on one of the survivors' injuries.

42. Tom O'Neal, "An Open Letter to Mab Segrest," *Shelby Star*, May 31, 1989.

43. Cash, 425.

11. A Journey We Make Daily

1. This dialogue is from a transcript of our conversation, which I taped. I have tightened the dialogue some, clearing the final version with her.

12. Epilogue

1. This phone call was precipitated by my most recent self-help venture, a weekend workshop called "The Forum," sponsored by Landmark Education. The point of the weekend was to learn to "put the past in the past" by recognizing the ways in which we conspire to keep conflicts in our lives going because there are payoffs, usually involving being right. Our instructions were to "get off it" with someone in our lives—parents were highly recommended targets—and we fanned out to pay phones, dimes hot in our hands, to make the kind of phone calls I did with my father. Landmark was formerly EST, which some people consider a cult. I found it very helpful. Like Alice Walker said, "Take what you need."

2. *N.C. State Data Center Newsletter*, October 1993, 6–7.

3. D.W. Whitehurst, letter to Valentine Mott, from St. Augustine, Florida, October 2, 1843, quoted in Wickman, 151.

Part Two: On Being White and Other Lies

1. James Baldwin, "On Being White and Other Lies," *Essence*, April 1984, 90–92.

2. Thanks especially to Jacqui Alexander for many careful readings of drafts and for her confidence that I would, indeed, someday, finish the essay in a useable form. Thanks also to Barbara Smith for close editing and encouragement and to Tobi Lippin and Peter Barnes for feedback and support.

1. Commerce Capitalism

1. Howard Zinn, *A People's History of the United States* (New York: Harper & Row, 1980), 24. The most recurrent explanations for the psychology of white racism (in distinction to its material base) draw heavily on Freudian theories of repression and projection, as do Rawick, Roediger, Takaki, and Jordan.

2. For more on the pre-capitalist "tendency to seize upon physical differences as the badge of innate mental and temporal differences" see Thomas Gossett, *Race: The History of an Idea in America* (1963; reprint, Dallas: Southern Methodist University Press, 1975), 3–16. "Prior to 1500 differential valorization of human races is hardly noticeable," historian Magnus Morner comments of "the hierarchic classification of human races dictated by European ethnocentricity" in *Race Mixture in the History of Latin America* (Boston: Little, Brown, 1967), 6. Michael Omi and Howard Winant agree: "Race consciousness, and its articulation in theories of race, is largely a modern phenomenon" dating to European explorers' "discoveries," in *Racial Formation in the United States* (1986; reprint, New York: Routledge, 1989), 58.

3. T. Walter Wallbank, Alastair M. Taylor, and George Barr Carson Jr., eds., *Civilization Past and Present*, 5th ed. (Chicago: Scott, Foresman, 1965), 2:280.

4. Zinn, 23.

5. Winthrop Jordan, *The White Man's Burden: Historical Origins of Racism in the United States* (London: Oxford University Press, 1974), 33. *White over Black: American Attitudes Toward the Negro 1550–1812* (Baltimore: Penguin, 1969), is a longer version of this excellent book, which was abbreviated in *The White Man's Burden* to make it more accessible to students. References are to *The White Man's Burden* unless otherwise specified.

6. Zinn, 26–28; "African slavery is hardly to be praised. But it was far different from plantation or mining slavery in the Americas, which was lifelong, morally crippling, destructive of family ties, without hope of any future" (27).

7. Marvin Harris, *Patterns of Race in the Americas* (1964; reprint, New York: W.W. Norton, 1974), 12.

8. Quoted in Gilberto Freyre, *The Masters and the Slaves* (New York: Knopf, 1956), 178.

9. Eduardo Galeano, *Open Veins of Latin America: Five Centuries of the Pillage of a Continent*, trans. Cedric Belfrage (New York: Monthly Review Press, 1973), 50.

10. Zinn, 29.

11. "The Columbus Letter of March 14th, 1493," quoted in Virgil J. Vogel, *This Country Was Ours: A Documentary History of the American Indian* (New York: Harper & Row, 1972), 34.

12. The Aztecs' account of the incident as given later to the priest-historian Bernardino Sahagún, quoted in Vogel, 35–36.

13. "The Narrative of Alvar Nuñez Cabeça de Vaca," quoted in Vogel, 37.

14. Zinn, 26–27.

15 Galeano, 33–34.

16. Harris, 12–14.

17. Jordan, *White Man's Burden*, 4–7.

18. Jordan, *White Man's Burden*, 17, 18, 22.

19. Mab Segrest and Leonard Zeskind, *Quarantines and Death: The Far Right's Homophobic Agenda* (Atlanta: Center for Democratic Renewal, 1989), 29.

20. See Mary Daly, *Gyn/Ecology: The Metaethics of Radical Feminism* (Boston: Beacon Press, 1978), n. 183.

21. E. William Monter, "Pedestal and Stake: Courtly Love and Witchcraft," in *Becoming Visible: Women in European History*, ed. Renate Bridenthal and Claudia Koonz (Boston: Houghton Mifflin, 1977), 133. Perhaps in the witch craze, the trajectory of European misogyny (a much longer story than that of the racism traced here) intersects with the trajectory of European racism in a way that we have not fully understood, as Harriet Desmoines suggested to me in response to this section of the essay—for example, in the breaking of the European peasant movement leading toward land enclosure (a technique used also against people of color to break up communal ownership and economic and spiritual connections to the land).

22. Ed Cohen, "Legislating the Norm," in "Displacing Homophobia," special issue of *South Atlantic Quarterly* 88, no. 1 (Winter 1989): 185–86.

23. Jordan, *White over Black*, 18.

24. Quoted in Jordan, *White over Black*, 41.

25. See, for example, Stanley Elkins, *Slavery: A Problem in American Institutional and Intellectual Life*, 2nd ed. (Chicago: University of Chicago Press, 1971), 38–44.

26. Harris, 37. See Patricia Williams, *The Alchemy of Race and Rights* (Cambridge, MA: Harvard University Press, 1991), for a brilliant examination of the history and implications her own "hybrid" origins.

27. Galeano, 91–93.

28. Galeano, 95.

29. "Rich Got Richer in '80s, Census Report Says," *Raleigh News and Observer,* January 11, 1991.

30. Jordan, *White Man's Burden,* 40, 44–45.

31. Elkins, 44–49.

32. Jordan, *White Man's Burden,* 47.

33. Quoted in Vincent Harding, *There Is a River: The Black Struggle for Freedom in America* (1981: reprint, New York: Random House, 1983), 27.

34. Jordan, *Black over White,* 93–95.

35. Jordan, *White Man's Burden,* 46, 57.

36. See Margo Adair, "The Subjective Side of Politics," unpublished essay. The People's Institute for Survival and Beyond, based in New Orleans (1444 N. Johnson St., New Orleans, LA 70116), shapes much of its work with white people against racism on this historical knowledge of the ideological construction of whiteness.

2. Industrial Capitalism

1. Article II, Section 2 of the U.S. Constitution tied representation and taxes to "the whole Number of free persons, including those bound to Service for a Term of Years, and excluding Indians not taxed, three-fifths of all other persons." The prohibition against abolishing the slave trade was in Article II, Section 9.

2. The *-s* was dropped and "Cobbs" became "Cobb."

3. John Hope Franklin, *From Slavery to Freedom: A History of Negro Americans,* 3rd ed. (New York: Random House, 1969), 147–49.

4. Franklin.

5. Franklin, 171.

6. Franklin, 178.

7. Franklin, 186.

8. Quoted in Jordan, 73.

9. Harris, 3–4.

10. Quoted in Richard Drinnon, *Facing West: The Metaphysics of Indian Hating and Empire Building* (Minneapolis: University of Minnesota Press, 1980), 42.

11. Quoted in Drinnon, 43–44.

12. Quoted in S. Lyman Taylor, *A History of Indian Policy* (Washington, DC: Bureau of Indian Affairs, 1973), 35.

13. Quoted in Drinnon, 86.

14. Quoted in Drinnon, 89.

15. Gossett, 231.

16. Quoted in Drinnon, 76–77.

17. Quoted in Drinnon, 179.

18. Quoted in Ronald T. Takaki, *Iron Cages: Race and Culture in Nineteenth Century America* (Seattle: University of Washington Press, 1979), 96.

19. Takaki, *Cages,* 101–2.

20. Quoted in Harding, 109–11.

21. Quoted in Harding, 95.

22. Jordan, *White over Black*, 194–95.

23. Paula Giddings, *When and Where I Enter: The Impact of Black Women on Race and Sex in America* (Toronto: Bantam, 1984), 48–50.

24. See Harding, chapter 9, where he quotes Delany: "We are politically not of them, but aliens to the laws and political privileges of the country" (174). Delany's emerging Black nationalism was influenced by the nationalism sweeping Europe. Delany prefigures Du Bois in his observation: "It would be duplicity longer to disguise the fact that the great issue, sooner or later, upon which must be disputed the world's destiny, will be the question of black and white, and every individual will be called upon for his identity with one or the other" (186).

25. Takaki, *Cages*, 75–79.

26. David Roediger, *The Wages of Whiteness: Race and the Making of the American Working Class* (London: Verso, 1991), 57, discusses the African American role as "anti-citizen."

27. Quoted in Gossett, 235.

28. Roediger, 95; see also George Rawick, *From Sundown to Sunup: The Making of the Black Community* (Westport, CT: Greenwood, 1972).

29. Quoted in Rudolfo Acuña, *Occupied America: A History of Chicanos*, 3rd ed. (New York: Harper & Row, 1988), 6.

30. Acuña, 1–2, 12.

31. See Acuña's chapter "Legacy of Hate: The Conquest of Mexico's Northeast."

32. Takaki, *Strangers from a Different Shore: A History of Asian Americans* (Boston: Little, Brown, 1989), 32–33.

33. Quoted in Takaki, *Strangers*, 22.

34. Takaki, *Strangers*, 79–81.

3. Finance Capitalism

1. Nell Irvin Painter, *Standing at Armageddon: The United States, 1877–1919* (New York: W.W. Norton, 1987), xvii, xx.

2. Painter, 21–22.

3. Omi and Winant, 64–65.

4. Robert J. Norrell, *Reaping the Whirlwind: The Civil Rights Movement in Tuskegee* (New York: Vintage, 1986), 10, 19–20.

5. C. Vann Woodward, *The Strange Career of Jim Crow*, 2nd ed. (London: Oxford University Press, 1966), 70.

6. In the *Slaughterhouse Cases* of 1873, in *U.S. v. Reese* in 1875, and in *U.S. v. Cruikshank* in 1876, the Supreme Court cut back sharply on privileges and immunities seen as under federal protection, limiting the scope of the Fourteenth and Fifteenth Amendments. The *Civil Rights Cases* of 1883 nullified portions of

the Civil Rights Act, the legislative enactment of the Fourteenth Amendment, saying that Congress could restrain states but not individuals from acts of racial discrimination and segregation. In *Hall v. De Cuir* (1877) and *Louisville, New Orleans and Texas Railroads v. Mississippi* (1890), the Court ruled that states first could not prohibit, then could require segregation, leading toward the 1896 *Plessy v. Ferguson* decision that "legislation is powerless to eradicate racial instincts" and "separate but equal" facilities were constitutional. *Williams v. Mississippi* (1898) "completed the opening of the legal road to proscription, segregation, and disfranchisement by approving the Mississippi plan for depriving Negroes of the franchise"(Woodward, 71). "Just as the Negro gained his emancipation and new rights through a falling out between white men, he now stood to lose his rights through the reconciliation of white men" (Woodward, 70).

7. Giddings, 27.

8. Manning Marable, *Race, Reform and Rebellion: The Second Reconstruction in Black America, 1945–1982* (Jackson: University of Mississippi Press, 1984), 8.

9. Woodward, 60–65.

10. Woodward, 79–80, 90.

11. Takaki, *Cages*, 219.

12. Painter, 162.

13. Takaki, *Strangers*, 28.

14. Takaki, *Strangers*, 31.

15. Painter, 163.

16. Acuña, 54–81.

17. Acuña, 90–91.

18. Acuña, 98, 103.

19. Quoted in Drinnon, 182.

20. Gossett, 233.

21. Quoted in Takaki, *Strangers*, 24.

22. Takaki, *Strangers*, 25.

23. Takaki, *Cages*, 217–19.

24. Quoted in Giddings, 66.

25. Commented Frances Ellen Harper, "The white women all go for sex, letting race occupy a minor position. Being black means that every white, including every white working-class woman, can discriminate against you." Quoted in Giddings, 68.

26. Quoted in Giddings, 91.

27. Giddings, 160.

28. Linda Gordon, *Woman's Body, Woman's Right* (New York: Grossman, 1976); see the section "Eugenists," 274–90, especially 281–82.

29. Painter, 147.

30. Quoted in Christine Bolt, *Victorian Attitudes to Race* (London: Routledge & Kegan Paul, 1976), 1–2.

31. *Journal of the Anthropological Society of London* (1864), i–xvii; quoted in Bolt, 20.

32. Robert Knox, *Anthropological Review*, VIII (1870), 51, 243–46, 456; quoted in Bolt, 22.

33. Charles Darwin, *The Descent of Man* (London: J. Murray, 1871), 2:225–26.

34. Quoted in Lucy S. Dawidowicz, *The War Against the Jews 1933–1945* (Toronto: Bantam, 1976), 41.

35. Quoted in Dawidowicz, 23–24.

36. Quoted in Dawidowicz, 14.

37. John D'Emilio and Estelle B. Freedman, *Intimate Matters: A History of Sexuality in America* (New York: Harper & Row, 1988), 227.

38. Havelock Ellis and John Addington Symonds, *Sexual Inversion* (London: Wilson & Macmillan, 1897; reprint, New York: Arno Press, 1975), 137. Ellis, according to Gordon, favorably reviewed eugenicist Lothrop Stoddard's *The Rising Tide of Color Against White Supremacy* in 1920 (Gordon, 283).

39. Painter, 149–50.

40. Quoted in Painter, 150.

41. Quoted in Painter, 147.

42. Harry Magdoff, *The Age of Imperialism: The Economics of U.S. Foreign Policy* (New York: Monthly Review Press, 1969), 85–88.

43. Magdoff, 40.

44. Zinn, 380–81, 386.

45. For one version of this story, see Robin D.G. Kelley, *Hammer and Hoe: Alabama Communists During the Great Depression* (Chapel Hill: University of North Carolina Press, 1990), 50–53. For another, see Theodore Rosengarten's *All God's Dangers: The Life of Nate Shaw* (New York: Knopf, 1974).

46. Quoted in Bertram Gross, *Friendly Fascism: The New Face of Power in America* (Boston: South End Press, 1982), 21.

47. Gross, 17.

48. Quoted in Gross, 25.

49. Quoted in Gross, 24.

50. Gross, 22.

51. Gross, 23.

52. Gross, 34–36.

53. See Magdoff, 91–99, on the dynamics of devaluation; the quote is from testimony before the Joint Economic Committee of the Congress of the United States, Hearings on the United States Balance of Payments, Washington, DC, 1963, Part I, 83–84 (Magdoff, 104–5).

54. Quoted in Magdoff, 49.

55. Magdoff, 51.

56. Quoted in Magdoff, 54.

57. *Recent Activities Against Citizens and Residents of Asian Descent, A Report of the U.S. Commission on Civil Rights*, Publication No. 88, 11–12.

58. Quoted in John Lukacs, *Immigration and Migration: A Historical Perspective* (Monterey, VA: American Immigration Control Foundation, 1986), 14–15.

59. U.S. Civil Rights Commission, 13.

60. Edward H. Spicer, *A Short History of the Indians of the United States* (New York: D. Van Nostrand, 1969), 113, 116.

61. Omi and Winant, 14–24.

62. Quoted in Zinn, 440.

63. Forman, 23–24, 25.

64. See Roediger, 6.

Part Three: A Bridge, Not a Wedge

1. Bennett Harrison and Barry Bluestone, *The Great U-Turn: Corporate Restructuring and the Polarizing of America* (New York: Basic Books, 1988), 8–11.

2. Ellen Teninty, "Corporate Taxes: The Return for Our Public Investment," *Equal Means*, Fall 1993, 28–29.

3. For the origins of the New Right and the Religious Right, see "The New Right and the Christian Right," in the National Gay and Lesbian Task Force's *Fight the Right Action Kit*, 1734 14th Street NW, Washington, DC 20009; 202-332-6483; see also *The Public Eye*, the newsletter of Political Research Associates, 678 Massachusetts Ave., Suite 702, Cambridge, MA 02139, especially "Constructing Homophobia," March 1993.

4. War Resisters League, *Guide to War Tax Resistance* (New York: War Resisters League, 1986), 21.

5. See the work of the Federation of Industrial Retention and Renewal, 3411 West Diversey, Room 10, Chicago, IL 60647; 312-278-5418.

6. *Free Trade Mailing*, newsletter of the North American Worker-to-Worker Network, Durham, NC, February 1993, 6.

7. *A Common Destiny: Blacks and American Society* (Washington, DC: National Academy Press, 1990), introduction.

8. "Best Cities for Business," *USA Today*, October 27, 1993.

9. See "The Christian Coalition" in National Gay and Lesbian Task Force, *Fight the Right Action Kit*.

10. At the conference, one gay man from New Orleans disagreed with this information, but a lesbian verified it as true from her experience handing out anti-Duke literature in the French Quarter.

11. Suzanne Pharr and Scot Nakagawa have done pioneering analysis and organizing against the religious right; see their articles in *Fight the Right Action Kit* and Pharr's analysis in the 1992 and 1993 copies of *Transformation*, a newsletter of the Women's Project, 2224 Main Street, Little Rock, AR 72206.

12. Omi and Winant, 11–25.

13. Derrick Bell, *Faces at the Bottom of the Well* (New York: Basic Books, 1992).

14. Russ Bellant in *Old Nazis, the New Right and the Republican Party* (Boston: South End Press, 1991) describes other characteristics of fascism: the use of violence to impose views on others and the dehumanizing and scapegoating of "enemies" as subhuman and conspiratorial; a cult of personality around a charismatic leader or elite whose authoritarian power replaces constitutional government; these leaders' exhortations for the masses to join a heroic mission, including appeals to the working class or farmers; abandonment of working-class alliances by ultimately forging an alliance with the elite; and the abandonment of any consistent ideology in the drive for state power. See also Segrest and Zeskind, *Quarantines and Death*, 22–23.

15. Margaret Randall, *Gathering Rage: The Failure of 20th Century Revolutions to Develop a Feminist Agenda* (New York: Monthly Review Press, 1992), 113. Randall enumerates other of "socialism's errors": "The treatment of certain unexamined beliefs as if they were an immutable science, a self-induced blindness toward, and fear of, groups whose liberation struggles threaten traditional leadership (notably women and gays), duplicity in terms of the internal line on the one hand and what you tell the people you're organizing on the other, a democratic centralism that retains all of the centralism and little of the democracy, personality cults, new class privilege, cronyism, and much else" (116).

16. *Building Just Relationships for the Next 500 Years*, report of the Southeast Regional Economic Justice Network Gathering, September 1992; prepared by Southerners for Economic Justice, P.O. Box 240, Durham, NC 27702; available for $10. I am indebted to SEJ and Leah Wise for much of my understanding of the contemporary economy.

17. Joy Harjo, "I Give You Back," *She Had Some Horses* (New York: Thunder's Mouth Press, 1983), 74.

Afterword

1. Richard A. Oppel Jr., "As Two Men Go Free, a Dogged Former Prosecutor Digs In," *New York Times*, September 8, 2014.

2. Julia Pierce, "Julian Pierce '76: An Attorney Who Was 'For the People,'" in *The Lumbee Indians: An Annotated Bibliography,* ed. Glenn Ellen Starr Starling, http://lumbee.library.appstate.edu/bibliography/pier001.

3. Joseph Neff, "28 Years Later, a Question Resurfaces: Who Killed Julian Pierce," *Raleigh News and Observer*, February 17, 2017. The online version of the article includes a five-minute interview with Julia Pierce, who is now a lawyer with the Indian Health Service: www.newsobserver.com/news/local/crime/article 133389784.htmlwww.newsobserver.com/news/local/crime/article133389784 .html.

4. Malinda Maynor Lowery, *The Lumbee Indians: An American Struggle* (Chapel Hill: University of North Carolina Press, 2018), 166–98.

5. Abby Phillip, "Suspect in Kansas City Shootings Will Face Hate Crime Charges," *Washington Post*, April 14, 2014.

6. On March 14, 2019, the SPLC board dismissed Morris Dees. SPLC president Richard Cohen explained on the website, "You may see in the news today that our co-founder, Morris Dees, is no longer working with the SPLC. . . . Our work is about the cause, not the person. We're committed to ensuring that our workplace embodies the values we espouse—truth, justice, equity, and inclusion. When one of our own fails to meet those standards, no matter his or her role in the organization, we take it seriously and must take appropriate action" (https://www.splcenter.org/news/2019/03/14/splc-statement-our-co-founder). Dees was ousted after a long history of complaints of sexual harassment and racial discrimination, including a staff hierarchy with people of color on the lower rungs. See Bob Moser, "The Reckoning of Morris Dees and the Southern Poverty Law Center," *New Yorker*, March 21, 2019. As Moser explains, exposés of such problems with Dees and SPLC emerged in the 1990s, along with assertions that he used his clients' names and stories in fund-raising solicitations, amassing millions that went to pay top staff big salaries but gave the defendants in whose names he raised money little compensation apart from the case the SPLC won. We had seen this in North Carolina when Dees defended Jimmy Pratt and Bobby Persons, two black prison guards who had armed White Patriots on their porches after they applied to take the sergeants' test in the prison where they worked. Dees chose his cases carefully for high impact and sure success—it was like shooting into a barrel, but nobody else was shooting there. Whenever individuals or groups told me they were contributing to SPLC, I suggested that their money would be much better spent supporting the local groups on the front lines and the national groups that supported them.

7. Don Terry, "Miller's Crossing," Hatewatch, June 16, 2014, 4, http://www.splcenter.org/blog/2014/06/16/millers-crossing.

8. See also Todd Heyward and Matt Comer, "Frazier Glenn Miller's Ties to a 1987 Triple Slaying: Did the Feds Protect a Killer," *Raw Story*, April 18, 2014.

9. Terry, "Miller's Crossing," 2.

10. Terry, "Miller's Crossing."

11. Gina Kolata, "Death Rates Rising for Middle-Aged White Americans, Study Finds," *New York Times*, November 2, 2015.

12. Joel Achenbach and Dan Keating, "New Research Identifies a 'Sea of Despair' Among White Working Class Americans," *Washington Post*, March 23, 2017.

13. Caitlin Dickson, "White Nationalists Reject Kansas City Suspect Frazier Glenn Miller," *Daily Beast*, April 15, 2014.

14. Don Terry, "Racists Express Support for Frazier Glenn Miller, Suspect in Deadly Kansas Shooting, on White Supremacist Forum," Hatewatch, April 15, 2014, http://www.splcenter.org/blog/2014/04/15/racists-express-support-for-frazier-glenn-miller-suspect-in-deadly-kansas-shooting-on-white-supremacist-forum.

15. Glenn Miller, *A White Man Speaks Out* (n.p.: White Patriot Party, 1999), n.p.

16. Miller, *A White Man Speaks Out*, n.p.

17. "Virginia Governor Defends Charlottesville Response: Militia Members Had 'Better Guns than Police,'" *Business Insider*, August 13, 2017.

18. John Ellston, "Eddie Hatcher's Last Stand?," *Indy Weekly*, October 11, 2000. See also the 1999 film by Taylor Sisk, *Takeover: The Trials of Eddie Hatcher*, and Bob Lederer, "Gay Political Prisoner Eddie Hatcher," *Out FM*, WBAI (New York), September 8, 2018.

Index

Publishing in the Public Interest

Thank you for reading this book published by The New Press. The New Press is a nonprofit, public interest publisher. New Press books and authors play a crucial role in sparking conversations about the key political and social issues of our day.

We hope you enjoyed this book and that you will stay in touch with The New Press. Here are a few ways to stay up to date with our books, events, and the issues we cover:

- Sign up at www.thenewpress.com/subscribe to receive updates on New Press authors and issues and to be notified about local events
- Like us on Facebook: www.facebook.com/newpressbooks
- Follow us on Twitter: www.twitter.com/thenewpress

Please consider buying New Press books for yourself; for friends and family; or to donate to schools, libraries, community centers, prison libraries, and other organizations involved with the issues our authors write about.

The New Press is a 501(c)(3) nonprofit organization. You can also support our work with a tax-deductible gift by visiting www.thenew press.com/donate.